CONVERSATIONAL SPANISH
FOR MEDICAL PERSONNEL

Allen S. Martin, MD
1005 Laximes Dr.
Goshen, IN

Please Keep in

Asg Director's office

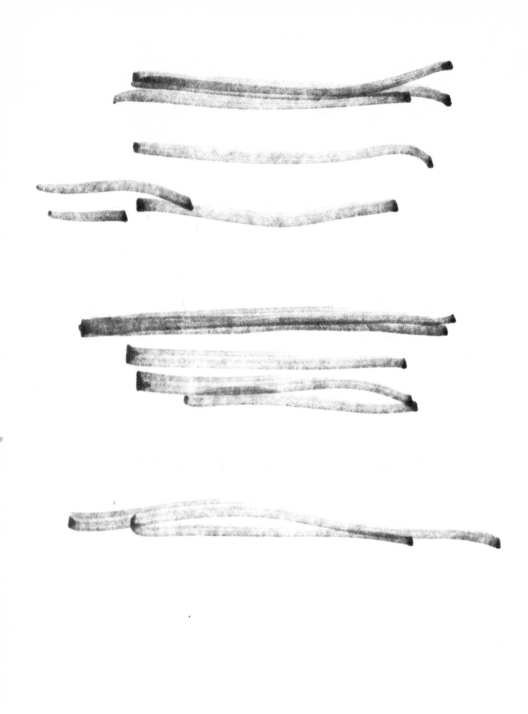

CONVERSATIONAL SPANISH FOR MEDICAL PERSONNEL

*Essential Expressions, Questions,
and Directions for Medical Personnel
to Facilitate Conversation with
Spanish-Speaking Patients
and Coworkers*

ROCHELLE K. KELZ, Ph.D.

Lecturer in Spanish | North Park College | Chicago, Illinois

A Wiley Medical Publication
JOHN WILEY & SONS
New York . London . Sydney . Toronto

Library of Congress Cataloging in Publication Data:

Kelz, Rochelle.
  Conversational Spanish for medical personnel.

  (A Wiley medical publication)
  1. Spanish language—Conversation and phrase books
(for medical personnel) I.   Title. [DNLM: 1. Medicine—
Phrase books—Spanish.   PC4121 K29c]
PC4120. M3K4   468′. 3′ 42102461   76-55722
IABN 0-471-02154-7

Printed in the United States of America
10 9 8 7 6 5 4

A Max y Melissa
que aún no comprenden por qué no puedo jugar
con ellos a cada rato

PREFACE

More than a dozen good Samaritans swarmed to the scene of an automobile wreck in Texas where a woman was quietly sitting behind the steering wheel. Most of the would-be helpers ignored her "No puedo mover las piernas." One woman, however, knew that this meant she couldn't move her legs, and stopped the good-willed but amateurish rescue effort so that the injured woman could be removed from the car by the ambulance assistants who soon arrived. Permanent spinal damage and perhaps even death were thus avoided because a passerby knew the correct Spanish words.

A San Diego physician took his month's vacation in central Peru, donating his medical skills to an impoverished area that could not possibly afford his talent if he charged his usual fee. Spanish did not come easily to him. He could have gotten by without any knowledge of Spanish because his Peruvian assistants spoke English quite well. But he learned how to greet his patients, thank them, bid them good-by, and added some Spanish medical terms to his vocabulary. A few words spoken in Spanish to a poor Peruvian make his eyes "light up like a full moon," he explained. He could tell that patients had more confidence in him after he spoke just a few words in their own language.

A nurse who works the night shift in one of Chicago's North Side hospitals empathizes with men whose wives are in the delivery room. For most of them it is a difficult experience; for those who speak only Spanish, it is pure agony. She speaks just a few phrases, like "Todo va bien" (All is going well) or "¿Le gustará café?" (Would you like coffee?), which bring smiles of relief from the fathers-to-be that she will remember forever.

These situations illustrate how a rudimentary understanding of medical Spanish has helped non-native Spanish-speaking citizens and medical personnel make life easier for themselves or others. Not many of us have the opportunity to save a life because we understand another language, but there are many times when we can make certain experiences more tolerable for ourselves and others. This book, as part of the trend in career education, is designed to eliminate any artificial separation between the academic and vocational worlds. As such, the goal of this work is to aid communication between medical personnel and Spanish-speaking people. Millions of Spanish-speaking persons who know little or no English live in the United States. Their inability to communicate poses a serious problem when these people seek medical attention.

Conversational Spanish for Medical Personnel : Essential Expressions, Questions, and Directions for Medical Personnel to Facilitate Conversation with Spanish-speaking Patients and Coworkers is a teaching manual that assists non-Spanish-speaking personnel in health-related fields in effective communication with Spanish-speaking patients and coworkers. While the book is not (nor is it meant to be) a grammar text, essential grammar, both in English and Spanish, is thoroughly explained to facilitate comprehension of the basic structures of speech in both languages. Often, medical personnel, though highly motivated, have minimal exposure to language study. But effective health care depends on efficient communication, and communication implies comprehension of certain grammar points not necessarily considered essential in traditional study of the Spanish language. Thus, the concise explanations of grammar points given in this book, illustrated by examples using medical vocabulary, reinforce active communication and aid in the ability to deal with occupational roles in the second language. The book also provides variations of Spanish words and phrases, listing many regionalisms, slang, and basic alternatives to the traditional expressions in an effort to avoid misunderstandings by medical practitioners or patients. At all times, the emphasis is on speaking to the sick patient—never on doing exercises in grammar.

The expressions appearing in this book are primarily those used in the Latin American countries located closest to the United States. Frequently these words or expressions are unknown or little used in Spain because many local Indian words enrich American Spanish. In addition, words and meanings often vary from one Spanish-speaking country to another. I have chosen the word or words most widely understood throughout the entire Spanish-speaking world. Most frequently these words or expressions derive from Spain. Words that are unique to one or two Latin American countries are noted as such so that people who deal with patients from that particular locality may acquire the necessary word or colloquialism, as well as the general term used elsewhere. The designation *Sp Am* is used with any variant current in a number of Spanish-American countries.

The English translations opposite the Spanish expressions are given principally for the benefit of English-speaking students but may also be used by Spanish-speaking medical personnel who wish to acquaint themselves with conversational usage in American English.

Chicago, Illinois   Rochelle K. Kelz, Ph. D.

CONTENTS

CONVERSATIONAL SPANISH FOR MEDICAL PERSONNEL

ONE

PRONUNCIATION
PRONUNCIACION

THE ALPHABET
EL ALFABETO

The Spanish alphabet has thirty letters. They are:

Letter	Name	Letter	Name	Letter	Name
A	ah	K	kah	RR	er-rray
B	bay	L	eh-lay	S	eh-say
C	say	LL	ĕl-yay	T	tay
CH	chay	M	ĕh-may	U	oo
D	day	N	eh-nay	V	bay or oo-bay
E	ay (ā)	Ñ	eh-nyay	W	do-blay bay or
F	eh-fay	O	oh		do-blay oo or
G	hay	P	pay		bay do-blay
H	ah-chay	Q	coo	X	eh-keys
I	ee (ē)	R	eh-ray	Y	ē grē-ay-gah
J	hoe-tah			Z	zeh-tah

GENERAL REMARKS
OBSERVACIONES GENERALES

Spanish is pronounced the way it is written. Spanish letters are treated as feminine nouns, and each has one sound except for C, D, E, G, N, O, S, X, and Y, which have at least two sounds. The letters K and W appear only in foreign words. The letter combinations $CH, LL, Ñ$, and RR each have one sound, are each considered to be one consonant, and are alphabetized as such. Excluding prefixes and suffixes, C, R, and L are the only three consonants that may be doubled in Spanish.

The Spanish alphabet is divided into vowels (**vocales**) and consonants (**consonantes**). The vowels A, E, I, O, and U are the same as in English. Y is a vowel when it is the last letter in a word and a consonant when it begins a word or a syllable. Thus, Y serves two functions. An example of Y's use as a vowel is **hoy** (today); as a consonant, **inyección** (injection).

All vowels in Spanish are short, pure sounds. A, I, and U each have one sound, although there will be slight variations according to placement within the phrase or word.

RULES OF PRONUNCIATION
REGLAS DE LA PRONUNCIACION

A[1] sounds like *A* in f*a*ther and is pronounced as a clipped *ah.* /a/

Examples :

adrenal adrenal   **aparato** apparatus

abdomen abdomen   **amígdala** tonsil

B is pronounced exactly like *V*. Thus the sounds of **a ver** and **haber** and **las aves** and **la sabes** are the same. Pronunciation of these two letters depends on their position in the word, phrase or sentence. When *B* appears at the beginning of a sentence, a breath group, or follows *M* or *N*, *B* has the *B* sound of *boy*. /b/

Examples :

brazo arm   **hombro** shoulder

bazo spleen   **miembro** limb

bostezar to yawn

Note that in all other positions, especially when the *B* or *V* occurs between two vowels (intervocalic), the sound softens. They should then be pronounced with less lip pressure. Do not quite close the lips, but allow air to escape through the slight opening between them. /ƀ/

Examples :

cabeza head   **aborto** abortion

C has two sounds.
1. Before *A, O, U*, or a consonant, *C* generally has a hard sound, as in *c*ap.[1] /k/

Examples :

carne flesh   **córnea** cornea

cadáver corpse   **clavículas** clavicles

cuerpo body   **cúbito** ulna

2. *C* before *E* or *I* is pronounced like the *C* in *c*ity throughout most of Latin America and in the southern part of Spain. In Spain, except Andalusia, *C* followed by *E* or *I* is pronounced approximately like *TH* in the English word *th*in. /s/ or /θ/ Castilian

---

[1] See **Dialectal Variations** on page 10.

Examples:

cintura waist	**cerebro** cerebrum
cirujano surgeon	**contracepción** contraception

CH[1] is pronounced as the *CH* of *ch*ild. /ĉ/

Examples:

mucho much, a lot	**chinelas** slippers
gancho clasp (for a dental bridge)	**chaleco** vest
noche night, evening	**chicle** chewing gum

D has two sounds.
1. At the beginning of a sentence, after a pause, an *N* or an *L* it is a hard, strongly dentalized sound. The tip of the tongue presses against the back of the upper front teeth. /d/

Examples:

domingo Sunday	**dolencia** ailment
dos veces al día twice a day	**indicación** indication

NOTE: Care must be taken to articulate this Spanish *D* as a dental sound, and not as an alveolar as it is in English. Intervocalic *D* in English, as in mu*dd*y, la*dd*er, is the equivalent of Spanish *R*.

2. In other positions, *D* approaches the *TH* of *th*e.[1] /đ/

Examples:

médicos physicians	**mojado** wet
codo elbow	**radio** radium
gordo obese	

E has two sounds.
1. When no other letter follows it in the syllable, it is like the long *A* sound in m*a*te. /e/

Examples:

higiene hygiene	**pelo** hair
teléfono telephone	**vena** vein

2. When followed by a consonant in the same syllable, *E* is like the *E* in m*e*t, especially before *RR*.[1] /ę/

Examples:

español Spanish   **estreñir** to constipate

papel paper   **empujar** to push

F[1] is pronounced essentially the same as in English. /f/

Examples:

afeitar to shave   **fumar** to smoke

familia family   **fémur** femur

G before *A, O, U* or a consonant has two sounds.
1. When initial after a pause or after *N*, the *G* is hard, like the *G* in *g*irls. /g/

Examples:

lengua tongue   **gotero** dropper

garganta throat   **glándulas** gland

2. In all other positions the *G* before *A, O, U*, or a consonant has the weaker *G* of English su*g*ar. The back of the tongue is raised toward the soft palate but does not touch it.[1] /ǥ/

Examples:

su gotero your dropper   **hago** I am doing. I am making.

las gafas the glasses

lentes

G before *E* or *I* is a soft guttural sound that does not exist in English. Formed in the back of the throat, it is like the *CH* in German A*ch* or in the Scottish Lo*ch*. /h/

Examples:

virgen virgin   **ginecólogo** gynecologist

vagina vagina   **gemelos** twins

Occasionally a silent *U* will precede the *E* or *I* to indicate that the *G* is hard as in English *g*uest.

Examples:

pagué paid   **cónyugue** spouse

To keep the *U* sound in the *gue* or *gui* combination, a dieresis (¨) is inserted over the *U*.

Examples:

ungüento ointment   **lingüística** linguistics
bilingüe bilingual

H is the only silent consonant.

Examples:

hormonas hormones   **hematólogo** hematologist
heroína heroin   **hígado** liver

I is like the *I* in mach*i*ne.   /i/

Examples:

miopia myopia   **infarto** infarct
irritación irritation   **interno** intern

J is pronounced just like the soft Spanish *G*.   /h/

Examples:

aguja needle   **joven** young person
juanete bunion   **jeringa** syringe

K is pronounced as in English.   /k/

Examples:

kilo kilo   **kilogramo** kilogram
kilómetro kilometer

L[1] is pronounced almost the same as in English, but with the tip of the tongue against the upper front teeth.   /l/

Examples:

líquido liquid   **laceración** laceration
lágrimas tears

LL[1] is considered to be one consonant in Spanish. In Mexico, many parts of South America, and in some parts of Spain it usually sounds like the *Y* of *yes*. In most parts of Spain, Paraguay, most of Peru, and in Bogota, Colombia *LL* approximates the *LLI* in the English word Wi*lli*am.   /y/ or /ḽ/ Castilian

Examples:

costilla rib	**cuchillada** gash
espaldilla shoulder blade	**llorar** to tear, to cry
mellizos twins	

M is pronounced essentially the same as in English.   /m/

Examples:

miope myopia	**metabolismo** metabolism
médula marrow	**mejilla** cheek

N has three pronunciations.
1. It is pronounced generally as in English. It is short and clipped.   /n/

Examples:

noche night	**novacaína** novocaine
nalgas buttocks	**negro** black

2. *N* is pronounced like *M* before *B*, *F*, *P*, *M*, and *V*.

Examples:

enfermo ill	**un viejo** an old man
enfermera nurse	**un brazo** an arm
un pulmón a lung	**un metatarso** a metatarsus

3. *N* assumes a nasal quality similar to English *N* in ri*ng* before *CA*, *CU*, *CO*, *K*, *G*, *J*, *QU*, or *HUE*.   /ŋ/

Examples:

un hueso a bone	**un cúbito** an ulna
un kilo one kilo	**estancado** stagnant
sangre blood	**estangurria** catheter
un jarro a pitcher	**estanquidad** watertightness

Ñ sounds like the *NI* in o*ni*on or the *NY* in ca*ny*on. It always begins a syllable. /ṇ/

Examples:

niño child

otoño fall, autumn

señor sir, Mr.

O has two pronunciations.

1. When it ends a syllable it is comparable to the English *O* in *o*ak.[1] /o/

Examples:

no no

enérgico energetic

emocional emotional

agotamiento exhaustion

muslo thigh

oreja ear

2. When followed by a consonant in the same syllable it sounds like *O* in *o*r. /ǫ/

Examples:

ombligo navel

órgano organ

hormona hormone

cónyugue spouse

P is pronounced as in English. /p/

Examples:

pañal diaper

pijama pajamas

pecho chest, breast

pestaña eyelash

In a few words the *P* before *S* is retained in print, but is silent. Some authorities now omit this initial *P*.

Examples:

psicología psychology

psiquíatra psychiatrist

psicoterapia psychotherapy

Q appears only before *UE* or *UI*. The *U* is always silent and the *Q* has a *K* sound. /k/

Examples:

quejar to complain

quijada jaw

bronquios bronchia

química chemistry

R[1] has two pronunciations.

1. It is slightly trilled when not in an initial position. /r/

Examples:

primo hermano   first cousin   **varicela**   chicken pox

urólogo   urologist

2. It is strongly trilled when initial or after *S*. $/\bar{r}/$

Examples:

roncha   rash   **roséola**   roseola

reumatismo   rheumatism   **los ricos**   the wealthy

RR[1] is very strongly trilled. *RR* often affects the sound of the vowel preceding it. $/\bar{r}/$

Examples:

sarro   tartar of the teeth   **gonorrea**   gonorrhea

diarrea   diarrhea

S has two pronunciations.

1. *S* is usually pronounced as *ESS* in the English dr*ess*. $/s/$

Examples:

saliva   saliva   **toser**   to cough

sudor   sweat

2. *S* before *B, D, G, L, M, N,* and *V* has the *Z* sound in toy*s*. $/z/$

Examples:

asma   asthma   **los dientes**   the teeth

desgana   loss of appetite

T is similar to English, but the tip of the tongue must go directly behind the upper front teeth. *T* is dental in Spanish, but alveolar in English; i.e., the tongue touches slightly above the gums. $/t/$

Examples:

té   tea   **tijeras**   scissors

teléfono   telephone   **asistente de hospital**   orderly

NOTE: The sound the English *T* sometimes has when it occurs between vowels (wa*t*er, clu*tt*er) is the equivalent of Spanish *R*.

U sounds like the *U* in r*u*le. /u/

Examples:

mujer woman   **champú** shampoo

pulso pulse   **cura** dressing

V[1] has the same sound as Spanish *B*. /b/ or /ƀ/

Examples:

vaginal vaginal   **vena** vein

vacunar to vaccinate   **la vena** the vein

verruga wart   **la vida** the life

W occurs only in foreign words and keeps the pronunciation of the original language. /w/

X has two pronunciations.

1. Before a consonant, it is usually a hissing *S* as in *s*it.[1] /s/

Examples:

excelente excellent   **ambidextro** ambidextrous

excepto except

2. Between vowels *X* is like the *X* in e*x*amine. /ǵs/

Examples:

sexual sexual   **tóxico** toxic

In Mexico the words *México, mexicano,* and *Texas* are written with an *X*, but pronounced with Spanish *J*. In Spain these words are spelled with a *J*.

Y[1] has three pronunciations.

1. As a consonant it is generally pronounced like the *Y* in *y*es. /y/

Examples:

yo I   **yeso** plaster

yodo iodine   **yerno** son-in-law

yeyuno jejunum

2. Consonantal *Y* is usually pronounced like the *J* in *j*udge when it follows an *N*. /ŷ/

Examples:

cónyugue spouse

inyectar to inject

inyección injection

3. When it stands alone or at the end of a word, *Y* is considered a vowel and is pronounced as the Spanish *I*. /i/

Examples:

y and

estoy I am

Z is pronounced the same way as *C* before *E* or *I*. Thus, in Spanish America and in southern Spain it has the *S* sound of *s*it. In central and northern Spain *Z* has the *TH* sound of *th*ink. /s/ or /θ/ Castilian

Examples:

embarazada pregnant

corazón heart

matriz womb

izquierdo, -a left

zurdo left-handed

pinzas nippers

DIALECTAL VARIATIONS OF SPANISH
VARIANTES DIALECTALES DE ESPAÑOL

In Spain any educated speaker can easily be understood by any other educated Spanish-speaker. This is due both to unanimity of linguistic standards and to uniformity of education. Dialectal differences are great, however, among the uneducated masses.

In Spanish America the Spanish differs from that of Spain principally in vocabulary and pronunciation. The most acceptable dialect of Spanish throughout Spanish America is apparently that spoken in southern Mexico, the Yucatan peninsula, Guatemala, Honduras, El Salvador, Nicaragua, Costa Rica, the interior of Venezuela, Ecuador, most of Colombia, Peru and Chile.[2]

The following discussion briefly describes dialectal variations that exist both in Spain and in Spanish America. Remember, any educated Spanish-speaker can easily understand and be understood by any other educated Spanish-speaker regardless of country of origin.

Vowels *Vocales*

A In central Mexico and parts of Ecuador, words with an unstressed *A* at the end are occasionally quite relaxed, almost to the *UH* sound, in rapid conversation.

---

[2] Pedro Henríquez Ureña, "Observaciones sobre el español de América," *Revista de filología española* VIII (1921): 357–390.

E   In the Caribbean region Spanish-speakers frequently use the pronunciation of the English *E* as in b*e*t, even when no other letter follows it in the syllable.

I   Has no important dialectal variations.

O   In parts of Cuba, Mexico, and Colombia a final unstressed *O* is pronounced as the *U* in English r*u*le. This usually does not cause confusion.

U   Has no important dialectal variations.

Consonants   *Consonantes*

C   In all dialects of Spanish the hard *C* sound at the end of a syllable, or at the end of a foreign word is often eliminated when it occurs in rapid speech.

doctor→dotor   doctor   **Nueva York→Nueva Yor**   New York

The syllable final hard *C* generally tends to voice to $|g|$:

doctor→dogtor   doctor   **técnico→tegnico.**   technician

CH   In Panama, Cuba and the Dominican Republic a variation of this sound (similar to English *sh*ell) is freely used in which the tongue assumes almost the same position as for the *CH*, except that the front of the tongue never touches the front palate.

D   Sometimes the intervocalic *D* completely disappears in all dialects of Spanish. Even educated Spanish-speakers will frequently drop it in words ending in -*ado*:

operado→operao   operated

It is usually eliminated when occurring at the end of a word:

Madrid→Madri   Madrid   **usted→uste**   you (formal, sing.)

The omission of this *D* in any other combination is considered substandard:

nada→naa or **na**   nothing

F   In many parts of Spanish America a rural variant of the *F* sound exists, particularly after the *M* sound and before the diphthong *UE*. This free variation is a softened *P*:

enfermo→epermo   ill   **fuerte→puerte**   strong

G   This sometimes disappears at the end of a syllable:

indigno→indino   unworthy

Many uneducated or rural Spanish-speakers will use dialectal variations of *GU* for *BU*. This is considered substandard Spanish and is indicated orthographically by the use of *GÜ*:

abuela→agüela   grandmother   **buenos días→güenos días**   good morning, good day, hello

Many educated speakers, however, will pronounce words with *HU* as though they were spelled *GU* or *GÜ*:

hueso→güeso bone **huele mal→güele mal** it smells bad

L When *L* occurs at the end of a syllable it is often replaced by *R* by uneducated Spanish-speakers in the Caribbean, along the coast of Colombia, and parts of Chile.

bolsillo→borsillo pocket

LL In Uruguay, Argentina and neighboring countries, *LL* sometimes sounds like *S* in pleasure and sometimes like *J* in *j*udge. In these countries the consonant Y has the *LL* pronunciation.

PS In Cuba, Central America, Colombia and Venezuela *PS* is pronounced *KS*:

peksi kola Pepsi Cola

PT is pronounced *KT* and visa versa:

apto→akto apt

R Many Spanish-speaking people, even educated speakers, in the Caribbean, the coastal region of Colombia and parts of Chile, will replace words with syllables ending with *R* with an *L*:

enfermo→enfelmo ill **carne→calne** meat

The sound of Spanish *R* is similar to the English *D* or *T* sounds of mu*dd*y, bu*dd*y, bu*t*ter, or wa*t*er. This frequently causes confusion in hearing and speaking for English speakers of Spanish:

cata **cada** **cara**
moto **modo** **moro**

RR Spanish-speakers in Cuba, Puerto Rico, Dominican Republic, Panama and coastal Colombia pronounce the *RR* so that the tongue strikes either the uvula or the velum. This type of sound exists in French (*rouge*) and German (*rot*).

S The Spanish spoken in Cuba, Puerto Rico, the Dominican Republic and the coastal regions of Chile, Argentina and Uruguay substitutes an aspirated *H* sound for both voiced and unvoiced *S*. This pronunciation is common among educated speakers, especially in rapid conversation:

espero→ehpero I am waiting **los codos→loh codos** the elbows

los chicos→loh chicos the children

V The occasional use of the *V* sound is not a matter of dialect. Rather, it is a hypercorrection. The *V* sound has never been used consistently in modern Spanish and is best avoided.

X   In Cuba, Puerto Rico, Dominican Republic, Venezuela and parts of Argentina and Uruguay *X* before a consonant has an aspirated *H* sound:

extraño→ehtraño   strange

Y   In eastern Argentina, Uruguay, and central Colombia *Y* is pronounced like the *S* in plea*s*ure.

DIPHTHONGS
DIPTONGOS

The vowels are divided into two groups:

strong vowels: A, E, O

weak vowels: U, I (Y)

Spanish vowels retain their basic sound when they form part of a diphthong, but they are pronounced more rapidly in succession and form one syllable. A diphthong consists of a strong and weak vowel, a weak and strong vowel, or two weak vowels in one syllable:

AU—about like "ow" in "cow."
primeros auxilios   first aid

UA—about like "wa" in "waffle."
sublingual   sublingual

AI or **AY**—about like "ai" in "aisle," or "y" in "rye."
traigo   I am bringing   **hay**   there is, there are

IA—about like "ya" in "yard."
arteria   artery

EU—an "e" plus "u" sound.
terapéutico   therapeutic

UE—about like "we" in "wet."
hueso   bone

EI or **EY**—about like "ei" in "eight" or "ey" in "they."
aceite   oil   **ley**   law

IE—about like "ye" in "yes."
diente   tooth

OI or **OY**—about like the "oy" in "toy."

oigo I hear   **hoy** today

IO—about like "yo" in "yoke."

ovar*io* ovary

UO—about like "wo" in "woke."

d*uo*deno duodenum

IU—about like "ew" in "chew."

d*iu*rético diuretic

UI or **UY**—like "we."

plasma sang*ui*neo blood plasma   **m*uy*** very

The stress in a diphthong is always on the strong vowel, or on the second of two weak ones.

The combinations *QUE, QUI, GUE,* or *GUI* are *not* diphthongs: the *U* is silent.

Two strong vowels never form a diphthong:

í-le-on ileum   **le-e** he reads

crá-ne-o skull

When the weak vowel in a strong and weak vowel combination is stressed, a written accent on the weak vowel breaks up the diphthong:

frí-o cold   **pa-ís** country

REMARKS CONCERNING THE FORMATION OF SOME SPANISH WORDS AND THEIR CORRESPONDING ENGLISH EQUIVALENTS

CORRESPONDENCIA DE PALABRAS

The Spanish ending *ción* corresponds to the English *tion*.

esterilización sterilization   **obfuscación** obfuscation
recuperación recuperation

The Spanish endings *dad* and *tad* correspond to the English *ty*.

dificultad difficulty   **sexualidad** sexuality
mortalidad mortality

The Spanish endings *dad* and *tad* may also correspond to the English *ness.*

enfermedad   illness

The Spanish endings *cia* and *cio* correspond to the English *ce.*

servicio   service   **edificio**   edifice

impotencia   impotence

The Spanish ending *cia* may also correspond to the English *tia.*

exodoncia   exodontia   **demencia**   dementia

ortodoncia   orthodontia

The Spanish endings *ia* and *io* correspond to the English *y.*

directorio   directory   **laboratorio**   laboratory

familia   family

The Spanish ending *ia* also corresponds to the English *y.*

disentería   dysentery   **histerectomía**   hysterectomy

vasectomía   vasectomy

The Spanish ending *oso* (*osa* in the feminine) corresponds to the English *ous.*

cautelosa (cautelosa)   cautious   **nervioso (nerviosa)**   nervous

generoso (generosa)   generous

The Spanish ending *ico* (*ica* in the feminine) corresponds of the English *ical.*

biológico (biológica)   biological   **físico (física)**   physical

The Spanish ending *itis* corresponds to the English *itis.*

mastitis   mastitis   **laringitis**   laryngitis

The Spanish ending *scopio* corresponds to the English *scope.*

microscopio   microscope   **estetoscopio**   stethoscope

The Spanish ending *ólogo* corresponds to the English *gist.*

patólogo   pathologist   **oftalmólogo**   ophthalmologist

neurólogo   neurologist

The Spanish ending *'tico* (*'tica* in the feminine) corresponds to the English *otic.*

narcótico   narcotic   **neurótico (neurótica)**   neurotic

The Spanish ending *logía* corresponds to the English *logy.*

serología   serology   **biología**   biology

The Spanish ending *ómetro* corresponds to the English *ometer*.

termómetro thermometer

esfigmomanómetro
sphygmomanometer

Many English words which begin with *s* and a consonant, insert *e* before the *s* for the corresponding Spanish word.

esfigmomanómetro
sphygmomanometer

escroto scrotum

esquisofrénico schizophrenic

English words that have the *ph* sound are spelled in Spanish with an *f*.

físico physical

flebitis phlebitis

fósforo phosphorus

The English vowel *y* is replaced in Spanish by the *i*.

esfigmomanómetro
sphygmomanometer

hímen
hymen

Many English words ending in silent *e*, drop the *e* and add *o* or *a* in Spanish.

medicina medicine

intenso (intensa) intense

caso case

dentífrico dentifrice

Many English words that end in a consonant add *o*, *a*, or *e* in Spanish.

accidente accident

víctima victim

mucho much

The endings *ar*, *er*, and *ir* are added to some English infinitives that end in a consonant to form the corresponding verbs in Spanish.

permitir permit

inyectar inject

comprender comprehend

Many English infinitives ending in silent *e*, drop the *e* and add *ar* or *ir* to form the Spanish equivalent.

terminar terminate

cauterizar cauterize

revivir revive

ACCENTUATION
ACENTUACION

Spanish words do not usually bear a written accent (´). Rules for determining the stressed syllable are clear:

1. Words ending in a vowel, an -*N*, or -*S*, stress the next to the last syllable:

a-ci-DO-sis acidosis **BUS-can** they are looking for

me-di-CI-na medicine

2. Words ending in a consonant other than -*N* or -*S*, are stressed on the last syllable:

pe-OR worst **es-pa-ÑOL** Spanish

3. Words that do not follow rules 1 and 2 must have a written accent mark (´) on the syllable stressed.

Á-ci-do acid **ac-NÉ** acne

tam-PóN tampon **MÉ-di-co** physician

NOTE: Spanish has only one written accent, which always indicates that the syllable bearing it is *stressed*.

1. Interrogative words are always accented:

¿qué? what? **¿cuánto?** how much?

¿cuándo? when?

2. A written accent differentiates similarly spelled words, usually monosyllabic, with different meanings:

él he **el** the

dé give (command) **de** of, from

sí yes **si** if

sé I know **se** himself, etc.

sólo only (adv.) **solo** alone (adj.)

The accent mark may be omitted over capital letters: PRONUNCIACION DE CONVERSACION MEDICA.

DIVISION OF WORDS INTO SYLLABLES
SEPARACION DE LAS SILABAS

Spanish words are syllabified according to simple but rigid rules:

1. A word has as many syllables as it has vowels, diphthongs, and triphthongs.

2. A single consonant, including *CH*, *LL*, *RR*, goes with the following vowel:

sa-rro tartar **ni-ño** little boy

mu-cha-cha girl

3. Two consonants are usually separated:

som-no-len-cia sleepiness   **a-del-ga-zar** to lose weight
bar-bi-lla chin

    A. An *L* or an *R* combined with another consonant goes with the following vowel in Spanish:

re-tra-í-do withdrawn   **pla-no** plain
sa-cro sacrum

    B. There is one exception: -*S* plus a consonant. Since this combination cannot begin a syllable, the -*S* goes with the preceding syllable:

as-cen-sor elevator   **es-to-ca-da** stab

4. Three consonants are usually divided after the first one, unless the second is an *S*:

in-gle groin   **abs-ten-ción** withdrawal
tem-blar to tremble

Practice *Práctica*

Rewrite the following words. Divide them into syllables and indicate the stressed syllable:
¿Cómo se divide en sílabas las palabras siguientes? Escríbalas de nuevo. Indique Vd. donde cae el acento.

limb **extremidad**	_____
menopause **menopausia**	_____
to masturbate **masturbar**	_____
crab louse **ladrilla**	_____
cramps **calambres**	_____
booster shot **reactivación**	_____
blood clot **coágulo de sangre**	_____
analgesic **analgésico**	_____
intramuscular shot	
inyección intramuscular	_____
reflex **reflejo**	_____
heart **corazón**	_____
stomach **vientre**	_____
uvula **campanilla**	_____
wrist **muñeca**	_____
skull **cráneo**	_____
navel **ombligo**	_____
coronary **coronaria**	_____
breastbone **esternón**	_____
adrenal gland **glándula suprarrenal**	_____
instep **empeine**	_____

Pronunciation Practice   *Práctica de la pronunciación*

Contrast the two sounds.   **Contraste los dos sonidos.**

Practice the contrasting *b* sounds.

		/b/	/ƀ/
vagina	the vagina	*vagina*	la *vagina*
beard	the beard	*barba*	la *barba*
mouth	the mouth	*boca*	la *boca*
I drink	I drink	*bebo*	yo *bebo*
he came	he came	*vino*	él *vino*
bladder	the bladder	*vejiga*	la *vejiga*

Practice the contrasting *d* sounds.

		/d/	/đ/
finger	my finger	*dedo*	mi *dedo*
weakness	the weakness	*debilidad*	la *debilidad*
pain	a little pain	*dolor*	poco *dolor*
doubt	the doubt	*duda*	la *duda*
slender		*delgado*	

Practice the contrasting *g* sounds.

		/g/	/ǵ/
it pleases	I like	*gusta*	me *gusta*
drop	a drop	*gota*	una *gota*
expenses	your expenses	*gastos*	sus *gastos*

Practice the contrasting *r* sounds.

		/r̄/	/r/
knee	the knee	**rodilla**	la **rodilla**
cold		**resfriado**	
diarrhea		**diarrea**	
	uterus		**útero**
rabies		**rabia**	
	urethra		**uretra**
rectum		**recto**	
	relative		**pariente**
kidney		**riñón**	
	ear		**oreja**
gonorrhea		**gonorrea**	
	nose		**nariz**

Reading Exercise   *Ejercicio de lectura*

Read the following aloud for pronunciation practice:

Un doctor me dijo que no podía quedarme en este lugar y que tendría que dormir más, hacer más ejercicios y comer menos.

—Pero, doctor, ¿adónde iré para vivir de este modo? No puedo dormir tanto si me despiertan temprano todos los días. Y no me gusta divertirme con deportes.

Lea en voz alta para la práctica:

A doctor told me that I could not remain in this place and that I would have to sleep more, do more exercises and eat less.

"But, Doctor, where will I go to live in this way? I can not sleep so much if they wake me up early every day. And I don't like to amuse myself with sports."

El perro de San Roque no tiene rabo
porque Ramón Ramírez se lo ha cortado.

Saint Roque's dog doesn't have a tail
because Ramón Ramírez cut it off.

PUNCTUATION
PUNCTUACION

Spanish punctuation is the same as English punctuation with the following exceptions:

1. A question has an inverted question mark (¿) at the beginning of the question as well as the regular question mark (?) at the end.

¿Dónde está el médico?   Where is the physician?

2. An inverted exclamation point (¡) precedes exclamations and a regular exclamation mark (!) concludes them.

¡Qué magnífica enfermera es!   What a magnificent nurse she is!

3. In quotations a dash (—) is generally used to indicate a change of speaker instead of quotation marks.

El doctor dijo:—¿Qué es lo que Vd.   The doctor said: "What is the matter
padece?—Siento mucha opresión   with you?" "I feel a lot of congestion in
en el pecho.—respondió Pablo.   my chest," responded Paul.

CAPITALIZATION
USO DE MAYUSCULAS

Capital letters are not used as frequently in Spanish as in English. Only proper nouns, and topographic nouns are capitalized.

The pronoun **yo** (I) is not capitalized, except at the beginning of a sentence.

The days of the week and the months of the year are not capitalized except at the beginning of a sentence.

Hoy es miércoles.   Today is Wednesday.

Es el veinte de agosto   It is the twentieth of August.

An adjective of nationality is not capitalized. Some authors capitalize adjectives of nationality used as nouns while others do not.

Dígalo Vd. en inglés.	Say it in English.
Hablo con un español. ⎫ **Le hablo a un Español.** ⎭	I am speaking to a Spaniard.

The following words are capitalized when they are abbreviated:

usted-Vd. (Ud.) ustedes-Vds. (Uds.)	you
senõr-Sr. señora-Sra. señorita-Srta.	Mr. Mrs. Miss

WORD ORDER IN A DECLARATIVE SPANISH SENTENCE
ORDEN DE LAS PALABRAS EN LA ORACION ENUNCIATIVA

A sentence is a group of words that expresses a complete thought. There are two parts to the sentence: the subject (noun or pronoun) and its modifiers, and the predicate (verb) and its modifiers.

Spanish word order is much more flexible than English word order. The meaning is not usually affected by a change in the order of the words.

El médico encuentra a las enfermeras en el hospital en la sala de emergencia	
En el hospital en la sala de emergencia el médico encuentra a las enfermeras.	
En el hospital el médico encuentra a las enfermeras en la sala de emergencia.	The physician meets the nurses in the hospital in the emergency room.
El médico encuentra en el hospital a las enfermeras en la sala de emergencia.	
Encuentra el médico a las enfermeras en el hospital en la sala de emergencía.	

It may be helpful to remember that the subject of the Spanish sentence, though it frequently precedes the verb, may follow it, especially when the subject is longer than the predicate.

Aquí se ven muchas operaciones.	Many operations are seen here.

The two parts of a compound verb are *never* separated.

Le haría daño a los ojos.	It would harm your eyes.

INTERROGATIVE WORD ORDER
INTERROGACION

A question is ordinarily formed in Spanish by placing the verb before the subject, which is done in English in the case of the verbs *be* and *have*, and the other auxiliary verbs.

Statement	*Question*
Usted es enfermera.	**¿Es usted enfermera?**

Declarative sentences may be turned into a question by using the expressions **¿verdad?** or **¿no es verdad?** or simply **¿no?** at the end of a statement.

Usted habla español, ¿verdad? You speak Spanish, don't you?

In questions the Spanish word order may be:

$$\text{Verb} + \begin{cases} \text{Adverb} \\ \text{Noun Object} \\ \text{Predicate Adjective} \end{cases} + \text{Subject}$$

If an interrogative word is used in the question, normally this word is placed in the same position as in the English sentence.

¿Por qué necesita primeros auxilios? Why do you need first aid?

NEGATION
NEGACION

To form a negative statement or question, place the word *NO* immediately before the verb.

¿Sufre Vd.?	Do you suffer?
Vd. no sufre.	You do not suffer. You are not suffering.
¿No sufre Vd.?	Don't you suffer?

No is used with other negative words, which come after the verb and which strengthen the negative sense of the sentence, unlike in English. If any negative word is used with **no** it must be placed after the verb, otherwise it must take the place of **no** immediately before the verb:

El doctor *no* llega *nunca* a tiempo.	The doctor never arrives on time.
El doctor *nunca* llega a tiempo.	
Ella *no* necesita *ninguna* medicina.	She does not need any medicine.
El nene *no* come *nada*.	The baby does not eat anything at all.

CHAPTER
TWO
COMMON EXPRESSIONS
EXPRESIONES CORRIENTES

GREETINGS

Good morning (good day).
And to you.
Good afternoon
  (used from noon till evening.)
Good afternoon (response).
Good evening.
Good evening (response).

INTRODUCTION

Hello (hi).
Let me introduce myself.

My name is _____.
I am _____.
What is your name?
I am glad to meet you.
I am glad to see you.
It's been a real pleasure.

I am pleased to meet you.
The pleasure is mine.

CONVERSATION

How are you?
How do you feel today?
How are things?
How goes it?
Fine, thank you.
Very well, thanks.
Marvelous, thanks.

SALUDOS

Buenos días.
Muy buenos.
Buenas tardes.

Muy buenas.
Buenas noches.
Muy buenas.

PRESENTACION

Hola.
Déjeme presentarme.
Permita usted que me presente.
Me llamo _____, para servirle.
Soy _____, para servirle.
¿Cómo se llama usted?
Me alegro de conocerle.
Me alegro de verle.
He tenido un verdadero gusto.
Tanto gusto.
Estoy encantado (-a) de conocerle.
El gusto es mío.

CONVERSACION

¿Cómo está usted?
¿Cómo se siente hoy?
¿Cómo le va?
¿Qué tal?
Bien, gracias.
Muy bien, gracias.
Maravilloso (-a), gracias.

So, so. (fair.)	**Así, así.**
	Regular.
	Pasándolo.
	Pasándola. (Mex.)
	Así no más. (Span. Am.)
Better than yesterday.	**Mejor que ayer.**
And (how are) you?	**¿Y usted?**
I am slightly ill.	**Estoy un poco enfermo (-a).**
	Estoy un poco malo (-a).
I feel blue.	**Tengo murria.**
I feel okay.	**Me siento bien.**
I feel bad.	**Me siento mal.**
I feel better.	**Me siento mejor.**
I feel worse.	**Me siento peor.**
I am sorry.	**Lo siento.**

FAREWELLS

DESPEDIDAS

Good bye.	**Adiós.**
	¡Que le vaya bien!
Well, good bye.	**Pues, adiós.**
So long. (see you later.)	**Hasta luego.**
	Hasta lueguito. (Chile, Arg.)
Till we meet again.	**Hasta la vista.**
Until tomorrow.	**Hasta mañana.**
"I'll see you."	**Nos veremos.**
	Nos vemos. (Mex.)
Until next time.	**Hasta la próxima vez.**
Come again.	**Vuelva otra vez.**
Regards to the family.	**Recuerdos a la familia.**

COURTESY

CORTESIA

Please.	**Por favor.**
Excuse me. (I must leave. I'd like to pass, etc.)	**Con permiso.**

Pardon (me). (for interrupting, but . . .)	**Perdón.**
	Perdóneme usted.
	Dispense usted.
You are welcome.	**De nada.**
Don't mention it.	**No hay de que.**
Gladly. (I'd be glad to.)	**Con mucho gusto.**
My deepest sympathy.	**Mi sentido pésame.**

COMMUNICATION

COMMUNICACION

Do you speak English?	**¿Habla usted inglés?**
Do you speak Spanish?	**¿Habla usted español?**
Do you understand English?	**¿Comprende usted inglés?**
Do you understand Spanish?	**¿Comprende usted español?**
Repeat, please.	**Repita, por favor.**
Please speak more slowly.	**Hable usted más despacio, por favor.**
	Favor de hablar más despacio.
Tell me, please.	**Dígame, por favor.**
	Favor de decirme.
What's the matter?	**¿Qué pasa?**
Do you need something?	**¿Necesita usted algo?**
Do you want something?	**¿Desea usted algo?**
How can I help you?	**¿En qué puedo servirle?**
How do you say _____?	**¿Cómo se dice _____?**
You say _____.	**Se dice _____.**
What does _____ mean?	**¿Qué quiere decir _____?**
It means _____.	**Quiere decir _____.**
Please speak louder.	**Hable usted en voz más alta, por favor.**
	Favor de hablar en voz más alta.

Exercise   *Ejercicio*

Practice these greetings and farewells with others in your class, making up your own variations.

Practique estos saludos y despedidas con la clase, creando nuevos diálogos.

Exercise   *Ejercicio*

The following is a conversation between a nurse and a patient in the hospital. Take the part of the nurse, filling in her comments and reactions. Use the new vocabulary that you have just learned.

Lo que sigue es una conversación entre una enfermera y una paciente en el hospital. Haga Vd. el papel de la enfermera, dando sus comentarios y sus reacciones. Use Vd. el nuevo vocabulario que acaba de aprender.

NURSE
Good morning, I am Mary, your nurse.

PATIENT
Good morning. I am Mrs. García.

NURSE
I am glad to meet you.

PATIENT
The pleasure is mine.

NURSE
How do you feel today?

PATIENT
Better than yesterday, but I still am slightly ill.

NURSE
What is the matter?

PATIENT
I have the chills.

NURSE
Do you need something?

PATIENT
I would like another blanket.

NURSE
Gladly.

PATIENT
Pardon me.

NURSE
Yes?

PATIENT
Do you understand Spanish?

NURSE
A little.

PATIENT
My family is coming this afternoon and they do not understand English.

NURSE
I will be pleased to meet them. So long.

PATIENT
Well, good bye.

ENFERMERA
_____

PACIENTE
Muy buenos. Me llamo señora García.

ENFERMERA
_____

PACIENTE
El gusto es mío.

ENFERMERA
_____

PACIENTE
Mejor que ayer, pero todavía un poco enferma.

ENFERMERA
_____

PACIENTE
Tengo escalofríos.

ENFERMERA
_____

PACIENTE
Me gustaría otra manta.

ENFERMERA
_____

PACIENTE
Perdóneme Vd.

ENFERMERA
_____

PACIENTE
¿Comprende Vd. español?

ENFERMERA
_____

PACIENTE
Mi familia vendrá esta tarde y ellos no comprenden inglés.

ENFERMERA
_____

PACIENTE
Pues, adiós.

CHAPTER

THREE

NUMERICAL EXPRESSIONS
EXPRESIONES NUMERICAS

NUMBERS

Cardinals

1	uno, un, una
2	dos
3	tres
4	cuatro
5	cinco
6	seis
7	siete
8	ocho
9	nueve
10	diez
11	once
12	doce
13	trece
14	catorce
15	quince
16	diez y seis, dieciséis
17	diez y siete, diecisiete
18	diez y ocho, dieciocho
19	diez y nueve, diecinueve
20	veinte
21	veintiuno, veintiún, veintiuna, veinte y uno veinte y un, veinte y una
22	veintidós, veinte y dos
23	veintitrés, veinte y tres
24	veinticuatro, veinte y cuatro
25	veinticinco, etc.
26	veintiséis
27	veintisiete
28	veintiocho
29	veintinueve
30	treinta
31	treinta y uno (un, una)

NUMEROS

Cardinales

32	treinta y dos, etc.
40	cuarenta
50	cincuenta
60	sesenta
70	setenta
80	ochenta
90	noventa
100	ciento, cien
105	ciento cinco
200	doscientos, -as
300	trescientos, -as
400	cuatrocientos, -as
500	quinientos, -as
600	seiscientos, -as
700	setecientos, -as
800	ochocientos, -as
900	novecientos, -as
999	novecientos noventa y nueve
1.000[1]	mil
1.009	mil nueve
2.000	dos mil
7.555	siete mil quinientos cincuenta y cinco
27.777	veintisiete mil setecientos setenta y siete
100.000	cien mil
1.000.000	un millón
2.000.000	dos millones
4.196.234	cuatro millones ciento noventa y seis mil doscientos treinta y cuatro

[1] Note that in Spanish a period is used to punctuate thousands; a comma is used as a decimal point.

Ordinals

Ordinales

1st	**primero**		6th	**sexto**
2nd	**segundo**		7th	**séptimo**
3rd	**tercero**		8th	**octavo**
4th	**cuarto**		9th	**noveno**
5th	**quinto**		10th	**décimo**

Ordinals above ten are rarely used; they are replaced by cardinals. When a cardinal is used for an ordinal, it is placed after the noun it modifies.

segunda lección   second lesson

lección doce   twelfth lesson

Fractions

Fracciones

$\frac{1}{2}$ un medio (la mitad) $\frac{4}{5}$ cuatro quintos

$\frac{1}{3}$ un tercio (la tercera parte) $\frac{9}{16}$ nueve dieciseisavos

$\frac{1}{4}$ un cuarto (la cuarta parte) $\frac{7}{20}$ siete veintavos

$\frac{2}{3}$ dos tercios $\frac{1}{50}$ un cincuentavo

$\frac{3}{4}$ tres cuartos $\frac{28}{75}$ veintiocho setentaicincoavos

NOTE: The numerator of a fraction is a cardinal number. The denominators from $\frac{1}{4}$ to $\frac{1}{10}$ are the corresponding ordinals. From $\frac{1}{11}$ to $\frac{1}{99}$, the denominators end in the suffix −AVO, which is added to the cardinal after the final *e* or *a* has been dropped. There are two exceptions to the apocopation of the final *e*—**siete** and **nueve.**

$\frac{2}{7}$ **dos sieteavos** $\frac{1}{19}$ **un diecinueveavo**

The word **parte(s)** may be used to express all fractions higher than, and including, one-third.

$\frac{4}{7}$ **las cuatro séptimas partes**

Decimals   *Números decimales*

Fractions which are in the form of so many tenths (**décimas**) or hundredths (**centésimas**) or thousandths (**milésimas**), etc. are called decimal fractions (**quebrados decimales**), from a Latin word for *ten*. The decimal point (**punto decimal**) marks off integers (units [**unidades**], tens [**decenas**], hundreds [**centenas**], etc.) from fractions (**fracciones decimales**).

Additional decimal equivalents are:

ten thousandths	**diezmilésimas**
hundred thousandths	**cienmilésimas**
millionths	**millonésimas**
ten millionths	**diezmillonésimas**
hundred millionths	**cienmillonésimas**

Spanish decimals are read in several ways. The number 12.435,678 can be expressed

12 unidades, 4 décimas, 3 centésimas, 5 milésimas, etc. or

12 unidades, 435,678 millonésimas or

12 unidades, 435 milésimas, 678 millonésimas.

Social security numbers *Números del seguro social*

The nine digits in the social security numbers are expressed in Spanish according to the following breakdown:

123-45-6789 = **123-45-67-89** or

ciento veintitrés, cuarenta y cinco, sesenta y siete, ochenta y nueve

Some Spanish-speakers will express their social security number as: **1-2-3-45-6-7-8-9** or **uno, dos, tres, cuarenta y cinco, seis, siete, ocho, nueve.**

Street addresses *Señas del domicilio*

Addresses in Spanish are given with the street number following the name of the street. Street directions is the last item mentioned:

651 West Main Avenue = **Avenida Main, número seiscientos cincuenta y uno, oeste.**

CONVERSION: FAHRENHEIT/CENTIGRADE
CONVERSION: FAHRENHEIT/CENTIGRADO

32 degrees (**grados**) Fahrenheit (**Fahrenheit**) (F) = 0° centigrade (**centígrado**)
Each centigrade degree is equal to 1.8 Fahrenheit degrees.

To change degrees F to degrees C, subtract 32 and multiply by $\frac{5}{9}$.

$(F - 32) \times \frac{5}{9} = C$

To change degrees C to degrees F, multiply by $\frac{9}{5}$ and add 32.

$(C \times \frac{9}{5}) + 32 = F$

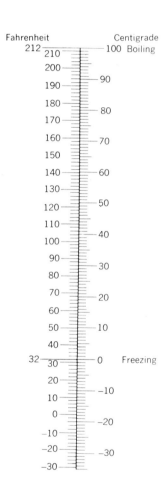

CONVERSION LIST

INDICE DE CONVERSIONES
DEL SISTEMA METRICO AL DECIMAL

1 centimeter (**centímetro**) = .393 inches (**pulgadas**)

1 inch = 2.54 centimeters

1 meter (**metro**) = $\begin{cases} 39.37 \text{ inches} \\ 3.28 \text{ feet (\textbf{pies})} \\ 1.093 \text{ yards (\textbf{yardas})} \end{cases}$

1 foot = .304 meters

1 yard = .914 meters

1 kilometer (**kilómetro**) = .621 miles

1 mile (**milla**) = 1.609 kilometers

1 gram (**gramo**) = .035 ounces (**onzas**)

1 ounce = 28.35 grams

1 kilogram (**kilo**) = $\begin{cases} 2.204 \text{ pounds (\textbf{libras})} \\ 35.273 \text{ ounces} \end{cases}$

1 pound = .453 kilograms (**kilogramos**)

1 liter (**litro**) = $\begin{cases} 2.113 \text{ pints (\textbf{pintas})} \\ 1.056 \text{ quarts (\textbf{cuartos})} \\ .264 \text{ gallons (\textbf{galones})} \end{cases}$

1 pint = .473 liters

1 quart = .946 liters

1 gallon = 3.785 liters

Centimeters   Inches

TELLING TIME

LA HORA

TELLING TIME	*LA HORA*
What time is it?	**¿Qué hora es?**
(An alternate phrase used frequently in Latin America.)	**(¿Qué horas son?)**
Do you know what time it is?	**¿Sabe usted la hora?**
I cannot say because I haven't any watch.	**No puedo decir porque no tengo reloj.**

It is one o'clock.	**Es la una.**
It is two o'clock.	**Son las dos.**
It is three o'clock.	**Son las tres.**
	Son las cuatro.

It is five o'clock.	**Son las cinco.**
It is six o'clock.	**Son las seis.**
	Son las siete.

It is eight o'clock.	**Son las ocho.**
It is nine o'clock.	**Son las nueve.**
It is ten o'clock.	**Son las diez.**
It is eleven o'clock.	**Son las once.**
	Son las doce.

It is one thirty.	**Es la una y media.**
It is 4:30.	**Son las cuatro y media.**
It is 11:30.	**Son las once y media.**
It is 1:15.	**Es la una y cuarto.**
It is 2:15.	**Son las dos y cuarto.**
It is 2:10.	**Son las dos y diez.**
It is 11:10.	**Son las once y diez.**

It is 10:10 pm.	**Son las veintidós y diez.**[2]

---

[2] Official time in Spain and other Spanish-speaking countries is expressed on a 24 hour basis. This applies to radio, television, train and airline schedules among other things. To figure out the equivalent time after 12 noon and before midnight (p.m.) you would need to subtract 12 hours. Thus, **las diecinueve** is 7:00 p.m., **las veintitrés** is 11:00 p.m.

Son las diez y veinte.

It is 12:05.   Son las doce y cinco.

It is 2:45.   Son las tres menos cuarto.

       Son las ocho menos cuarto.

Son las diez menos cuarto.

It is 6:55. (It is five to seven.)   Son las siete menos cinco.

Es la una menos veinte.

It is 6 a.m.   Son las seis de la mañana.

It is 5 p.m. (in the afternoon).   Son las cinco de la tarde.

It is 8 p.m. (in the evening).   Son las ocho de la noche.

It is exactly three o'clock.   Son las tres en punto.

It is approximately nine.   Son las nueve, más o menos.

It is noon.   Es mediodía.

It is midnight.   Es medianoche.

At 3:00.   A las tres.

At 5:05.   A las cinco y cinco.

At 12:50 (at ten to one).   A la una menos diez.

My watch is slow.   Mi reloj se atrasa.

My watch is fast.   Mi reloj se adelanta.

My watch has stopped.   Mi reloj ha parado.

Practice   *Práctica*

¿Qué hora es?

_____   _____   _____

_____   _____   _____

_____   _____   _____

_____   _____   _____

NOTES ON TELLING TIME
OBSERVACIONES ACERCA DE LA HORA

The verb **ser** is always used in telling time. The singular verb **es** is used to express one o'clock; from two o'clock on, the plural verb **son** is used. Note that the definite article **la** stands for **la hora**, and **las** stands for **las horas**. These definite articles are loosely translated as *o'clock*. **Media** ($\frac{1}{2}$) is a feminine adjective that agrees with the understood **hora**; **cuarto** ($\frac{1}{4}$) is a masculine noun and therefore does not have to agree in gender with **hora**. To express time from the hour to the half hour, minutes are added to the hour by **y**. When the number of minutes past the hour is greater than thirty, minutes are subtracted from the next hour, using the word **menos**. Thus, "six thirty-eight" becomes "seven minus twenty-two." Remember that from 12:31 to 1:30 the singular verb **es** and the article **la** are used.

Colloquially it is acceptable to say "**Faltan diez para las diez**" instead of "**Son las diez menos diez**."

The Spanish "day" is divided into **mañana**, (from sunrise to noon), **tarde** (from noon to sunset), and **noche** (from sunset to midnight). When the hour is specified, **de** must be used to translate *in* and *at* in the expressions **de la mañana**, etc. When there is no definite hour specified, **por** is used for *in* or *at*: **por la mañana** (in the morning), **por la tarde** (in the afternoon, evening) and **por la noche** (in the evening, at night).

ADDITIONAL EXPRESSIONS OF TIME
MAS EXPRESIONES HORARIAS

today **hoy**	monthly **mensual, mensualmente**
yesterday **ayer**	yearly **anual, anualmente**
tomorrow **mañana**	year round **todo el año**
tonight **esta noche**	during the day **durante el día**
now **ahora**	first time **primera vez**
the day after tomorrow **pasado mañana**	last time **última vez**
	once **una vez**
the day before yesterday **anteayer**	once a day **una vez al día**
a week from today **hoy en ocho**	twice a day **dos veces al día**
two weeks from today **hoy en quince**	three a day **tres veces al día**
	four a day **cuatro veces al día**
every other day **cada tercer día**	every hour **a cada hora**
month **mes**	every two hours **cada dos horas**
week **semana**	constantly **constantemente**
year **año**	occasionally **a veces**
next week **la semana que viene**	often **a menudo**
next month **el mes que viene**	on time **a tiempo**
next year **el año que viene**	per day **al (por) día**
minute **minuto**	per month **al (por) mes**
daily **diario**	per week **a (por) la semana**
weekly **semanal**	as of now **por ahora**

at bedtime   **al acostarse**

upon getting up   **al levantarse**

at the same time   **a la vez**

from time to time   **de vez en cuando**

by that date   **para esa fecha**

immediately, at once   **en seguida**

lately   **últimamente**

moment   **momento**

second   **segundo**

before meals   **antes de comer**

after meals   **después de comer**

a short while ago   **hace poco**

in a few minutes, shortly   **dentro de poco**

by then   **para entonces**

since when?   **¿desde cuándo?**

for how long?   **¿por cuánto tiempo?**

for many years   **por muchos años**

for the time being   **por ahora**

how often?   **¿cada cuánto tiempo?, ¿con qué frecuencia? ¿cada qué tiempo?**

how many times?   **¿cuántas veces?**

early   **temprano**

late   **tarde**

THE CALENDAR
EL CALENDARIO

Days of the week   *Los días de la semana*

Sunday   **el domingo**

Monday   **el lunes**

Tuesday   **el martes**

Wednesday   **el miércoles**

Thursday   **el jueves**

Friday   **el viernes**

Saturday   **el sábado**

Seasons   *Las estaciones*

spring   **la primavera**

summer   **el verano**

autumn   **el otoño**

winter   **el invierno**

Months of the year   *Los meses del año*

January   **enero**

February   **febrero**

March   **marzo**

April   **abril**

May   **mayo**

June   **junio**

July   **julio**

August   **agosto**

September   **septiembre**

October   **octubre**

November   **noviembre**

December   **diciembre**

Observe that in Spanish the months, seasons and days of the week are not capitalized.

The masculine definite article is used with the days of the week except when the days of the week are preceded by the adjectives **cada, muchos, pocos**, by any number, or by the verb **ser**. When the English *on* is expressed or implied before a day of the week or month, the definite article **el** (or **los**) is used.

on Saturday   **el sábado**   on April 23   **el veintitrés de abril**

on Wednesdays   **los miércoles**

In expressing dates, **primero** is used for the first day of the month. All other days of the month are counted in Spanish by the cardinal numbers, preceded by the definite article. The month and year, when expressed, are connected with the date by the preposition **de**:

on April 1   **el primero de abril**   January 7, 1970   **el siete de enero de mil novecientos setenta**

When the month is omitted, it is common to place the word **día**, *day*, before the number.

Today is the 23rd.   **Hoy es el día veintitrés.**

There are several ways to ask the day of the month. All are acceptable. When answering, the response should use the same terms as the question.

What day of the month is it?

- **¿A cuántos estamos?**
- **¿A cómo estamos?**
- **¿Cuál es la fecha?**
- **¿Qué fecha tenemos?**
- **¿Qué día del mes tenemos?**
- **¿Qué día del mes es hoy?**
- **¿A qué fecha estamos?**
- **¿A qué día del mes estamos?**

(Today) It is the 23rd of April

- **Hoy es el veintitrés de abril.**
- **Tenemos el veintitrés de abril.**
- **Estamos a veintitrés de abril.**

MORE CALENDAR VOCABULARY
MAS VOCABULARIO DEL CALENDARIO

birthday   **cumpleaños** (m, sg)   day   **día** (m)

calendar   **calendario** (m)   daylight   **luz de día** (f)

century   **siglo** (m)   eve   **víspera** (f)

date   **fecha** (f)   fortnight   **quincena** (f) holiday **fiesta** (f); **día de fiesta** (m); **día festivo** (m)

Christmas **Navidad** (f)

Christmas Eve **Nochebuena** (f)

Easter **pascua de resurrección** (f), **pascua florida** (f), **pascua de flores** (f)

Independence Day (USA) **día de la independencia** (m)

Labor Day (USA) **día del trabajo** (m)

Memorial Day (USA) **día (de recordación) de los caídos** (m)

New Year's Eve **víspera de año nuevo** (f)

Pentecost **pascua del espíritu santo** (f), **pascua de Pentecostés** (f)

hour, time **hora** (f)

daylight saving time **hora de verano** (f)

standard time **hora legal** (f), **hora normal** (f)

minute **minuto** (m)

midnight **medianoche** (f)

month **mes** (m)

noon **mediodía** (m)

week **semana** (f)

weekend **fin de semana** (m)

workday **día de trabajo** (m), **día laborable** (m)

saint's day **(día del) santo** (m)

year **año** (m)

fiscal year **año económico** (m)

leap year **año bisiesto** (m)

school year **año escolar** (m), **año lectivo** (m)

Spanish Refrain

Treinta días tiene noviembre,
con abril, junio y septiembre;
veintiocho tiene uno,
y los demás treinta y uno.

Exercise *Ejercicio*

Answer in Spanish.
Conteste Vd. en español.

1. ¿Qué día es hoy? (Hoy es lunes, etc. . . .)
2. ¿Qué día es mañana?
3. ¿Qué día fue (was) ayer?
4. Si hoy es lunes, ¿qué día es mañana? (Si hoy es lunes, mañana es . . .)
5. Si hoy es lunes, ¿qué día fue ayer?
6. Si hoy es jueves, ¿qué día es mañana?
7. Si hoy es miércoles, ¿qué día fue ayer?
8. Si hoy es martes, ¿qué día es pasado mañana?
9. Si hoy es martes, ¿qué día fue anteayer?
10. Si hoy es domingo, ¿qué día es pasado mañana?
11. ¿Cuáles son (Which are) los meses de la primavera? ¿del verano? ¿del otoño? ¿del invierno?
12. ¿En qué mes estamos ahora?
13. ¿Cuál es la fecha de hoy?
14. ¿En qué mes celebramos (do we celebrate) la Navidad? ¿La independencia de los Estados Unidos (United States)?
15. ¿En qué mes tiene Vd. su cumpleaños (do you have your birthday)? (Tengo mi cumpleaños en . . .)

FOUR

ANATOMICAL VOCABULARY
VOCABULARIO ANATOMICO

PARTS OF THE BODY

LAS PARTES DEL CUERPO

Miscellany	*Miscelánea*
artery	**arteria** (f)
articulation	**articulación** (f); **coyuntura** (f)
blood	**sangre** (f)
body	**cuerpo** (m)
bone	**hueso** (m)
capillary	**capilar** (m)
cartilage	**cartílago** (m)
circulation	**circulación** (f)
cholesterol	**colesterol** (m); **grasa en las venas** (f)
epidermis	**epidermis** (f)
fibroid	**fibroideo** (adj)
flesh	**carne** (f)
hormone	**hormona** (f); **hormón** (m)
joint	**articulación** (f); **coyuntura** (f)
ligament	**ligamento** (m)
limb	**miembro** (m); **extremidad** (f)
lingual	**lingual** (adj)
marrow	**médula** (f)
membrane	**membrana** (f)
mole, birthmark	**lunar** (m)
muscle	**músculo** (m)
nerve	**nervio** (m)
olfactory	**olfatorio** (adj)
organ	**órgano** (m)
periosteum	**periostio** (m)
perspiration	**sudor** (m)
pore	**poro** (m)
pulse	**pulso** (m)
senses	**sentidos** (m)
sensorial	**sensorial** (adj)
skeleton	**esqueleto** (m)
skin	**piel** (f)
tactile	**tácil** (adj)

tendon	**tendón** (m)
tissue	**tejido** (m)
valve	**válvula** (f)
vein	**vena** (f)

The head

La cabeza

Adam's apple	**nuez de Adán** (f)
aqueous humor	**humor acuoso** (m)
base of the cranium	**base del cráneo** (f)
beard	**barba** (f)
blood vessel	**vaso sanguíneo** (m)
brains	**sesos** (m)
cell	**célula** (f)
ciliated cell	**célula ciliada** (f)
cerebrum	**cerebro** (m)
chamber	**cámara** (f)
anterior	**anterior** (adj)
posterior	**posterior** (adj)
cheek	**mejilla** (f)
cheek bone	**pómulo** (m)
chin	**barbilla** (f); **mentón** (m)
chorioid	**coroides** (f, sg)
ciliary body	**cuerpo ciliar** (m)
cone	**cono** (m)
conjunctiva	**conjuntiva** (f)
cornea	**córnea** (f)
crystalline	**cristalino** (m)
ear	**oreja** (f)
auditory	**auditivo** (adj)
ear (organ of hearing)	**oído** (m)
external ear	**oído externo** (m)
external ear canal	**conducto auditivo externo** (m)
lobe of the ear	**pulpejo** (m)
eardrum	**tímpano** (m)
middle ear	**oído medio** (m)
anvil (incus)	**yunque** (m)

hammer (malleus)	**martillo** (m)
stirrup (stapes)	**estribo** (m)
inner ear	**oído interno** (m)
cochlea	**cóclea** (f); **caracol** (m)
semicircular canal	**conducto semicircular** (m)
earwax	**cerumen** (m); **cera de los oídos** (f); **cerilla** (f)
Eustachian tube	**trompa de Eustaquio** (f)
saccule	**sáculo** (m)
eye	**ojo** (m)
eyeball	**globo del ojo** (m); **globo ocular** (m)
eyebrow	**ceja** (f)
eyelash	**pestaña** (f)
eyelid	**párpado** (m)
face	**cara** (f); **rostro** (m)
features	**facciones** (f)
forehead	**frente** (f)
fossa	**fosa** (f)
fovea centralis	**fóvea central** (f)
frontal	**frontal** (adj)
ganglion	**gánglio** (m)
hair	**cabello** (m); **pelo** (m)
jaw	**mandíbula** (f); **quijada** (f)
jaw bone	**mandíbula** (f)
iris	**iris** (m)
lachrymal	**lagrimal** (adj)
larynx	**laringe** (f)
lens (of eye)	**cristalino** (m)
lip	**labio** (m)
lymph glands	**glándulas linfáticas** (f)
maxillar	**maxilar** (adj)
moustache	**bigote** (m); **mostacho** (m)
mouth	**boca** (f)
mucus	**moco** (m)
nape (of neck)	**nuca** (f)
nose	**nariz** (f)

nostril	**fosa nasal** (f); **ventana de la nariz** (f); **ventanilla de la nariz** (f)
occipital	**occipital** (adj)
optic nerve	**nervio óptico** (m)
parotid gland	**glándula parótida** (f)
pharynx	**faringe** (f)
pupil	**pupila** (f)
pituitary gland	**glándula pituitaria** (f)
retina	**retina** (f)
rod	**bastoncillo** (m)
saliva	**saliva** (f)
salivary gland	**glándula salival** (f)
scalp	**piel de la cabeza** (f); **cuero cabelludo** (m)
sclera	**esclerótica** (f)
sinus	**seno** (m)
skin (of the face)	**cutis** (m)
skull	**cráneo** (m)
socket (of the eye)	**cuenca** (f)
submaxillary gland	**glándula submaxilar** (f)
sublingual gland	**glándula sublingual** (f)
suture	**sutura** (f); **comisura** (f)
tear duct	**conducto lagrimal** (m)
tear gland	**glándula lagrimal** (f)
temple	**sien** (f)
throat	**garganta** (f)
tongue	**lengua** (f)
tonsils	**amígdalas** (f)
tooth	**diente** (m)
top of the skull	**tapa de los sesos** (f)
uvula	**campanilla** (f); **úvula** (f); **galillo** (m) (coll)
vitreous humor	**humor vítreo** (m)
vocal cord	**cuerda vocal** (f)
wrinkle	**arruga** (f)

THE HEAD

Hair

Forehead

Eyebrow

Eyelash

Nose

Mouth

Chin

Temple

Eye

Cheek

Ear

Jaw

Neck

PARTS OF AN EAR

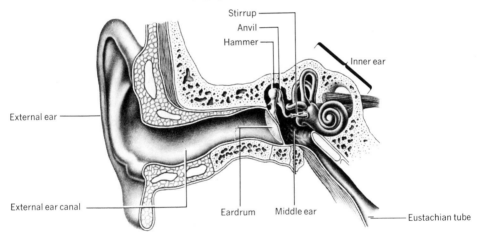

Stirrup

Anvil

Hammer

Inner ear

External ear

External ear canal

Eardrum

Middle ear

Eustachian tube

PARTS OF AN EYE

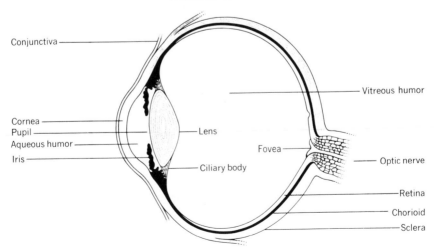

Conjunctiva

Vitreous humor

Cornea

Pupil

Aqueous humor

Iris

Lens

Fovea

Ciliary body

Optic nerve

Retina

Chorioid

Sclera

49

The trunk	El tronco
abdomen	**abdomen** (m); **vientre** (m)
anus	**ano** (m)
back	**espalda** (f)
backbone	**columna vertebral** (f)
belly	**barriga** (f); **panza** (f, coll)
bile	**bilis** (f)
bladder	**vejiga** (f); **vesícula** (f)
bosom	**senos** (m, pl)
bowel	**intestino inferior** (m)
bowels	**entrañas** (f)
breast	**pecho** (m); **teta** (f, slang); **busto** (m)
breastbone	**esternón** (m)
bronchia	**bronquios** (m)
buttock	**nalga** (f); **sentadera** (f); **anca** (f)
cervix	**cervix** (f); **cuello de la matriz** (m)
chest	**pecho** (m); **tórax** (m)
clitoris	**clítoris** (m); **bolita** (f, slang); **pelotita** (f, slang)
coccyx	**cóccix** (m)
collar bone	**clavícula** (f)
colon	**colon** (m)
coronary	**coronario** (adj)
crotch	**entrepiernas** (f, pl)
diaphragm	**diafragma** (m)
disc	**disco** (m)
slipped disc	**disco desplazado** (m)
duodenum	**duodeno** (m)
epididymis	**epidídimo** (m)
esophagus	**esófago** (m)
flank	**costado** (m)
Fallopian tubes	**trompas de Falopio** (f); **tubos** (m)
gallbladder	**vesícula biliar** (f)
gland	**glándula** (f)
adrenal	**glándula suprarrenal** (f)
carotid	**glándula carótidea** (f)

endocrine	**glándula endocrina** (f)
lymph	**glándula linfática** (f)
mammary	**glándula mamaria** (f)
parathyroid	**glándula paratiroides** (f)
prostate	**próstata** (f); **glándula de la próstata** (f); **glándula prostática** (f)
sebaceous	**glándula sebácea** (f)
sweat	**glándula sudorípara** (f)
thyroid	**glándula tiroides** (f)
gastric juice	**jugo gástrico** (m)
genitals	**órganos genitales** (m); **partes** (f, slang)
glans (penis)	**glande** (m); **bálano** (m); **cabeza** (f, slang)
heart	**corazón** (m)
heart valve	**válvula del corazón** (f)
hip	**cadera** (f)
ileum	**íleon** (m)
intestines	**intestinos** (m)
jejunum	**yeyuno** (m)
kidney	**riñón** (m)
lap	**regazo** (m)
liver	**hígado** (m)
loin	**lomo** (m)
lung	**pulmón** (m)
marrow	**médula** (f)
myocardium	**miocardio** (adj)
neck	**cuello** (m); **pescuezo** (m)
navel	**ombligo** (m)
nipple (female)	**pezón** (m); **chichi** (m, slang)
nipple (male)	**tetilla** (f)
ovary	**ovario** (m)
pancreas	**páncreas** (m)
pelvis	**pelvis** (f)

penis	**pene** (m); **miembro** (m); **pito** (m, slang); **verga** (f, slang); **pija** (f, Arg., slang)
pubis	**pubis** (m)
rectum	**recto** (m)
rib	**costilla** (f)
sacroiliac	**sacroilíaco** (adj)
sacrum	**sacro** (m)
sciatic	**ciático** (adj)
scrotum	**escroto** (m)
semen	**semen** (m); **esperma** (f)
seminal vesicle	**vesículo seminal** (m)
shoulder blade	**espaldilla** (f); **omóplato** (m)
side	**costado** (m); **lado** (m)
skin	**piel** (f)
spinal column	**columna vertebral** (f); **espina dorsal** (f)
spinal cord	**médula espinal** (f)
spleen	**bazo** (m)
stomach	**estómago** (m); **vientre** (m)
stomach (pit of)	**boca del estómago** (f)
testicle	**testículo** (m); **huevos** (m, pl, slang); **compañones** (m, pl, slang)
thorax	**tórax** (m)
thymus	**timo** (m)
thyroid	**tiroides** (m)
ureter	**uréter** (m)
urethra	**ureta** (f); **canal** (m)
uterus	**útero** (m); **matriz** (f)
vagina	**vagina** (f); **panocho** (m, slang)
vas deferens	**conducto deferente** (m)
vertebra	**vértebra** (f)
waist	**cintura** (f)
womb	**matriz** (f); **útero** (m)

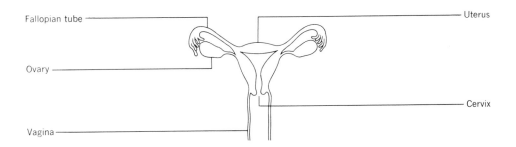

Fallopian tube

Ovary

Vagina

Uterus

Cervix

FEMALE GENITOURINARY SYSTEM
SIDE VIEW

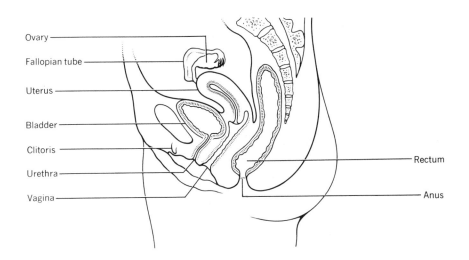

Ovary

Fallopian tube

Uterus

Bladder

Clitoris

Urethra

Vagina

Rectum

Anus

Upper extremities	Las extremidades superiores
arm	**brazo** (m)
armpit	**sobaco** (m); **axila** (f)
back of the hand	**dorso de la mano** (m)
cuticle	**cutícula** (f)
elbow	**codo** (m)
finger	**dedo** (m)
thumb	**pulgar** (m); **dedo gordo** (m)

53

MALE GENITOURINARY SYSTEM
FRONT VIEW

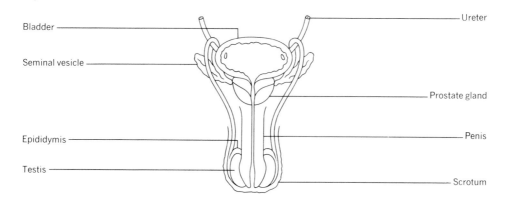

Bladder

Seminal vesicle

Epididymis

Testis

Ureter

Prostate gland

Penis

Scrotum

MALE GENITOURINARY SYSTEM
SIDE VIEW

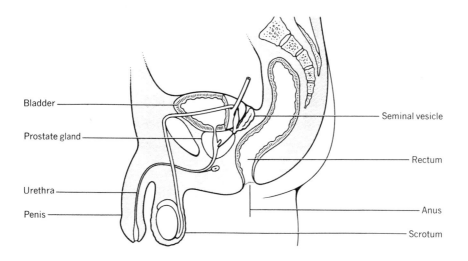

Bladder

Prostate gland

Urethra

Penis

Seminal vesicle

Rectum

Anus

Scrotum

ball of thumb	**pulpejo** (m)
index	**índice** (m)
middle finger	**dedo del medio** (m); **dedo del corazón** (m)
ring finger	**dedo anular** (m)
little finger	**meñique** (m)
fleshy tip of the finger	**yema** (f)
knuckle	**nudillo** (m)
fist	**puño** (m)

forearm	**antebrazo** (m)
hand	**mano** (f)
hangnail	**padastro** (m, coll); **cutícula desgarrada** (f)
humerus	**húmero** (m)
nail	**uña** (f)
palm of the hand	**palma de la mano** (f)
phalanx	**falange** (f)
radius	**radio** (m)
ulna	**cúbito** (m)
wrist	**muñeca** (f)

Lower extremities — *Las extremidades inferiores*

ankle	**tobillo** (m)
big toe	**dedo grueso** (m)
bunion	**juanete** (m)
calf of the leg	**pantorrilla** (f)
callus	**callo** (m)
femur	**fémur** (m)
fibula	**peroné** (m)
foot	**pie** (m)
groin	**ingle** (f)
heel	**talón** (m)
hip	**cadera** (f)
ingrown nail	**uña encarnada** (f); **uña enterrada** (f); **uñero** (m)
instep	**empeine** (m)
knee	**rodilla** (f)
knee (back of the)	**corva** (f)
kneecap	**rótula** (f); **choquezuela** (f)
leg	**pierna** (f)
shin	**espinilla** (f)
shin bone	**tibia** (f)
sole of the foot	**planta del pie** (f)
tendon	**tendón** (m)
thigh	**muslo** (m)

**THE HUMAN BODY
FRONT VIEW**

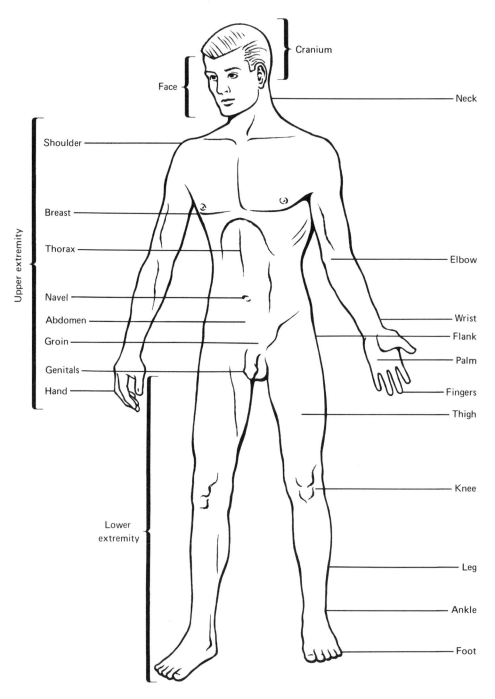

Cranium

Face

Neck

Shoulder

Breast

Thorax

Navel

Abdomen

Groin

Genitals

Hand

Upper extremity

Elbow

Wrist

Flank

Palm

Fingers

Thigh

Knee

Lower
extremity

Leg

Ankle

Foot

THE HUMAN BODY
REAR VIEW

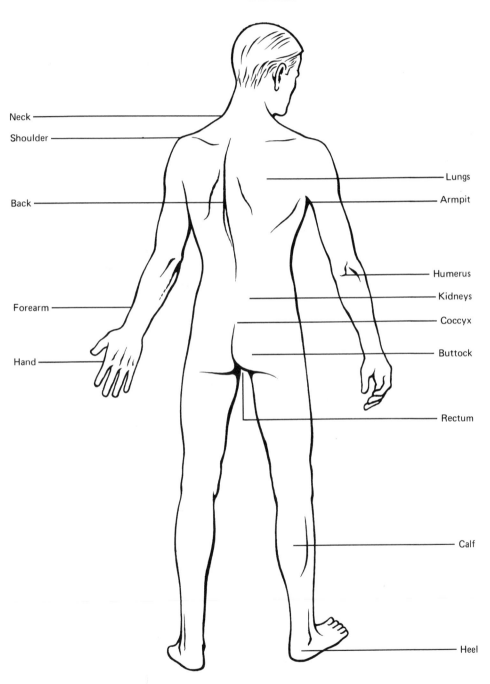

Neck

Shoulder

Back

Forearm

Hand

Lungs

Armpit

Humerus

Kidneys

Coccyx

Buttock

Rectum

Calf

Heel

DENTAL VOCABULARY	VOCABULARIO DENTAL
abscess	**absceso** (m)
acrylic	**acrílico** (adj)
amalgam	**amalgama** (f)
artificial, false teeth	**dientes postizos** (m)
block the nerve, to	**obstruir el nervio**
bite, to	**morder**
bridge (dental)	**puente** (m)
fixed dental bridge	**puente fijo** (m)
removable bridge	**puente movible** (m)
brush one's teeth, to	**cepillarse los dientes**
burr	**fresa** (f)
canker sore	**ulceración** (f); **postemilla** (f)
capillaries	**capilares** (m); **vaso capilar** (m)
caries	**caries** (f)
cavity	**carie** (f); **diente picado** (m); **diente cariado** (m); **cavidad** (f) **picadura** (f)
cementum	**cemento** (m)
chew, to	**mascar**
clasp	**gancho** (m)
cleaning	**limpieza** (f)
crown	**corona** (f)
acrylic jacket crown	**corona acrílica** (f)
porcelain jacket crown	**corona de porcelana** (f)
deaden the nerve, to	**adormecer el nervio**
dental artery	**arteria dental** (f)
dental drill	**taladro** (m)
dental floss	**hilo dental** (m); **seda encerada** (f)
dental forceps	**pinzas** (f, pl); **tenazas de extracción** (f, pl)
dental hygienist	**higienista dental** (m or f)
dental nerve	**nervio dental** (m)
dental office	**clínica dental** (f)
dental vein	**vena dental** (f)
dentine	**dentina** (f)

denture	**dentadura (postiza)** (f)
full denture	**dentadura completa** (f)
partial denture	**dentadura parcial** (f)
diet, liquid	**dieta de líquidos** (f)
drill	**taladro** (m)
drill, to	**perforar; taladrar**
emesis basin	**riñonera** (f)
enamel	**esmalte** (m)
extraction	**extracción** (f)
fauces	**fauces** (f, pl)
feel nothing, to	**no sentir nada**
file down, to	**limar**
fill, to	**empastar; tapar; calzar; emplomar** (Arg) **orificar**
fill with gold, to	
filling	**empaste** (m); **empastadura** (f); **relleno** (m); **tapadura** (f); **emplomadura** (f, Arg)
frenum of the tongue	**frenillo** (m)
gargle (liquid)	**gargarismo** (m)
gargle, to	**hacer gárgaras**
gold	**oro** (m)
gums	**encías** (f)
headrest	**apoyo para la cabeza** (m)
immobilization	**inmovilización** (f)
impaction	**impacción** (f)
impression	**impresión** (f)
inlay	**incrustación** (f); **orificación** (f)
jaw	**quijada** (f); **mandíbula** (f)
broken jaw	**quijada rota** (f); **mandíbula rota** (f)
nerve	**nervio** (m)
novocaine	**novocaína** (f)
numb	**entumecido** (adj); **adormecido** (adj)
occlusion	**oclusión** (f)
palate	**paladar** (m)
plaque	**placa** (f)
plate	**placa** (f)

polish, to	**limar**
porcelain	**porcelana** (f)
pressure	**presión** (f)
exert pressure on, to	**ejercer presión sobre**
sensations, pressure	**sensaciones de ser apretado**
pull out, to	**extraer**
pulp	**pulpa** (f)
pulpotomy	**pulpotomía** (f)
put to sleep, to	**adormecer por anestesia**
pyorrhea	**piorrea** (f)
reimplantation	**reimplantación** (f); **reinjertación** (f)
remove the nerve, to	**sacarle el nervio a alguien; matarle el nervio a alguien**
ridge	**elevación** (f); **reborde** (m)
rinse, to	**enjuagarse**
roof of the mouth	**cielo de la boca** (m); **paladar** (m)
root	**raíz** (f)
root canal	**canal radicular** (m)
root canal work	**extracción del nervio** (f); **curación del nervio** (f)
saliva	**esputo** (m); **saliva** (f); **expectoración** (f)
set a fracture, to	**reducir una fractura; componer una fractura**
show one's teeth, to	**enseñar los dientes** (coll.); **mostrar los dientes**
side	**lado** (m)
upper right side	**lado derecho superior** (m)
lower right side	**lado derecho inferior** (m)
upper left side	**lado izquierdo superior** (m)
lower left side	**lado izquierdo inferior** (m)
smooth, to	**limar**
sodium pentothal	**pentotal de sodio** (m)
spit in the bowl, to	**escupir en la taza**
straighten the teeth, to	**enderezar los dientes**
surface	**superficie** (f)

suture (dental)	**sutura** (f)
tartar	**sarro** (f)
teeth	**dientes** (m)
bicuspids	**bicúspides** (m); **premolares** (f)
canine, eyeteeth	**canino** (m); **colmillo** (m)
deciduous teeth	**dientes de leche** (m, pl)
incisors, front teeth	**incisivos** (m)
even teeth	**dientes parejos** (m)
molars	**molares** (m)
third molar	**tercer molar** (m)
stained teeth	**dientes manchados** (m)
white teeth	**dientes blancos** (m)
wisdom teeth	**muelas del juicio** (f); **muelas cordales** (f)
temporary filling	**empaste provisional** (m)
tingling	**hormigueo** (m)
tooth	**diente** (m)
baby tooth	**diente mamón** (m); **diente de leche** (m)
back tooth	**muela** (f)
impacted tooth	**diente impactado** (m)
large, misshapen tooth	**diente de ajo** (m, coll)
lower tooth	**diente inferior** (m)
neck of tooth	**cuello** (m)
toothache	**dolor de muelas** (m); **dolor de dientes** (m); **odontalgia** (f)
upper tooth	**diente superior** (m)
toothbrush	**cepillo de dientes** (m)
toothpaste	**pasta de dientes** (f); **pasta dentífrice** (f)
toothpick	**palillo de dientes** (m); **mondadientes** (m)
tooth socket	**alvéolo** (m)
waterpick	**limpiador de agua a presión** (m)
wire, to	**atar con alambre**

PARTS OF A TOOTH

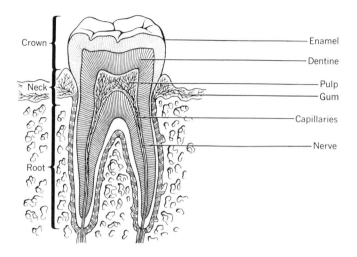

Crown

Enamel

Dentine

Neck

Pulp

Gum

Root

Capillaries

Nerve

SELF-TEST ANATOMICAL DIAGRAMS
EXAMEN DE SI MISMO ESQUEMAS ANATOMICOS

The diagrams below correspond to those appearing on the previous pages. Fill in the Spanish names for each body part indicated.

Los esquemas de abajo corresponden a los de las páginas anteriores. Completen con nombres españoles para cada parte del cuerpo humano indicada.

LA CABEZA

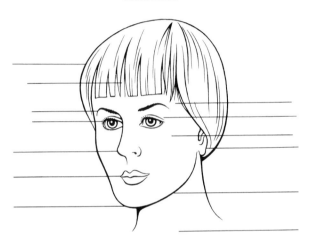

PARTES DE UN OIDO

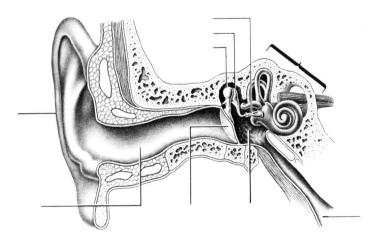

PARTES DE UN OJO

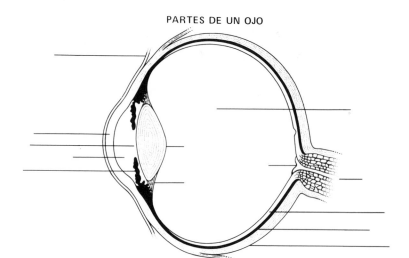

SISTEMA GENITOURINARIO DE HOMBRES
VISTA ANTERIOR

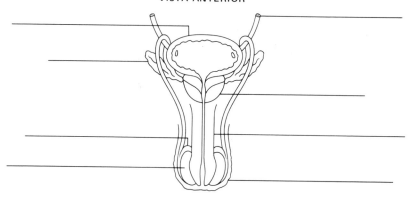

SISTEMA GENITOURINARIO DE HOMBRES
VISTA DE PERFIL

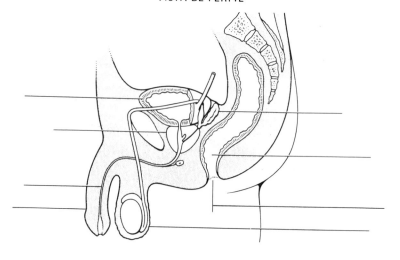

PARTES DE UN DIENTE

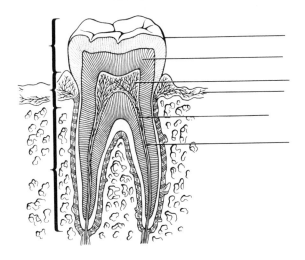

SISTEMA GENITOURINARIO DE MUJERES
VISTA ANTERIOR

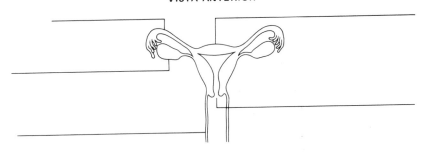

SISTEMA GENITOURINARIO DE MUJERES
VISTA DE PERFIL

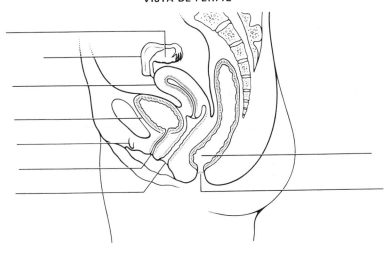

EL CUERPO HUMANO
VISTA ANTERIOR

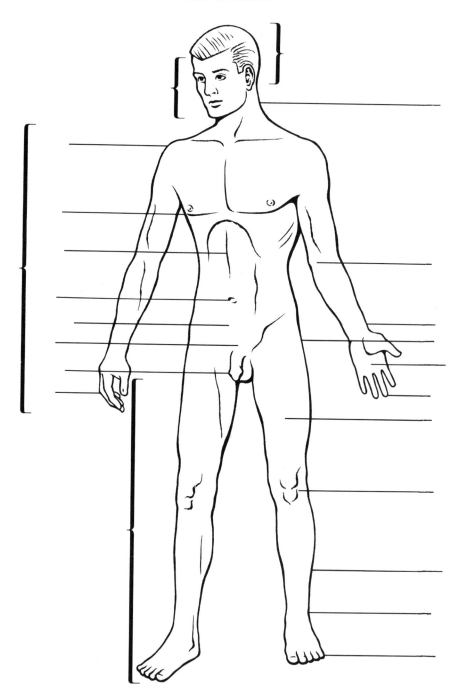

EL CUERPO HUMANO
VISTA POSTERIOR

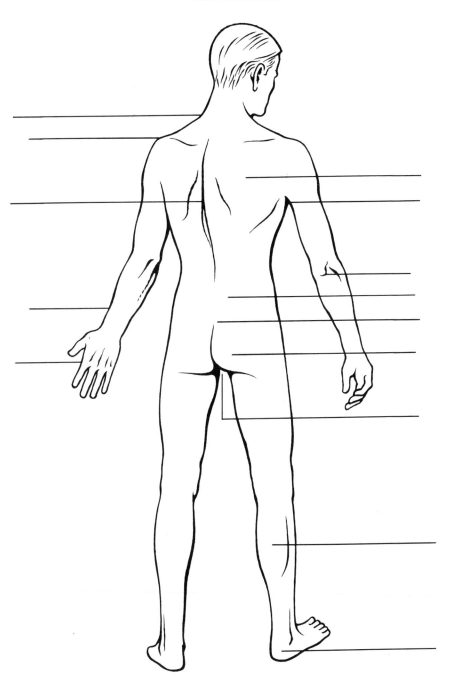

FIVE

CONVERSATIONS FOR MEDICAL AND PARAMEDICAL PERSONNEL

CONVERSACIONES PARA PERSONAL MEDICO Y PARAMEDICO

PRESENT ILLNESS[1]

ENFERMEDAD ACTUAL

1. What is wrong with you?

2. Did you have an accident?

3. When did it occur?

4. Where did it happen?

5. Were you hurt at work?

6. What is the name of your employer?

7. What is the address of your employer?

8. Did you faint before the accident?

9. Did you faint after the accident?

10. Did you have a dizzy spell before the accident?

11. Did you lose consciousness after the accident?

12. How long?

13. How did this illness begin?

14. When were you first taken sick?

15. Are you in pain?

1. **¿De qué se queja Vd.?**
   ¿Qué le pasa a Vd.?
   ¿Qué le sucede a Vd.?

2. **¿Tuvo Vd. un accidente?**
   ¿Sufrió Vd. un accidente?

3. **¿Cuándo ocurrió?**

4. **¿Dónde ocurrió?**

5. **¿Fue lastimado en el trabajo?**
   ¿Se lastimó en el trabajo?
   ¿Fue herido en el trabajo?

6. **¿Para qué compañía trabaja Vd.?**
   ¿Dónde trabaja Vd.?
   ¿Quién le emplea?

7. **¿Cuál es la dirección de su trabajo?**
   ¿Dónde está Vd. empleado (empleada)?

8. **¿Se desmayó Vd. antes del accidente?**

9. **¿Se desmayó Vd. después del accidente?**

10. **¿Tuvo Vd. mareos antes del accidente?**
    ¿Se sintió Vd. mareado antes del accidente?

11. **¿Perdió Vd. el conocimiento después del accidente?**

12. **¿Por cuánto tiempo?**

13. **¿Cómo empezó esta enfermedad?**
    ¿Cómo ha empezado esta enfermedad?

14. **¿Cuándo ha empezado esta enfermedad?**

15. **¿Siente Vd. dolor?**

[1] Students may find it helpful to refer to the Spanish Verb Section, pages 291–300.

16. When did your pains begin?

16. ¿Cuándo empezaron sus dolores?

17. Where is the pain?

17. ¿Qué le duele?
¿Dónde le duele?
¿Dónde siente Vd. el dolor?

18. In the head?

18. ¿En la cabeza?

19. In the abdomen?

19. ¿En el abdomen?

20. In the chest?

20. ¿En el pecho?

21. In the side?

21. ¿En el lado?
¿En su costado?

22. Which one?

22. ¿En qué lado?

23. In the shoulder blades?

23. ¿En los hombros?

24. In the back?

24. ¿En la espalda?

25. In the legs?

25. ¿En las piernas?

26. In the bones?

26. ¿En los huesos?

27. Here?

27. ¿Aquí?

28. Are you in pain now?

28. ¿Tiene Vd. dolores ahora?
¿Siente Vd. dolores ahora?
¿Sufre Vd. de dolor ahora?

29. Show me where it hurts you.

29. Enséñeme dónde le duele.

30. Is it a constant pain or does it come and go?

30. ¿Es un dolor constante, o va y vuelve? o le va y se le quita?

31. Is it dull, sharp, steady pain, or a feeling of pressure?

31. ¿Es un dolor sordo, agudo, continuo, o una sensación de presión?

32. Do you have pain here?

32. ¿Siente Vd. dolor aquí?
¿Le duele aquí?

33. Has the pain eased a great deal?

33. ¿Ha disminuido mucho el dolor?

34. How long have you had the pain?

34. ¿Desde cuándo tiene Vd. el dolor?

35. The pain is very strong at night.

35. El dolor es mayor durante la noche.
El dolor aumenta en la noche.

36. More during the daytime.

36. Mayor durante el día.

37. Do you have a lot of pain in your left (right) leg?

37. ¿Le duele mucho la pierna izquierda (derecha)?

38. Does it hurt more when I press, or when I stop pressing suddenly?

39. Does it hurt only where I am pressing, or somewhere else?

40. I will not hurt you.

41. It is not painful.

42. Tell me when you feel pain.

43. Have you had a heart attack?

44. When did you have your first attack?

38. **¿Le duele más cuando le comprimo o cuando dejo de comprimir rápidmente?**

39. **¿Le duele solamente donde aprieto, o en otros lugares más?**

40. **No voy a hacerle daño.**

41. **No le va a doler.**

42. **Avíseme cuando sienta dolor.**

43. **¿Sufrió Vd. un ataque cardíaco?**

44. **¿Cuándo sufrió Vd. su primer ataque?**

Review

Learn the Following Dialogue

DOCTOR
Good afternoon. What is wrong with you?
PATIENT
I don't feel well.
DOCTOR
Did you have an accident?
PATIENT
Yes, a large box fell on my head.

DOCTOR
When did it occur?
PATIENT
It happened at my factory during lunch.

DOCTOR
What is the name of your employer?
PATIENT
D & D Fabrics.
DOCTOR
What is the address of your employer?
PATIENT
2312 East Noyes, Evanston.

DOCTOR
Did you faint after the accident?
PATIENT
I suddenly lost consciousness.
DOCTOR
How long?
PATIENT
A minute.

Repaso

Aprenda el diálogo siguiente

DOCTOR
Buenas tardes. ¿De qué se queja Vd.?

PACIENTE
No me siento muy bien.
DOCTOR
¿Tuvo Vd. un accidente?
PACIENTE
Sí, una caja grande se me cayó en la cabeza.
DOCTOR
¿Cuándo ocurrió?
PACIENTE
Tuvo lugar en la fábrica donde trabajo, a mediodía.
DOCTOR
¿Quién le emplea?
PACIENTE
D & D Fabrics.
DOCTOR
¿Cuál es la dirección de su trabajo?
PACIENTE
Calle Noyes veintitrés doce Este, Evanston.
DOCTOR
¿Se desmayó Vd. después del accidente?
PACIENTE
De repente perdí el conocimiento.
DOCTOR
¿Por cuánto tiempo?
PACIENTE
Un minuto.

DOCTOR
Are you in pain now?

PATIENT
Yes, and I feel dizzy.

DOCTOR
Where is the pain? Show me.

PATIENT
My head and neck hurt me.

DOCTOR
Is it a constant pain or does it come and go?

PATIENT
It is a constant pain.

DOCTOR
Is it dull, sharp, steady, or a feeling of pressure?

PATIENT
It is a sharp pain in my head and a feeling of pressure on my neck.

DOCTOR
Has the pain eased a great deal?

PATIENT
It is better.

DOCTOR
We must have more information. Please give the nurse the information she requests. You will also need some tests before we can make a diagnosis.

DOCTOR
¿Siente Vd. dolor ahora?

PACIENTE
Sí, y me siento mareado.

DOCTOR
¿Dónde le duele? Enséñeme.

PACIENTE
Me duelen la cabeza y el cuello.

DOCTOR
¿Es un dolor constante, o va y vuelve?

PACIENTE
Es un dolor constante.

DOCTOR
¿Es un dolor sordo, agudo, continuo, o una sensación de presión?

PACIENTE
En la cabeza es un dolor agudo, y en el cuello, una sensación de presión.

DOCTOR
¿Ha disminuido mucho el dolor?

PACIENTE
Es mucho mejor.

DOCTOR
Debemos tener más informaciones. Tenga la bondad de contestar a las preguntas de la enfermera. Además, Vd. necesitará algunos análisis antes de que podamos hacer un diagnóstico.

PAST MEDICAL HISTORY[2]

1. Have you ever had:

   Rheumatic fever
   Measles

   German measles

   Scarlet fever

   Mumps

PREVIA HISTORIA MEDICA

1. ¿Ha sufrido Vd. alguna vez de:
   ¿Ha padecido Vd. alguna vez de:

   fiebre reumática
   sarampión
   rubéola
   sarampión alemán
   fiebre de tres días
   fiebre escarlatina
   paperas
   farfoyota (Puerto Rico)
   bolas (slang)

[2] See Chapter 8 for a fuller list of Key Diseases.

Typhoid fever	**fiebre tifoidea**
Polio	**polio**
Chicken pox	{ **varicela** **viruelas locas** (slang)
Cholera	**cólera**
Diphtheria	**difteria**
Small pox	**viruela**
Whooping cough	{ **tos ferina** **tos convulsiva** **coqueluche** (gall.)
Chronic tonsilitis	**amigdalitis crónica**
Chronic laryngitis	**laringitis crónica**
Tuberculosis	**tuberculosis**
Amebic dysentery	**disenteria amebiana**
High blood pressure	{ **hipertensión arterial** **presión arterial alta**
Low blood pressure	{ **hipotensión arterial** **presión arterial baja**
Diabetes	**diabetes**
Goiter	{ **bocio** **buche** (slang)
Anemia	{ **anemia (un número bajo de** **los glóbulos rojos)**
Venereal disease	{ **enfermedades venéreas** **secreta** (slang)
Gonorrhea	{ **gonorrea** **purgación** (slang)
Syphilis	{ **sífilis** **sangre mala** (slang)
Heart disease	{ **enfermedades cardíacas** **enfermedad del corazón** **cardiopatías**
Any kidney ailment	{ **cualquier enfermedad del** **riñón**
Kidney stones	**cálculos en el riñón**
Gall bladder attack	{ **ataque de la vesícula** **derrame de bilis** **ataque vesícular**
Gall stones	**cálculos en la vejiga**
Appendicitis	**apendicitis**
Jaundice	{ **derrame biliar** **ictericia** **piel amarilla** (coll.)
Hepatitis	**hepatitis**

Allergies	**alergias**
Hay fever	**fiebre del heno**
Sinusitis	**sinusitis**
Arthritis	**artritis**
Cystitis	**cistitis (infección de la vejiga)**
Spastic colon	{ **colon espástico** / **colitis mucosa**
Pneumonia	**neumonia**
Emphysema	**enfisema**
Varicose veins	{ **venas varicosas** / **venas inflamadas**
Brain stroke	{ **derrame cerebral** / **embolia cerebral** / **parálisis** / **hemorragia vascular** / **vascular hemorrage**
Blurred vision	**vista borrosa**
Parkinson's disease	{ **la parálisis agitante** / **la enfermedad de Parkinson**
Chorea (any spastic paralysis)	{ **corea** / **el mal** o **la danza** o **el baile de San Vito** o **de San Guido**
Tetanus	{ **tétanos** / **el mal de arco** (slang)
Pancreatitis	**pancreatitis**
Cirrhosis	**cirrosis del hígado**
Epileptic attacks	{ **ataques epilépticos** / **convulsiones**
Ulcers (stomach or duodenal)	**úlceras de estómago** o **duodeno**
Mononucleosis	**mononucleosis infecciosa**
Large boils	**furúnculos grandes** ,
Cancer	**cáncer**
Tropical diseases	**enfermedades tropicales**
Diverticulitis	{ **diverticulitis** / **colitis ulcerosa**
Any previous surgery	{ **cualquier cirugía anterior** / **cirugía previa**

2. Do you have problems with your thyroid gland?

2. ¿**Tiene Vd. problemas con la glándula tiroides?**
¿**Tiene Vd. problema de tiroides?**

3. What immunizations have you had?
Cholera
Yellow fever
Tetanus
Polio

Measles

3. ¿Qué clase de inmunizaciones ha tenido Vd.?
cólera
fiebre amarilla
tétanos
polio(melitis)—(la vacuna oral)
sarampión

4. Were you vaccinated against small pox?

4. ¿Le vacunaron contra la viruela?

5. Did you get an inoculation for typhoid?

5. ¿Le pusieron una inoculación contra el tifus?

6. Were there many people in your town with that disease?

6. ¿Había mucha gente en su pueblo con esa enfermedad?

7. Do you have asthma?

7. ¿Sufre Vd. de asma?
¿Ha padecido Vd. de asma?
¿Sufre Vd. de fatiga? (Coll.)

8. Are you allergic to

Any food
Penicillin
Aspirin
Sulfa
Sleeping pills
Dust or pollen
Animals

Insect bites

8. ¿Tiene Vd. alergias a...?
¿Es Vd. alérgico (alérgica) a...?
¿Padece Vd. de alergias a...?
alguna comida
penicilina
aspirina
sulfas
píldoras para dormir
polvo o polen
animales
⎰ mordeduras de insectos
⎱ picaduras de insectos

9. Do you have any drug reactions?

9. ¿Tiene Vd. alguna sensibilidad a productos químicos?

10. Have you been hospitalized within the last five years?

10. ¿Ha estado Vd. hospitalizado por cualquier razón durante los últimos cinco años?

11. Why?

11. ¿Por qué?

12. When did you come here (to the hospital) for the first time?

12. ¿Cuándo vino Vd. aquí (al hospital) por primera vez?

13. How long had you been in the hospital?

13. ¿Cuánto tiempo hacía que Vd. estaba[3] en el hospital?

14. How long have you been in the hospital?

14. ¿Cuánto tiempo lleva Vd. internado?

[3] See Chapter 9, page 295.

15. When was the last time you saw a doctor?

15. ¿Cuándo fue la última vez que visitó Vd. a un médico?
¿Cuándo fue la última vez que ha visitado a un médico?
¿Cuándo fue la última vez que ha visto a un médico?

16. How long had you been sick?

16. ¿Cuánto tiempo hacía que estaba enfermo (enferma)?[3]
¿Cuánto tiempo lleva Vd. de estar enfermo (enferma)?

17. What was the name of the medicine that the doctor gave you?

17. ¿Cómo se llama la medicina que el médico le recetó?
¿Cuál era el nombre de la medicina que le recetó el médico?

18. Are you taking any medicine, or are you undergoing any medical treatment at present?

18. ¿Toma Vd. alguna medicina o está siguiendo algún tratamiento médico actualmente?

19. How many pills do you have at home?

19. ¿Cuántas píldoras tiene Vd. en casa?

20. Do you travel much abroad?

20. ¿Viaja Vd. mucho al extranjero?

21. How do you travel? By plane, train, boat, or car?

21. ¿Por qué medio viaja Vd.?
¿Por avión, por tren, por barco, en auto?

22. How long do you spend away from the USA?

22. ¿Cuánto tiempo pasa Vd. fuera de los Estados Unidos?

23. Where do you stay?

23. ¿Dónde se queda Vd.?

24. Were you wounded while in the military service?

24. ¿Fue Vd. herido o inhabilitado mientras que estuvo en el servicio militar?

Although the drills that follow are designed to be done actively in class by the instructor and the students, they are arranged so that the student may do them individually outside the class. The student must cover the drill with a card, move the card down the page until the first question or response is visible, make the appropriate answer aloud, and then move the card down until the correct answer appears. This procedure is followed until the end of the drill, when the student may repeat the drill (for additional practice) or go on to the next one.

[3] See Chapter 9, page 295.

Exercise   *Ejercicio*

Ask the following questions using the cues in parenthesis:

¿Ha sufrido Vd. alguna vez de tuberculosis?
  (reumatismo)

¿Ha sufrido Vd. alguna vez de reumatismo?
  (fiebre tifoidea)

¿Ha sufrido Vd. alguna vez de fiebre tifoidea?
  (tos ferina)

¿Ha sufrido Vd. alguna vez de tos ferina?
  (derrame biliar)

¿Ha sufrido Vd. alguna vez de derrame biliar?
  (enfisema)

¿Ha sufrido Vd. alguna vez de enfisema?
  (alergias)

¿Ha sufrido Vd. alguna vez de alergias?
  (enfermedades venéreas)

¿Ha sufrido Vd. alguna vez de enfermedades venéreas?
  (vista borrosa)

¿Ha sufrido Vd. alguna vez de vista borrosa?
  (rubéola)

¿Ha sufrido Vd. alguna vez de rubéola?
  (varicela)

¿Ha sufrido Vd. alguna vez de varicela?

Exercise   *Ejercicio*

Ask the hypothetical patients about immunizations, using the cues in parenthesis:

¿Fue inmunizado Roberto contra la difteria?
  (la viruela)

¿Fue inmunizado Roberto contra la viruela?
  (Roberto y Pablo)

¿Fueron inmunizados Roberto y Pablo contra la viruela?
  (la varicela)

¿Fueron inmunizados Roberto y Pablo contra la varicela?
  (María)

¿Fue inmunizada María contra la varicela?
  (la fiebre escarlatina)

¿Fue inmunizada María contra la fiebre escarlatina?
  (la difteria)

¿Fue inmunizada María contra la difteria?
  (el nene)

¿Fue inmunizado el nene contra la difteria?
  (la cólera)

¿Fue inmunizado el nene contra la cólera?
  (las chicas)

¿Fueron inmunizadas las chicas contra la cólera?
  (el tifus)

¿Fueron inmunizadas las chicas contra el tifus?

REVIEW OF SYSTEMS

General

1. How much do you normally weigh?

2. Do you have chills?

3. Do the chills come every day?

    every other day?
    every three days?

4. Are you hot or cold frequently?

5. Are you nervous?

6. Are you depressed?

Practice

With a friend practice the following dialogue until you have mastered it.

DOCTOR
Good Afternoon, Mr. González. I would like you to answer my questions to the best of your ability.

MR. GONZÁLEZ
Okay, Doctor.

DOCTOR
How much do you normally weigh?

MR. GONZÁLEZ
140 pounds.

DOCTOR
What was your maximum body weight, and when was that?

MR. GONZÁLEZ
A year ago I weighed 175 pounds.

REPASO DE SISTEMAS

General

1. **¿Cuánto pesa Vd. por lo regular?**

2. **¿Tiene Vd. escalofríos?**

3. **¿Siente Vd. los escalofríos todos los días?**
   cada dos días?
   cada tres días?

4. **¿Tiene Vd. calor o frío con frecuencia?**

5. **¿Está Vd. nervioso (nerviosa)?**

6. **¿Está Vd. deprimido (deprimida)?**
   ¿Sufre Vd. de depresiones severas?

Práctica

Con un amigo practique Vd. el diálogo siguiente hasta que lo sepa por memoria.

DOCTOR
Buenas tardes, señor González. Quiero que Vd. conteste a mis preguntas lo mejor posible.

SR. GONZÁLEZ
Muy bien, doctor.

DOCTOR
Por lo regular, ¿cuánto pesa Vd.?

SR. GONZÁLEZ
Ciento cuarenta libras.

DOCTOR
¿Cuál fue su peso máximo, y cuándo pesaba eso?

SR. GONZÁLEZ
Hace un año pesé ciento setenta y cinco libras.

DOCTOR
Then you have lost a lot of weight?

MR. GONZÁLEZ
Yes, I have lost thirty-five pounds.

DOCTOR
What was your minimum body weight, and when?

MR. GONZÁLEZ
When I was in the army I weighed only 130 pounds.

DOCTOR
When were you in the army?

MR GONZÁLEZ
I was in the army from 1972–1974. I was in the DMZ for a year.

DOCTOR
Were you ever ill while in the army?

MR. GONZÁLEZ
Never.

DOCTOR
Do you sweat much?

MR. GONZÁLEZ
No, I sweat very little.

DOCTOR
Do you have chills?

MR. GONZÁLEZ
Yes, I often have the chills.

DOCTOR
Do the chills come every day?

MR. GONZÁLEZ
I have the chills every other day, usually in the evening.

DOCTOR
Are you nervous?

MR. GONZÁLEZ
Yes, I am very nervous, and I eat little.

DOCTOR
Very well, let's find out more about the problem.

DOCTOR
Entonces, ¿ha perdido mucho peso últimamente?

SR. GONZÁLEZ
Sí, he perdido treinta y cinco libras.

DOCTOR
¿Cuál fue su peso mínimo, y cuándo?

SR. GONZÁLEZ
Cuando estaba en el ejército pesaba solamente ciento treinta libras.

DOCTOR
¿Cuándo estaba en el ejército?

SR. GONZÁLEZ
Estuve en el ejército desde mil novecientos setenta y dos hasta setenta y cuatro. Estuve en la zona desmilitarizada en Vietnam por un año.

DOCTOR
¿Sufrió Vd. enfermedades mientras estaba en el ejército?

SR. GONZÁLEZ
Nunca.

DOCTOR
¿Suda Vd. mucho?

SR. GONZÁLEZ
No, sudo muy poco.

DOCTOR
¿Tiene Vd. escalofríos?

SR. GONZÁLEZ
Sí, a menudo tengo escalofríos.

DOCTOR
¿Siente Vd. los escalofríos todos los días?

SR. GONZÁLEZ
Siento los escalofríos cada dos días, generalmente por la noche.

DOCTOR
¿Está Vd. nervioso?

SR. GONZÁLEZ
Sí, estoy muy nervioso, y como poco.

DOCTOR
Muy bien. Vamos a averiguar cuál es el verdadero carácter de su problema.

Skin, Hair

7. Do you have any bleeding problems if you cut yourself?

8. How long does it last?
9. Does this happen frequently?
10. Do you have any rash on your *face*?
11. How long have you had this rash?
12. Does it irritate much?
13. Did you take anything for it?

14. Do you have chronic skin diseases, like psoriasis or seborrhea?

15. Do you have any black or dark red moles that have changed in size?
16. Do you have any moles that bleed?
17. Do you break out in hives?

18. Are you losing your hair?
19. Does your scalp itch?

Head

20. Do you get headaches?

21. Do you get migraines?
22. Do you ever feel dizzy?

La piel, el pelo

7. **¿Tiene Vd. problemas de**
{ **echar sangre**
sangrar
si se corta?

8. **¿Cuánto tiempo le dura?**
9. **¿Ocurre con frecuencia?**
10. **¿Tiene Vd. alguna erupción en *la cara*?**
11. **¿Desde cuándo tiene Vd. esta erupción?**
12. **¿Le irrita mucho?**
13. **¿Ha tomado Vd. algo para curarlo?**

14. **¿Sufre Vd. de enfermedades crónicas de la piel, como**
{ **psoriasis**
la sarna (slang) } **o seborrea?**

15. **¿Tiene Vd. lunares negros o marrones que han sufrido cambios?**
16. **¿Tiene Vd. lunares que sangran?**
17. **¿Brota Vd. urticarias severas en la piel?**

18. **¿Está Vd. perdiendo el pelo?**
19. **¿Le pica la cabeza?**

La cabeza

20. **¿Tiene Vd. dolores de cabeza?**
¿Tiene Vd. jaquecas?
¿Le duele la cabeza?
¿Le dan dolores de cabeza?

21. **¿Tiene Vd. migrañas?**
22. **¿Tiene Vd. vértigo alguna vez?**
¿Suele Vd. tener mareos?
(coll.)

23. How long do you feel dizzy?

23. **¿Cuánto tiempo le duran los mareos?**

Review

Practice the following dialogue:

DOCTOR
Do you have any bleeding problems, Mr. Gómez?

MR. GÓMEZ
No, Doctor, I don't have any bleeding problems if I cut myself.

DOCTOR
How long have you had this rash on your face?

MR. GÓMEZ
I have had it for a month.

DOCTOR
Does it irritate much?

MR. GÓMEZ
Yes, it itches me, but I don't scratch.

DOCTOR
Did you take anything for it?

MR. GÓMEZ
Yes, I have been using a gray ointment.

DOCTOR
Discontinue using the ointment for now.

MR. GÓMEZ
What should I use?

DOCTOR
After I do some more tests, I will give you a prescription. Do you get headaches?

MR. GÓMEZ
I do; I have an awfully bad headache now.

DOCTOR
How long do the headaches generally last?

MR. GÓMEZ
All day. The pain is especially bad over my left eye.

DOCTOR
Do you ever feel nauseated while you have a headache?

Repaso

Practique Vd. el diálogo siguiente.

DOCTOR
¿Tiene Vd. problemas de sangrar, señor Gómez?

SR. GÓMEZ
No, doctor, no tengo problemas de sangrar si me corto.

DOCTOR
¿Desde cuándo tiene Vd. esta erupción en la cara?

SR. GÓMEZ
La tengo desde hace un mes.

DOCTOR
¿Le irrita mucho?

SR. GÓMEZ
Sí, me irrita, pero no me rasco.

DOCTOR
¿Ha tomado Vd. algo para curarla?

SR. GÓMEZ
Sí, he usado una pomada gris.

DOCTOR
Discontinúe Vd. el uso de la pomada para ahora.

SR. GÓMEZ
¿Qué debo usar?

DOCTOR
Después de hacerle algunas pruebas más, le daré una receta. ¿Tiene Vd. dolores de cabeza?

SR. GÓMEZ
Los tengo; me duele muchísimo la cabeza ahora.

DOCTOR
Generalmente, ¿cuánto tiempo le duran los dolores de cabeza?

SR. GÓMEZ
Por lo común, todo el día. El dolor es aún más fuerte encima del ojo izquierdo.

DOCTOR
Mientras que tiene dolor de cabeza, ¿tiene náusea alguna vez?

MR. GÓMEZ
Yes, Doctor, and sometimes I vomit.

DOCTOR
What do you do for the headache?

MR. GÓMEZ
I usually take two aspirins every three hours and stay in bed until I feel better.

DOCTOR
Very well, Mr. Gómez.

SR. GÓMEZ
Sí, doctor, y a veces vomito.

DOCTOR
¿Qué hace para su jaqueca?

SR. GÓMEZ
Por lo regular tomo dos aspirinas cada tres horas y guardo cama hasta que me sienta mejor.

DOCTOR
Muy bien, señor Gómez.

Eyes

24. Do you wear glasses?

25. Do you wear contact lenses?

26. Do you sometimes see things double?

27. Do you have blurred vision?

28. Do you see things through a mist?

29. Do your eyes burn?

30. Do your eyes water much?

31. Your eyes seem inflamed (red).

32. Do you have eyestrain?

33. Do you have eyeaches?

34. Do you have a discharge from your eyes?

35. Does your eyeball feel as if it were swollen?

36. How long have your eyelids been swollen?

37. When did your eyes begin to look yellow?

Los ojos

24. **¿Usa Vd. anteojos?** (general term)
    ¿Usa Vd. lentes? (Mex)
    ¿Usa Vd. espejuelos? (Cuba)

25. **¿Usa Vd. lentes de contacto?**

26. **¿Ve Vd. las cosas doble algunas veces?**

27. **¿Ve Vd. borroso?**

28. **¿Ve Vd. nubladas las cosas como a través de una neblina?**

29. **¿Le arden los ojos?**

30. **¿Le lagrimean mucho los ojos?**

31. **Sus ojos parecen inflamados (rojos).**

32. **¿Sufre Vd. de cansancio de ojos?**

33. **¿Sufre Vd. de dolores de ojos?**

34. **¿Le supuran los ojos?**

35. **¿Le siente el ojo hinchado?**

36. **¿Desde cuándo tiene Vd. los párpados hinchados?**

37. **¿Cuándo empezaban sus ojos a tener este color amarillo?**

38. Did you ever have trouble with your vision?

38. ¿Ha tenido alguna vez dificultades con su $\begin{cases} \text{vision?} \\ \text{vista?} \end{cases}$

Review

Practice the following dialogue.

DR. JONES
Hello, Mr. García. Please be seated.

MR. GARCÍA
Thank you, Doctor.

DR. JONES
What seems to be your trouble?

MR. GARCÍA
My eyes hurt me.

DR. JONES
When were your eyes examined last?

MR. GARCÍA
About three years ago.

DR. JONES
Did you ever have trouble with your vision?

MR. GARCÍA
Yes, I had astigmatism in the left eye and they gave me a prescription for glasses.

DR. JONES
Do you still wear glasses now?

MR. GARCÍA
No, I don't wear them because I lost my glasses last year and I didn't have enough money to buy new ones.

DR. JONES
Do you feel pain in your right eye?

MR. GARCÍA
No, but my left eye hurts me, and I often have bad headaches.

DR. JONES
Oh, really? Do you ever have eyeaches too?

Repaso

Pratique Vd. el diálogo siguiente.

DR. JONES
Buenas tardes, señor García. Siéntese Vd. por favor.

SR. GARCÍA
Gracias, doctor.

DR. JONES
Vamos a ver, ¿cuál parece ser la molestia?

SR. GARCÍA
Me duelen los ojos.

DR. JONES
¿Cuánto tiempo hace que se examinó la vista?

SR. GARCÍA
Hace tres años, más o menos.

DR JONES
¿Ha tenido alguna vez dificultades con su vista?

SR. GARCÍA
Sí, tenía astigmatismo en el ojo izquierdo y me dieron una prescripción para anteojos.

DR. JONES
¿Todavía lleva los anteojos?

SR. GARCÍA
No, no los llevo porque se me perdieron los anteojos el año pasado y no tuve bastante dinero para comprar otros nuevos.

DR. JONES
¿Siente dolor en el ojo derecho?

SR. GARCÍA
No, pero me duele el izquierdo, y muchas veces tengo horribles dolores de cabeza.

DR. JONES
¿De veras? ¿Sufre de dolores de ojos también?

MR. GARCÍA

My left eye aches me only when I read for a long time, and only at night.

DR. JONES

Do you sometimes see things double?

MR. GARCÍA

No. When I have eyeaches I see things as though through a mist.

DR. JONES

Do your eyes burn?

MR. GARCÍA

No.

DR. JONES

Do your eyes water much?

MR. GARCÍA

Yes, very often my eyes water a lot.

DR. JONES

Your left eye seems inflamed now. Did anything get into your eye?

MR. GARCÍA

I don't think so.

DR. JONES

Does your eyeball feel as if it were swollen?

MR. GARCÍA

I don't understand. My left eye hurts me.

DR. JONES

Very well. Let me see your eyes, and I will examine them.

SR. GARCÍA

Me duele el ojo izquierdo solamente cuando leo por mucho tiempo y entonces solamente por la noche.

DR. JONES

¿Ve Vd. las cosas doble algunas veces?

SR. GARCÍA

No. Cuando sufro de dolores de ojos veo nubladas las cosas como a través de una neblina.

DR. JONES

¿Le arden los ojos?

SR. GARCÍA

No.

DR. JONES

¿Le lagrimean mucho los ojos?

SR. GARCÍA

Sí, muy a menudo me lagrimean mucho los ojos.

DR. JONES

El ojo izquierdo parece inflamado ahora. ¿Le entró algo en el ojo?

SR. GARCÍA

Creo que no.

DR. JONES

¿Le siente el ojo hinchado?

SR. GARCÍA

No comprendo. El ojo izquierdo me duele.

DR. JONES

Muy bien. Déjeme ver sus ojos, y los examinaré.

Ears

39. Do you ever have middle or inner ear infections?

40. Are you (tone-deaf) hard of hearing, or deaf?

41. Do you wear a hearing aid?

42. Do you have any hearing problems?

Los oídos

39. **¿Tiene Vd. alguna vez infecciones del oído medio o interno?**

40. **¿Es Vd. duro de oído, o sordo (sorda)?**

41. **¿Lleva Vd. un aparato auditivo?**

42. **¿Tiene Vd. problemas de oído?**
    ¿Padece Vd. de defectos de la audición?

43. Do your ears run?

43. **¿Le supuran los oídos?**
¿Le sale material de los oídos?

44. Do you have a discharge from your left (right) ear?

44. **¿Le supura el oído izquierdo (derecho)?**

45. Do you usually get earaches?

45. **¿Le duelen con frecuencia los oídos?**

46. Are your ears clogged?

46. **¿Siente Vd. los oídos**
⎰taponados?
⎱tapados? (Mex.)

47. Do your ears ring?

47. **¿Siente Vd. un tintineo en los oídos?**
¿Le rumban a Vd. los oídos?
¿Tiene Vd. como campanillas en los oídos?

48. Do you have ringing in your right (left) ear?

48. **¿Le rumba el oído derecho (izquierdo)?**

49. Do you ever have dizzy spells?

49. **¿Tiene Vd. vértigo alguna vez?**
¿Suele Vd. tener mareos? (coll.)
¿Tiene Vd. episodios de mareos?

50. Do you ever feel dizzy on getting up quickly from bed?

50. **¿Tiene Vd. mareos al levantarse de la cama rápido?**

Nose and sinuses

La nariz y los sienes

51. Do you have a stuffed nose?

51. **¿Tiene Vd. la nariz obstruida?**

52. Does your nose feel clogged?

52. **¿Tiene Vd. la nariz** ⎰**tapada?** (Mex) **tupida?** **taponada?**

53. Do you have a cold?

53. **¿Tiene Vd. un resfriado?**
¿Tiene Vd. un catarro? (head cold)
¿Está Vd. resfriado(-a)?
¿Está Vd. catarrado(-a)?

54. Did you catch cold?[4]

54. **¿Se ha resfriado Vd.?**
¿Se acatarró Vd.?

---

[4] When a person sneezes, Spanish-speaking people often say "¡Jesus!" The phrase originated in the Middle Ages as a supplication for divine help in time of trouble.

55. How many colds did you have last year?

55. ¿Cuántos { resfríos / resfriados / catarros } ha tenido Vd. el año pasado?

56. Do you have nose bleeds?

56. ¿Le sangra la nariz a veces? ¿Presenta Vd. sangrado nasal?

57. Do you have a running nose?

57. ¿Le fluye a Vd. la nariz? ¿Moquea Vd.? (slang)

58. Do you have problems smelling?

58. ¿Tiene Vd. problemas olfatorios?

Mouth and throat

La boca y la garganta

59. Are you frequently hoarse?

59. ¿Tiene Vd. ronquera a menudo? ¿Está Vd. ronco (ronca) con frecuencia?

60. Does your tongue feel swollen, thick, or rough?

60. ¿Le siente la lengua hinchada, gruesa, o dura?

61. Does your tongue feel furry?

61. ¿Es su lengua con costra? ¿Se forman incrustaciones en su lengua?

62. How long has your tongue been that color?

62. ¿Desde cuándo tiene la lengua de ese color?

63. Does your tongue burn?

63. ¿Le arde la lengua?

64. Can you taste anything?

64. ¿Puede Vd. saborear algo?

65. Do you have a sour taste in your mouth?

65. ¿Siente Vd. un sabor agrio de boca? ¿Tiene Vd. una acidez en la boca?

66. Do you have sore throats?

66. ¿Suele Vd. tener la garganta dolorida? ¿Le duele la garganta con frecuencia?

67. Does your throat hurt when you swallow?

67. ¿Le duele la garganta cuando Vd. traga? ¿Tiene Vd. dolores o dificultades al tragar?

68. Does your tongue feel sore?

68. ¿Tiene Vd. la lengua dolorida?

69. Do your gums bleed frequently?

69. ¿Le sangran las encías frecuentemente?

70. Do you have infections of the gum?

70. ¿Tiene Vd. infecciones de las encías?

71. Do you have a toothache?

71. ¿Tiene Vd. dolor de muelas?

Neck

El cuello

72. Can you swallow?

72. ¿Puede Vd. tragar?

Breasts

Los pechos

73. Do you have a discharge from your nipples?

73. ¿Le supuran los pezones?

74. What color is the discharge from your nipples?

74. ¿De qué color es la material que sale de los pezones?

75. Have you noticed any lumps in your breasts?

75. ¿Se ha fijado Vd. en
{ algún tumor
alguna protuberancia }
de los pechos?
¿Ha notado { alguna bolita
algún tumorcito }
en la mama? (coll.)

76. Your breasts are swollen. Do they hurt when you have your period?

76. Vd. tiene los pechos hinchados. ¿Le duelen durante la regla?

77. Do your breasts begin to swell before your periods?

77. ¿Empiezan a hincharse los pechos antes de la regla?

78. Have your nursed your child?

78. ¿Ha dado de mamar a su criatura?

79. Did you nurse your child?

79. ¿Amamantó a su criatura?

80. How long have you been nursing?

80. ¿Desde cuánto tiempo da Vd. el pecho?

81. How long did you nurse?

81. ¿Desde cuánto tiempo dió Vd. el pecho?

Respiratory

Respiratorio

82. Can you breathe well?

82. ¿Puede Vd. respirar bien?

83. Do you have any difficulty in breathing?

83. ¿Tiene Vd. alguna dificultad para respirar?

84. How long can you hold your breath?

84. ¿Durante cuánto tiempo puede Vd. retener la respiración?

85.	Try it.	85.	**Pruébalo.**	
86.	Are you short of breath?	86.	**¿Le falta la respiración?**	
87.	Do you perspire a lot, especially at night?	87.	**¿Suda Vd. mucho, sobre todo por la noche?**	
88.	Do you cough a lot?	88.	**¿Tiene Vd. mucha tos?** **¿Tose Vd. mucho?**	
89.	How long have you been coughing?	89.	**¿Desde cuándo tiene Vd. tos?** **¿Desde cuándo tose Vd.?**	
90.	Does it hurt when you cough?	90.	**¿Le duele { cuando tose? / al toser?**	
91.	Are you coughing from an allergy?	91.	**¿Tose Vd. por alguna alergia?**	
92.	Do you cough up phlegm?	92.	**Al toser, ¿arroja Vd. flemas?**	
93.	What color is the phlegm? clear gray or white yellow or green red maroon or black	93.	**¿De qué color son las flemas? incolora gris o blanca amarilla o verde roja marrón o negra**	
94.	Do you cough up blood?	94.	**Al toser, ¿arroja Vd. sangre?**	
95.	Do you spit blood?	95.	**¿Escupe Vd. sangre?**	
96.	Do you wheeze?	96.	**¿Le silba a Vd. el pecho?** **¿Le sale un silbido al respirar?**	
97.	When was your last chest x-ray?	97.	**¿Cuándo fue su última radiografía del pecho (de los pulmones)?**	
98.	What were the results?	98.	**¿Cuáles fueron los resultados?**	

Review

Practice the following dialogue.

DR. SMITH
When did your illness begin, Mrs. Navas?

MRS. NAVAS
It began Wednesday evening.

DR. SMITH
Did you have any fever?

MRS. NAVAS
Yes, I had 102.

Repaso

Practique Vd. el diálogo siguiente.

DR. SMITH
¿Cuándo empezó su enfermedad, señora Navas?

SRA. NAVAS.
Empezó el miércoles por la noche.

DR. SMITH
¿Tuvo Vd. fiebre?

SRA. NAVAS
Sí, ciento dos grados Fahrenheit.

DR. SMITH
How long did the fever last?

MRS. NAVAS
For almost two days.

DR. SMITH
Did you vomit?

MRS. NAVAS
Yes, I vomited a lot, and I also coughed quite a bit.

DR. SMITH
How long have you been coughing?

MRS. NAVAS
For about a day.

DR. SMITH
Does it hurt when you cough?

MRS NAVAS
Yes, my chest hurts, and so does my throat.

DR. SMITH
Do you cough up phlegm?

MRS. NAVAS
Sometimes.

DR. SMITH
What color is the phlegm?

MRS. NAVAS
I am not sure. I think the phlegm is yellow.

DR. SMITH
Does anything else hurt you?

MRS. NAVAS
Right now my throat is sore.

DR. SMITH
Are you hoarse frequently?

MRS. NAVAS
Usually not.

DR. SMITH
Does your throat hurt when you swallow?

MRS. NAVAS
Yes, and it is difficult for me to swallow.

DR. SMITH
I am going to give you a prescription for two medicines. One is for lozenges. Take one every four hours. The other is for a cough medicine. Take two teaspoonsful after every meal and at bedtime. Call me tomorrow.

DR. SMITH
¿Por cuánto tiempo tuvo fiebre?

SRA. NAVAS
Por casi dos días.

DR. SMITH
¿Vomitó Vd.?

SRA. NAVAS
Sí, vomité mucho y también tosía bastante.

DR. SMITH
¿Desde cuándo tose Vd.?

SRA. NAVAS
Hace como un día.

DR. SMITH
¿Le duele al toser?

SRA. NAVAS
Sí, me duele el pecho, y la garganta también.

DR. SMITH
Al toser, ¿arroja Vd. flemas?

SRA. NAVAS
A veces.

DR. SMITH
¿De qué color son las flemas?

SRA NAVAS
No estoy segura. Creo que las flemas son amarillas.

DR. SMITH
¿Le duele algo más?

SRA. NAVAS
Ahorita tengo la garganta dolorida.

DR. SMITH
¿Está Vd. ronca con frecuencia?

SRA. NAVAS
Generalmente no.

DR. SMITH
¿Le duele la garganta al tragar?

SRA. NAVAS
Sí, y no puedo tragar muy bien.

DR. SMITH
Voy a darle unas recetas para dos medicinas. Una es para pastillas. Tome una cada cuatro horas. La otra es para un jarabe para la tos. Tome dos cucharaditas después de cada comida y al acostarse. Llámeme mañana.

Cardiovascular

99. Do you feel (very) weak?

100. Do you have pains in your chest?

101. In what part of the chest?

102. In the middle, more towards the left side, more towards the right side?

103. Under the breastbone?

104. Does the pain extend to the arms, to the shoulders, to the neck?

105. Does the pain extend to the back or neck?

106. How long does the pain last?

107. Does your heart beat rapidly or irregularly?

108. Can you remember ever having had irregular heart beats, or very rapid heart beats?

109. When?

110. Do you have difficulty breathing through your nose when you walk?

111. Have you noticed any shortness of breath lately?

112. Do you get short of breath when you climb stairs? When you walk?

113. How many flights of stairs can you climb without being short of breath?

Cardiovascular

99. ¿Se siente (muy) débil?

100. ¿Tiene Vd. dolores en el pecho?
¿Ha estado teniendo dolores en el pecho?

101. ¿En qué parte del pecho?

102. ¿En el medio, más hacia el lado izquierdo, más hacia el lado derecho?

103. ¿Debajo del esternón?

104. ¿Se extiende el dolor algunas veces hacia los brazos, hacia los hombros, o hacia el cuello?

105. ¿Se extiende el dolor hacia la espalda o el cuello?

106. ¿Cuánto tiempo dura el dolor?

107. ¿Le late el corazón rápidamente o con irregularidad?

108. ¿Puede Vd. recordar haber tenido alguna vez latidos irregulares o palpitaciones muy rápidas del corazón?

109. ¿Cuándo?

110. ¿Tiene Vd. dificultad en respirar por la nariz al caminar?

111. ¿Ha notado si ha tenido falta de aliento últimamente?

112. ¿Le falta el aliento cuando sube Vd. por las escaleras? ¿Cuando camina?

113. ¿Cuántos pisos puede Vd. subir sin que le falte el aliento?
¿Cuántas escaleras puede Vd. subir sin tener falta de aliento?

114. Did you ever have shortness of breath at night?

115. Do you awaken in the night because of shortness of breath?

116. How many pillows do you use to sleep on?

117. Can you lay flat on the bed without pillows and not be short of breath?

118. Is any part of your body swollen?

119. How long has it been swollen like this?

120. How many days?

121. How many weeks?

122. Are your ankles swollen in the morning when you awaken?

123. Do you have a heart murmur or hypertension?

124. When did you last have an electrocardiogram?

125. What were the results?

114. ¿Ha tenido falta de aliento por la noche?

115. ¿Se despierta Vd. por la noche por falta de respiración?

116. ¿Cuántas almohadas usa Vd. para dormir?

117. ¿Puede Vd. acostarse sobre la cama sin almohadas, y no tener falta de aliento?

118. ¿Tiene Vd. alguna parte del cuerpo hinchada?

119. ¿Desde cuándo está hinchado así?
¿Cuánto tiempo está hinchado así?

120. ¿Cuántos días?

121. ¿Cuántas semanas?

122. ¿Tiene Vd. los tobillos hinchados por la mañana al despertarse?

123. ¿Tiene Vd. un murmullo de corazón o padece Vd. de la hipertensión?

124. ¿Cuándo fue la última vez que le hicieron un electrocardiograma?

125. ¿Cuáles fueron los resultados?

Gastrointestinal

126. Do you eat between meals?

127. Do you drink a lot of liquids?

128. Do you drink milk?

129. How much?

130. Do you drink alcoholic beverages?

131. How many do you drink?

Gastrointestinal

126. ¿Come Vd. algo entre comidas?

127. ¿Toma Vd. muchos líquidos?

128. ¿Bebe Vd. leche?

129. ¿Cuánta?

130. ¿Toma Vd. algunas bebidas alcohólicas?

131. ¿Cuánto bebe Vd.?

132.	What type of alcoholic beverage do you drink?		132.	**¿Qué tipo (clase) de bebida alcohólica toma Vd.?**
133.	How much coffee or tea do you drink?		133.	**¿Cuántas tazas de café o de té bebe Vd.?**
134.	What type of coffee do you drink, regular or decaffeinated?		134.	**¿Qué clase de café toma Vd., regular o descafeinado?**
135.	How much water do you drink daily?		135.	**¿Cuántos vasos de agua bebe Vd. diariamente?**
136.	How much pop do you drink?		136.	**¿Cuántas bebidas gaseosas toma Vd. diariamente, como una Coca-Cola?**
137.	What foods disagree with you?		137.	**¿Qué alimentos le caen mal?**
138.	Do you get gas pains?		138.	**¿Suele Vd. tener aire (flato)?**
139.	Do you belch (burp) a lot?		139.	**¿Eructa Vd. mucho?**
140.	Do you get heartburn?		140.	**¿Suele tener ardor de estómago?** **¿Tiene Vd. molestias en la parte superior del abdomen?**
141.	Do you have an upset stomach after eating fried or fatty foods?		141.	**¿Se siente descompuesto (descompuesta) del estómago después de comidas fritas o con grasa?**
142.	What exactly happens?		142.	**¿Qué le pasa exactamente?**
143.	Do you have frequent stomach aches (bellyaches)?		143.	**¿Suele tener dolor de estómago (de vientre) a menudo?** **¿Tiene Vd. dolor de estómago (de vientre) con frecuencia?**
144.	Do you feel nauseated?		144.	**¿Tiene Vd. ganas de vomitar?**
145.	Are you nauseated?		145.	**¿Tiene náusea(s)?**
146.	Are you going to vomit?		146.	**¿Va a vomitar?**
147.	Did you vomit?		147.	**¿Vomitó?**

Review

Practice the following dialogue.

DR. BURNS
    What is your problem, Miss Mendoza?

Repaso

Practique el diálogo siguiente.

DR. BURNS
    ¿Qué le sucede a Vd., señorita Mendoza?

MISS MENDOZA
My stomach bothers me frequently.

DR. BURNS
How much do you weigh?

MISS MENDOZA
125 pounds.

DR. BURNS
What is your occupation?

MISS MENDOZA
I am a beautician.

DR. BURNS
Do you like working in a beauty shop?

MISS MENDOZA
Yes, but the hours are very long.

DR. BURNS
Generally what hours do you work?

MISS MENDOZA
I work on Sundays from 10 until 3 in the afternoon, and on Tuesdays, Wednesdays and Thursdays I work from 9 until 6. On Fridays and Saturdays I work from 9 until 10 in the evenings.

DR. BURNS
How many meals do you normally eat?

MISS MENDOZA
Well, I always eat a good breakfast. Orange juice, two eggs, ham, some toast and coffee.

DR. BURNS
Do you eat lunch?

MISS MENDOZA
Usually I just drink black coffee all day long.

DR. BURNS
What about supper?

MISS MENDOZA
I am generally too tired to cook, so I have a hamburger and french fries, and a coke, or else fried chicken and french fries.

DR. BURNS
Do you have an upset stomach after eating such a supper?

SRTA. MENDOZA
Me molesta mucho el estómago con frecuencia.

DR. BURNS
¿Cuánto pesa Vd.?

SRTA. MENDOZA
Ciento veinticinco libras.

DR. BURNS
¿Cuál es su ocupación?

SRTA. MENDOZA
Soy peluquera.

DR. BURNS
¿Le gusta trabajar en un salón de belleza?

SRTA. MENDOZA
Sí, pero las horas son larguísimas.

DR. BURNS
Por lo común, ¿cuáles son las horas que trabaja?

SRTA. MENDOZA
Los domingos trabajo desde las diez hasta las tres de la tarde, y los martes, miércoles y jueves, trabajo desde las nueve hasta las seis. Los viernes y los sábados trabajo desde las nueve de la mañana hasta las diez de la noche.

DR. BURNS
¿Cuántas comidas toma Vd. al día?

SRTA. MENDOZA
Pues, siempre desayuno bien. Jugo de naranja, dos huevos, jamón, unas tostadas y café.

DR. BURNS
¿Almuerza Vd.?

SRTA. MENDOZA
Generalmente solamente bebo café puro todo el día.

DR. BURNS
¿Y para la cena?

SRTA. MENDOZA
Con frecuencia estoy tan cansada que no tengo ganas de cocinar. Así compro una hamburguesa y papas fritas y una Coca, o pollo frito con papas fritas.

DR. BURNS
¿Se siente descompuesta del estómago después de comer tal cena?

MISS MENDOZA
Frequently my stomach hurts me after the chicken.

DR. BURNS
What exactly happens.

MISS MENDOZA
I have sharp pains here.

DR. BURNS
Do you drink milk?

MISS MENDOZA
I drink coffee because I don't like milk.

DR. BURNS
What type of coffee do you drink, regular or decaffeinated?

MISS MENDOZA
I drink regular.

DR. BURNS
How many cups do you drink daily?

MISS MENDOZA
I drink between fifteen and twenty.

DR. BURNS
How much water do you drink daily?

MISS MENDOZA
I almost never drink water.

DR BURNS
Do you drink much pop?

MISS MENDOZA
Sometimes while I am working I drink two or three cans of pop.

DR. BURNS
Do you burp a lot?

MISS MENDOZA
Only after drinking the pop.

DR. BURNS
Do you get heartburn often?

MISS MENDOZA
Yes, I usually have heartburn after drinking too much coffee, or late in the evening after supper.

DR. BURNS
You must eat more regularly—three meals a day, and you must drink more water and less coffee. Here is a list of foods which you should eat daily.

SRTA. MENDOZA
Después del pollo muchas veces me duele el estómago.

DR. BURNS
¿Qué le pasa exactamente?

SRTA. MENDOZA
Sufro de dolores agudos aquí.

DR. BURNS
¿Bebe Vd. leche?

SRTA. MENDOZA
Tomo café porque no me gusta leche.

DR. BURNS
¿Qué clase de café toma Vd., regular o descafeinado?

SRTA. MENDOZA
Tomo regular.

DR. BURNS
¿Cuántas tazas de café bebe Vd. al día?

SRTA. MENDOZA
Tomo entre quince y veinte.

DR. BURNS
¿Cuántos vasos de agua bebe Vd. diariamente?

SRTA. MENDOZA
Casi nunca bebo agua.

DR. BURNS
¿Toma Vd. muchas bebidas gaseosas?

SRTA. MENDOZA
A veces mientras trabajo bebo dos o tres botes de soda.

DR. BURNS
¿Eructa Vd. mucho?

SRTA. MENDOZA
Solamente después de beber soda.

DR. BURNS
¿Suele tener ardor de estómago a menudo?

SRTA. MENDOZA
Sí, por lo regular suelo tener ardor de estómago después de beber demasiado café o muy tarde por la noche después de la cena.

DR. BURNS
Vd. debe comer con más regularidad—tres comidas al día y debe beber más agua y menos café. Aquí tiene una lista de las comidas que debe tomar diariamente.

148. Are you vomiting blood?

149. Do you keep vomiting?

150. Do you need a pan?

151. How are your stools?

152. Do you move your bowels regularly?

153. Did you move your bowels yet?

154. Do you have diarrhea?

155. Is it diarrhea with mucus?

156. Have you ever had typhoid fever?

157. Are you constipated?

158. Do you have blood in your stools?

159. Have you noticed the color of your stools?

160. Is your stool dark black or light gray?

161. Do you often take laxatives?

162. Have you ever had hemorrhages?

163. Do you have hemorrhoids?

164. Do you have bleeding hemorrhoids?

165. Do you have rectal bleeding?

148. **¿Vomita Vd. sangre?**
¿Está vomitando sangre?

149. **¿Sigue Vd. vomitando?**

150. **¿Necesita el bacín?**

151. **¿Cómo son sus evacuaciones?**

152. **¿Evacua Vd. con regularidad?**
¿Va Vd. al inodoro con regularidad?
¿Obra Vd. con regularidad?
(Mex.)

153. **¿Ya evacuó Vd.?**
¿Obró ya? (Mex.)
¿Hizo caca ya? (slang)

154. **¿Tiene Vd. diarrea?**
¿Tiene el chorrillo? (slang)
¿Tiene la cursera? (slang)
¿Están sus intestinos corrientes? (Mex.)

155. **¿Es diarrea con moco?**

156. **¿Ha tenido alguna vez la fiebre tifoidea?**

157. **¿Está Vd. estreñido (estreñida)?**

158. **¿Tiene sangre en las deposiciones intestinales?**

159. **¿Se ha fijado Vd. en el color de sus evacuaciones?**

160. **¿Son sus evacuaciones negras o grises claras?**

161. **¿Suele Vd. tomar laxantes?**

162. **¿Ha tenido Vd. hemorragias?**

163. **¿Padece Vd. de hemorroides?**
¿Sufre Vd. de almorranas?

164. **¿Tiene Vd. hemorroides sangrantes?**

165. **¿Le sale sangre por el ano?**
¿Echa sangre del recto?

166.	Have you ever had a (an inguinal) hernia?	166.	**¿Ha tenido alguna vez una hernia (una quebradura) inguinal (en la ingle)?**
167.	Have you ever had a barium x-ray where you swallowed barium or where you had a barium enema?	167.	**¿Le han hecho alguna vez una prueba de bario donde Vd. tragó el bario o donde le hicieron una lavativa de bario?**
168.	Have you ever had a gastrointestinal x-ray?	168.	**¿Le han hecho una radiografía gastrointestinal?**
169.	Have you ever had a gallbladder x-ray?	169.	**¿Le han hecho alguna vez radiografía de la vesícula biliar?**
170.	What were the results?	170.	**¿Cuáles fueron los resultados?**
171.	Have you ever been told you have gallstones?	171.	**¿Le han dicho a Vd. alguna vez que tiene cálculos en la vesícula biliar?**

Genitourinary

Génitourinario

172.	Can you urinate?	172.	**¿Puede Vd. orinar?**
173.	When you urinate do you notice a delay in beginning?	173.	**Al orinar, ¿ha notado Vd. una demora en comenzar a orinar?**
174.	Are you unable to control your urine?	174.	**¿Tiene Vd. pérdidas involuntarias de orina?**
175.	How long has it been since you have urinated?	175.	**¿Desde cuándo no orina Vd.?**
176.	What color is your urine?	176.	**¿De qué color es la orina?**
177.	How frequently do you urinate?	177.	**¿Con qué frecuencia orina Vd.?**
178.	How much do you urinate?	178.	**¿Cuánto orina Vd?**
179.	When you urinate do you pass a lot or a little urine?	179.	**Al orinar, ¿pasa mucha o poca orina?**
180.	Do you awaken in the night to urinate?	180.	**¿Se despierta Vd. por la noche para orinar?** **¿Se levanta Vd. de la cama para orinar por la noche?**
181.	How often?	181.	**¿Cuántas veces?**
182.	Did you urinate?	182.	**¿Orinó Vd.?** **¿Hizo pipi?** (slang)

183.	Does it hurt when you urinate?		183.	**¿Le duele cuando orina Vd.?**
184.	Is there a burning sensation when you urinate?		184.	**¿Hay un ardor (quemazón) al orinar?**
185.	Do your ankles swell when you don't urinate?		185.	**¿Hinchan los tobillos cuando no orina Vd.?**
186.	Do you have pus in your urine?		186.	**¿Orina Vd. con pus?** **¿Tiene Vd. pus en la orina?**
187.	Do you have blood in your urine?		187.	**¿Tiene Vd. sangre en la orina?**
188.	Does your urine look bloody?		188.	**¿Le parece que tiene sangre en la orina?**
189.	Your kidneys aren't functioning.		189.	**Sus riñones no funcionan.**
190.	Do you usually get backaches?		190.	**¿Suele Vd. tener dolores de espalda?**
191.	Have you ever had kidney stones?		191.	**¿Ha tenido alguna vez cálculos en los riñones?**

Review

Practice the following dialogue.

DR. GREEN
What is your problem, Miss Ruiz?

MISS RUIZ
I am having problems with my urine.

DR. GREEN
Can you urinate?

MISS RUIZ
Oh, yes, Doctor, but I am unable to control my urine.

DR. GREEN
How long has it been since you have urinated?

MISS RUIZ
About five minutes.

DR. GREEN
How frequently do you urinate?

MISS RUIZ
I feel like I have to urinate every few minutes.

DR. GREEN
When you urinate, do you pass a lot or a little urine?

Repaso

Practique Vd. el diálogo siguíente.

DR. GREEN
¿Cuál es su problema, señorita Ruiz?

SRTA. RUIZ
Tengo problemas al orinar.

DR. GREEN
¿Puede Vd. orinar?

SRTA. RUIZ
Ah, sí, doctor, pero tengo pérdidas involuntarias de orina.

DR. GREEN
¿Desde cuándo no orina Vd.?

SRTA. RUIZ
Casi cinco minutos.

DR. GREEN
¿Con qué frecuencia orina Vd.?

SRTA. RUIZ
Me parece que tengo que orinar cada cuantos minutos.

DR. GREEN
Al orinar, ¿pasa mucha o poca orina?

MISS RUIZ
I only pass a few drops, but I feel like I have to go.

DR GREEN
Does it hurt when you urinate?

MISS RUIZ
I don't think so.

DR. GREEN
Is there a burning sensation when you urinate?

MISS RUIZ
No.

DR. GREEN
I am going to give you a prescription for some pills. Take one pill after each meal and at bedtime. Drink two glasses of water with each pill.

MISS RUIZ
Yes, Doctor.

DR. GREEN
These pills may turn your urine different colors. Do not be afraid.

Genitourinary (Men)

192. Do you get pains in the testicles?

193. Have you ever been impotent or sterile?

194. Do you have a discharge from your penis?

195. Have you ever had prostatitis (inflamed prostate)?

Genitourinary (Women)

196. When was your last menstrual period?

SRTA. RUIZ
No paso más que unas gotas, pero me parece que tengo que orinar.

DR. GREEN
¿Le duele cuando orina Vd.?

SRTA. RUIZ
Creo que no.

DR. GREEN
¿Hay un ardor al orinar?

SRTA. RUIZ
No.

DR. GREEN
Le daré una prescripción para unas píldoras. Tome una después de cada comida y antes de acostarse. Trague esta medicina con dos vasos de agua cada vez.

SRTA. RUIZ
Sí, doctor.

DR. GREEN
Estas píldoras puedan cambiar su orina a varios colores. No se preocupe Vd.

Génitourinario (para hombres)

192. **¿Suele Vd. tener dolores**
   de los testículos?
   de los huevos? (slang)
   de los compañones? (slang)

193. **¿Ha padecido alguna vez de la impotencia o de la esterilidad?**

194. **¿Le supura el pene?**

195. **¿Ha padecido alguna vez de prostatitis (la prostata agrandada)?**

Génitourinario (para mujeres)

196. **¿Cuándo fue su última menstruación?** (general)
   ¿Cuándo fue su último período? (coll.)
   ¿Cuándo fue su última administración? (Mex.)
   ¿Cuándo fue su última regla? (Mex. & P.R.)

197. How long did it last?

198. How often do you get your periods?

199. How many days does it last?

200. How old were you when you first began to menstruate?

201. Have your periods always been regular up to now?

202. Have you ever had menstrual problems?

203. How is your mood during your menstrual flow?

204. Describe your menstrual flow.

205. Do you spot between periods (or after menopause)?

206. Do you ever hemorrhage then?

207. Are you bleeding heavily?

208. How many sanitary pads or tampons did you use during your last menstrual cycle?

209. Do you have vaginal secretions?

210. Are they watery?

211. Are they thick and yellow?

212. Are they thick and white?

213. Are they frothy and greenish?

214. Do you suffer from prolapse of the uterus?

215. When was your last pap smear?

197. **¿Cuánto tiempo le duró?**

198. **¿Cada cuánto le baja a Vd. la menstruación?**
¿Cada cuánto menstrua Vd.?

199. **¿Por cuántos días pierde Vd. sangre?**
¿Por cuántos días le dura?

200. **¿A qué edad tuvo su primera menstruación (regla)?**

201. **¿Han sido regulares sus reglas hasta ahora?**

202. **¿Ha tenido alguna vez desórdenes menstruales?**

203. **¿Cuál es su tipo de humor durante la menstruación?**

204. **Describa Vd. su hemorragia menstrual.**

205. **¿Tiene Vd. manchas de sangre entre períodos menstruales? (después de menopausia?)**

206. **¿Tiene Vd. hemorragia con sangre obscura o sangre roja entonces?**

207. **¿Está sangrando mucho?**

208. **¿Cuántas toallas higiénicas ha usada Vd. en su última menstruación?**

209. **¿Tiene Vd. secreciones vaginales?**

210. **¿Son aguachentas?**

211. **¿Son espesas y amarillas?**

212. **¿Son espesas y blancas?**

213. **¿Son espumosas y verdosas?**

214. **¿Padece Vd. de la matriz caída?**

215. **¿Cuándo le han tomado un extendido vaginal para el test de Papanicolau?**

216.	Have you ever been pregnant?	216.	¿Ha estado embarazada alguna vez? ¿Ha estado encinta alguna vez?
217.	Are you pregnant now?	217.	¿Está Vd. embarazada en este momento?
218.	How many months?	218.	¿Cuántos meses?
219.	Have you ever had an abortion or miscarriage?	219.	¿Ha tenido alguna vez un aborto inducido o espontáneo, o un mal parto?
220.	Was the birth natural or induced?	220.	¿Fue el parto natural o provocado?
221.	Was the delivery normal or did they use instruments?	221.	¿Fue un parto normal o usaron forceps?
222.	Was the delivery by caesarean section?	222.	¿Fue el parto por operación cesárea?

Practice

Read the following aloud both for fluency and comprehension. Then answer the questions based on the passage.

From the age of puberty until a woman enters menopause, she menstruates monthly. Once a month an egg is formed by the woman's ovaries and if the woman does not become pregnant, the lining of the uterus is cast off and replaced each month. This reproductive process, because it is repeated regularly every month, is called a menstrual cycle. The menstrual cycle is measured from the first day of menstruation to the first day of the next menstruation. Usually these cycles are 28 days long. Some women have longer menstrual cycles, others shorter ones. The menstrual cycle is controlled by hormones.

These hormones cause one of the ovaries to produce an egg each month. The hormones also cause changes in the lining of the uterus. If an egg is fertilized by sperm from a man, the egg attaches itself to the lining of the uterus.

If the egg is not fertilized the lining of the uterus is shed, accompanied by a flow of blood. The flow of blood passes from the uterus out through the vagina. This flow lasts from three to five days. Hormone secretions begin with the next menstrual cycle.

1. How long are menstrual cycles on the average?
2. What does the ovary produce?
3. How long does the flow of blood last?

Práctica

Lea lo que sigue en voz alta para fluidez y comprehensión. Entonces conteste Vd. a las preguntas que siguen.

Desde la edad de pubertad hasta el cambio de vida, una mujer menstrua una vez al mes. Una vez cada mes un óvulo se forma y a menos que la mujer esté embarazada, el forro o recubrimiento interior del útero es expulsado y reemplazado cada mes. Este proceso reproductivo, a causa de la repetición regular cada mes, se llama un ciclo menstrual. El ciclo mentrual empieza el primer día de la menstruación y dura hasta el primer día de la próxima menstruación. Generalmente estos ciclos duran veintiocho días. Para algunas mujeres estos ciclos duran más, para otras duran menos tiempo. El ciclo menstrual es controlado por unas hormonas.

Estas hormonas hacen que uno de los ovarios produzca un óvulo cada mes. Estas hormonas también producen cambios en el forro del útero. Si un óvulo es fertilizado por los espermatozoides de un hombre, el óvulo fertilizado se adhiere al forro del útero.

Si el óvulo no es fertilizado, el recubrimiento interior del útero es expulsado, acompañado de un flujo de sangre. El flujo sangrado pasa desde el útero hasta la vagina. El sangrado menstrual dura de tres a cinco días. La secreción de hormonas comienza de nuevo al empezar la menstruación.

1. ¿Por cuántos días duran los ciclos menstruales por lo regular?
2. ¿Qué produce un ovario?
3. ¿Por cuántos días duran el flujo sanguíneo?

Genitourinary (Venereal)	*Génitourinario (venérea)*
223. Have you ever had any venereal disease (syphilis, gonorrhea)?	223. **¿Ha padecido Vd. alguna vez de cualquier enfermedad venérea (sífilis, gonorrea)**
224. Did you receive treatment?	224. **¿Recibió Vd. tratamiento?**
225. When? Where?	225. **¿Cuándo? ¿Dónde?**

Extremities

Las extremidades

226. Are your joints stiff in the morning?	226. **¿Siente Vd. rígidas sus articulaciones por la mañana? ¿Están rígidas las co(y)junturas por la mañana?** (Coll.)
227. Have you had aches in your joints during the last year?	227. **¿Ha tenido Vd. dolores en las articulaciones durante el último año?**
228. Which joints are painful?	228. **¿Cuáles son las articulaciones que le duelen?**
229. Are your knees and wrists swollen or only your ankles and knees?	229. **¿Tiene Vd. las rodillas y las muñecas hinchadas o solamente los tobillos y las rodillas hinchados?**

Neurological

Neurológico

230.　Do you feel (very) weak?

230.　¿Se siente (muy) débil?

231.　Do you ever feel dizzy (giddy)?

231.　¿Suele Vd. tener mareos? (Coll.)
¿Tiene Vd. vértigo alguna vez?

232.　Do you have fainting spells?

232.　¿Ha tenido Vd. desmayos?
¿Suele Vd. tener desvanecimientos?

233.　Are you subject to them?

233.　¿Se desmaya Vd. con frecuencia?

234.　Do you feel like falling?

234.　¿Se siente Vd. como si se caería?

235.　Do you have convulsions?

235.　¿Le ha ocurrido a Vd. tener convulsiones o haber estado inconsciente?
¿Suele Vd. tener convulsiones?

236.　Do you see double?

236.　¿Ve Vd. doble?
¿Ve Vd. bizco? (Cent. Am.)
¿Ve Vd. las cosas doble?

237.　Do you have blurred vision?

237.　¿Ve Vd. borrosamente?
¿Ve Vd. borroso?

238.　Have you ever lost consciousness?

238.　¿Perdió Vd. el sentido alguna vez?

239.　For how long?

239.　¿Por cuánto tíempo?

240.　How frequently does this happen?

240.　¿Con qué frecuencia ocurre?

241.　Do you have tingling sensations?

241.　¿Tiene Vd. hormigueos?

242.　Do you have numbness in your hands or feet?

242.　¿Tiene Vd. $\begin{cases} \text{entumecimiento} \\ \text{calambres} \end{cases}$ en las manos o los pies?

243.　Have you been sleeping on your arm?

243.　¿Ha dormido Vd. encima del brazo?

244.　Are some of the fingers numb?

244.　¿Tiene Vd. algunos de los dedos adormecidos?

245.　Come see me if your fingers become numb.

245.　Venga a verme si se le adormecen los dedos.

Musculoskeletal

246. Do you have any swelling?

247. Do you have a herniated disc?

248. Do you have varicose veins?

249. Have you had any pain in your back?

250. Where?

251. Have you been bothered recently by muscle spasms?

Muscular-esquelético

246. ¿Se le hincha a Vd. alguna parte del cuerpo?

247. ¿Tiene Vd. una hernia del disco intervertebral?

248. ¿Tiene Vd. las venas inflamadas o venas varicosas?

249. ¿Ha tenido Vd. algún dolor de espalda?

250. ¿Dónde?

251. ¿Ha tenido Vd. recientemente molestias o dolores en los músculos?

PERSONAL HISTORY

1. What is your name?[5]

2. Where do you live?[6]

HISTORIA PERSONAL

1. ¿Cómo se llama Vd.?[5]

2. ¿Dónde vive Vd.?[6]

[5] Persons of Spanish descent frequently have names that, upon first glance, seem confusing to English-speaking Americans. Often they have several given names or **nombres de pila** (**nombres de bautismo**). Moreover, both paternal and maternal surnames are retained. The paternal surname precedes the maternal one. Neither is ever considered to be a middle name. Only in the case of an illegitimate child is the maternal surname alone used. Sometimes these family names are connected by the conjunction **y** (and), or by a hyphen; generally they are not. Occasionally, the maternal family name is abbreviated, in which case the first initial of the mother's last name follows the father's last name. In cases where the paternal family name is extremely common (the Spanish equivalent of "Smith" or "Jones") it is either abbreviated or omitted. Thus, in the case of Jaime José Alfredo Fernández y García, the first three names are given names, Fernández is the surname of the father, and García is the surname of the mother.
    In addition, the following variations may be found:
      Jaime José Alfredo Fernández García
      Jaime José Alfredo Fernández G.
      Jaime José Alfredo Fernández
      Jaime José Alfredo F. García
      Jaime José Alfredo García
      Jaime José Alfredo Fernández-García
    A Spanish woman upon her marriage drops her mother's maiden name and replaces it with that of her husband, prefixed by **de**. Thus, María Fernández y Montero becomes María Fernández de González upon her marriage to Juan Carlos González y Ortiz. Should her husband die, she is known as María Fernández Vda. de González. (**Vda.** = **viuda** = widow)
    A number of Spanish surnames include the preposition **de**, with or without a definite article, **el**, etc. At one time the preposition **de** indicated nobility, but no such distinction is made now and the use of **de** is optional. However, some families still retain it as part of the surname: del Campo, de la Torre, de la Rosa.
    Many famous people, for somewhat diverse reasons, use only one family name. The great Spanish writer Benito Pérez Galdós is known to most as Galdós. Federico García Lorca also retained his maternal name, and is best known as Lorca. However, Jacinto Benavente y Martínez, Miguel de Unamuno y Jugo, and Miguel de Cervantes Saavedra are all known by their paternal surname.

[6] See above page 33.

3. What is your telephone number[7]

3. **¿Cuál es el número de teléfono de su casa, por favor?**[7]

4. How old are you?

4. **¿Cuántos años tiene Vd.? ¿Qué edad tiene Vd.?** (Coll.)

5. What is your birthdate?[8]

5. **¿Cuál es la fecha de su nacimiento?**[8]

6. Where were you born?

6. **¿Dónde nació Vd.?**

7. Are you single or married?

7. **¿Es Vd. soltero (soltera) o casado (casada)?**

8. Are you divorced?

8. **¿Es Vd. divorciado (divorciada)?**

9. Are you a widow?

9. **¿Es Vd. viuda?**

10. Are you a widower?

10. **¿Es Vd. viudo?**

11. Do you have any children?

11. **¿Tiene Vd. algunos hijos?**

12. How many?

12. **¿Cuántos?**

13. How old is she/he (are they)?

13. **¿Cuántos años tiene(n)? ¿Qué edad tiene(n)?** (Coll.)

14. What do you do? (How do you earn a living?)

14. **¿Cómo gana Vd. la vida? ¿Qué clase de trabajo tiene Vd.?**

15. What is your occupation?[9]

15. **¿Cuál es su ocupación?**[9]

16. Are you happy in your work?

16. **¿Tiene Vd. satisfacción en el trabajo?**

17. What is your religion?[10]

17. **¿Cuál es su religión?**[10]

18. What is your nationality?[11]

18. **¿Cuál es su nacionalidad?**[11]

19. How much education do you have?

19. **¿Cuántos años de la escuela cumplió Vd.?**

[7] Local telephone numbers in many Spanish-speaking countries are composed of between two and seven digits:

> Costa Rica—6 digits
> El Salvador—6 digits
> Guatemala—2-6 digits
> Philippines—4-7 digits
> Spain—6-7 digits
> Venezuela—4-6 digits

Inhabitants tend to express their telephone numbers in groups of twos. Thus, 230695→23-06-95. If the telephone number contains an odd number of digits, the first number is given separately whereas the remaining digits are grouped in twos: 7123445→7-12-34-45.

Some Spanish-speakers adopt the U.S. custom of expressing all digits as units numbers: 525-4123→-5-2-5-4-1-2-3.

[8] In Spanish-speaking countries it is customary to celebrate both one's birthday and one's saint's day, the **día de su santo**, the day of the saint after whom one is named.

[9] See **Occupations**, pages 227ff.

[10] See **Religions**, page 254.

[11] See **Nationalities**, page 251.

20. Are you allergic to any medication? To any food? To dust or pollen?

21. Do you have hay fever?

22. How much do you normally weigh?

23. Have you gained or lost much weight recently, suddenly?

24. Do you have a good appetite?

25. During the last year have you noticed an increase in your desire for sweets?

26. How many meals do you eat daily?

27. What do you eat for breakfast? lunch? dinner?

28. Do you eat between meals?

29. How much butter do you eat daily?

30. How many eggs?

31. Do you drink coffee or tea?

32. How much coffee and tea do you drink a day?

33. Do you drink regular or decaffeinated coffee?

34. How much water do you drink daily?

35. Do you drink alcoholic beverages?

36. What type of alcoholic beverage do you generally buy?

37. How long does a bottle of alcohol last you?

38. How often during the week do you drink alcoholic beverages?

20. ¿Es Vd. alérgico (alérgica) a alguna medicina? ¿a alguna comida? ¿a polvo o a polen?

21. ¿Tiene Vd. la fiebre del heno?

22. Por lo regular, ¿cuánto pesa Vd.?

23. ¿Ha ganado o perdido peso últimamente, de repente?

24. ¿Tiene Vd. buen apetito?

25. ¿Ha observado Vd. durante el último año un aumento de apetito por dulces?

26. ¿Cuántas comidas toma Vd. al día?

27. ¿Qué toma Vd. para el desayuno? ¿para el almuerzo? ¿para la cena?

28. ¿Toma Vd. algo entre comidas?

29. ¿Cuánta mantequilla come Vd. al día?

30. ¿Cuántos huevos come Vd. por semana?

31. ¿Toma Vd. café o té?

32. ¿Cuántas tazas de café o de té bebe Vd. al día?

33. ¿Toma Vd. café regular o descafeinado?

34. ¿Cuántos vasos de agua bebe Vd. al día?

35. ¿Toma Vd. algunas bebidas alcohólicas?

36. ¿Qué tipo de bebida alcohólica compra Vd. por lo regular?

37. ¿Cuánto tiempo le queda una botella de alcohol?

38. ¿Cuántos días de la semana toma Vd. bebidas alcohólicas?

39.	Do you sleep well?		39.	**¿Duerme Vd. bien?**
40.	What time do you go to bed?		40.	**¿A qué hora se acuesta por la noche, por lo regular?**
41.	What time do you get up in the morning?		41.	**¿A qué hora se despierta por la mañana, por lo regular?**
42.	It is important to rest more.		42.	**Es importante descansar más.**
43.	Do you walk a lot at home?		43.	**¿Camina Vd. mucho en casa?**
44.	Do you walk a lot outside of the house?		44.	**¿Camina Vd. mucho afuera de la casa?**
45.	How many blocks do you walk on the average during the day?		45.	**¿Cuántas manzanas camina Vd. promedio durante el día?**
46.	Do you do your own shopping?		46.	**¿Va Vd. de compras sí mismo (misma)?**
47.	Do you smoke?		47.	**¿Fuma Vd.?**
48.	How much?		48.	**¿Cuántos cigarrillos al día?**
49.	If you smoke (or have smoked) how many years have you been smoking?		49.	**Si Vd. fuma (o ha fumado antes) ¿por cuántos años ha venido haciéndolo?**
50.	I advise you to stop smoking or at least to reduce it to a minimum.		50.	**Le aconsejo que deje de fumar o que lo reduzca a un mínimo.**
51.	Do you use drugs regularly? Are you a drug addict?		51.	**¿Es Vd. adicto al uso de drogas? ¿Es Vd. drogadicto? ¿Acostumbra Vd. a tomar alguna droga? ¿Es Vd. un adicto? ¿Toma Vd. alguna droga?**
52.	How much money do you spend daily on your drug habit?		52.	**¿Cuánto dinero gasta Vd. por día para sus drogas?**
53.	Do you smoke marijuana?		53.	**¿Fuma Vd. la mariguana?**
54.	Do you take morphine?		54.	**¿Ingiere Vd. morfina? ¿Se administra Vd. morfina? ¿Es Vd. adicto a morfina?**
55.	Do you use heroin, cocaine, LSD?		55.	**¿Toma Vd. heroína, cocaína, drogas alucinantes? LSD?**
56.	Do you use amphetamines?		56.	**¿Usa Vd. las anfetaminas?**
57.	Are you using barbiturates without medical supervision?		57.	**¿Toma Vd. los barbitúricos sin supervisión médica?**

58. Do you use

    antihistamines?

    aspirin

    sleeping pills

    birth control pills

    diet pills

    laxatives

    diuretics

    medication for diabetes

    digitalin or nitroglycerin

    antacids

    antibiotics

    tranquilizers

    vitamins

    thyroid pills

    cortisone

58. **¿Ha tomado Vd.**

    antihistamínicos?

    aspirinas

    píldoras para dormir (sedativos)

    píldoras para control de embarazo

    píldoras para dieta

    laxantes

    píldoras diuréticas

    medicación para diabetes

    digitalina o nitroglicerina

    antiácidos

    antibióticos

    tranquilizantes

    vitaminas

    medicación tiroides

    cortisona

59. How would you describe the feelings that you experience during coitus?

59. **¿Cómo describiría Vd. las sensaciones que tiene durante el coito (relación sexual)?**

Exercise   *Ejercicio*

¿Cómo se dice en español?

1. I normally weigh 125 pounds.
2. John eats three meals daily.
3. We never drink water.
4. The girl drinks coffee but I drink milk.
5. I have been smoking for five years.
6. I get up at 8 in the morning.
7. Paul goes to sleep at midnight.
8. You do not smoke now.
9. Why do you use barbiturates?
10. The widow has seven children.

FAMILY HISTORY

1. Are your parents alive?

2. What did your mother die from?

HISTORIA FAMILIAL

1. **¿Todavía están vivos sus padres?**
    ¿Todavía viven sus padres?

2. **¿De qué murió su madre?**

3.	What did your father die from?	3.	¿De qué murió su padre?
4.	How old were your grandparents when they died, or are they still alive?	4.	¿Cuántos años tenían sus abuelos cuando murieron, o viven todavía? ¿A qué edad murieron sus abuelos, o están vivos todavía?
5.	What did your grandmother die from?	5.	¿De qué murió su abuela?
6.	What did your grandfather die from?	6.	¿De qué murío su abuelo?
7.	What was your mother's maiden name?	7.	¿Cuál era el nombre de soltera de su madre?
8.	Where were you born?	8.	¿Dónde nació Vd?
9.	Where were your parents born?	9.	¿Dónde nacieron sus padres?
10.	Do you have any brothers/sisters?	10.	¿Tiene Vd. algunos hermanos? ¿hermanas?
11.	How many?	11.	¿Cuántos? ¿Cuántas?
12.	Is there any family history of blood disease?	12.	¿Hay alguna historia en su familia de enfermedades de la sangre?
13.	Is there a history of lung trouble or diabetes?	13.	¿Hay alguna historia de problemas pulmonares o de diabetes?

14.	Does anyone in your family suffer from asthma or hay fever?
	    extreme obesity
	    cancer or leukemia
	    heart attack
	    angina (pectoris)
	
	    chronic anemia
	
	    stroke
	    thyroid problems
	    stomach or duodenal ulcers
	
	    peptic ulcer
	    gall stones
	
	    kidney stones
		14.	¿Padece alguien de su familia de asma o de fiebre del heno?
			    obesidad extremada
			    cáncer o leucemia
			    ataque al corazón
			    angina del pecho
			    { anemia crónica
			     sangre pobre (slang)
			    parálisis
			    enfermedad de la tiroides
			    úlceras de estómago o duodenales
			    úlcera péptica
			    cálculos en la vesícula
			    { cálculos en los riñones
			     cálculos renales

15.	Whom can we call in case of emergency?	15.	¿A quién podemos llamar en caso de emergencia?

PREPARATION FOR PHYSICAL EXAMINATION

PREPARACION POR EL RECONOCIMIENTO FISICO

1. Take off your clothes, please.

2. Please take off your clothes down to your waist.

3. Please take off your clothes from the waist down.

4. Please take off your girdle and bra.

5. Lower your trousers, please.

6. Please hang your clothes over there.

7. Put on the gown, please.

8. Sit on the table, please.

9. Please lie down on the examining table.

10. The doctor will examine you now.

11. The doctor wants to examine your arm.

12. Just relax.

13. Please turn face up.

14. Please turn face down.

15. I am going to touch your knee with an instrument.

---

1. **Desvístase Vd., por favor. Favor de desvestirse.**

2. **Desvístase Vd. hasta la cintura, por favor. Quítese Vd. la ropa hasta la cintura, por favor**

3. **Desvístase Vd. de la cintura para abajo, por favor.**

4. **Quítese Vd. la faja y el { sostén, por favor. ajustador portabustos** (slang)

5. **Bájese Vd. los pantalones, por favor.**

6. **Cuelgue Vd. la ropa ahí, por favor.**

7. **Póngase Vd. la bata, por favor.**

8. **Siéntese Vd. sobre la mesa, por favor.**

9. **Acuéstese Vd. sobre la mesa de reconocimiento, por favor.**

10. **El doctor le (la) examinará ahora.**

11. **El doctor quiere examinarle el brazo.**

12. **Relaje Vd. el cuerpo. Relájese Vd.**

13. **Póngase Vd. boca arriba, por favor.**

14. **Póngase Vd. boca abajo, por favor.**

15. **Voy a tocar su rodilla con un instrumento.**

PHYSICAL EXAMINATION

RECONOCIMIENTO FISICO

Head

1. Bend your head to the right, please.

2. Bend your head to the left, please.

3. Bend your head forward.

4. Bend your head backwards.

5. Turn your head to the right; to the left.

6. Turn your head.

La cabeza

1. **Doble Vd. la cabeza a la derecha, por favor.**

2. **Doble Vd. la cabeza a la izquierda, por favor.**

3. **Doble Vd. la cabeza hacia adelante.**

4. **Doble Vd. la cabeza hacia atrás.**

5. **Vuelva Vd. la cabeza hacia la derecha; hacia la izquierda.**

6. **Gire Vd. la cabeza.**

Eyes

7. Let me see your eyes, please.

8. Look up.

9. Look down.

10. Keep looking at my nose.

11. Follow my finger with your eyes without moving your head.

12. Open your eyes more. (Wider).

13. Can you see this?

14. Do you see this?

Los ojos

7. **Déjeme ver sus ojos, por favor.**
   Déjeme mirar sus ojos.

8. **Mire Vd. hacia arriba.**
   Mire Vd. para arriba.

9. **Mire Vd. hacia abajo.**
   Mire Vd. para abajo.

10. **Míreme Vd. en la nariz.**

11. **Siga Vd. mi dedo con los ojos sin mover la cabeza.**

12. **Abra Vd. los ojos más.**

13. **¿Puede Vd. ver esto?**

14. **¿Ve Vd. esto?**

Ears

15. I am going to touch you with an instrument.

16. Do you hear this tuning fork vibrating?

17. Tell me if it seems sharper to you on the left side than on the right.

Los oídos

15. **Voy a tocarle con un instrumento.**

16. **¿Oye Vd. este diapasón vibrar?**

17. **Dígame Vd. si le parece más agudo en el lado izquierdo que en el derecho.**

18. Is this louder in the right ear than in the left?	18. ¿Oye Vd. mejor en el oído derecho que en el izquierdo?
19. Is there any difference?	19. ¿Hay alguna diferencia?
20. Call me if there is any change.	20. Avíseme Vd. si hay algún cambio.

Mouth and Throat / *La boca y la garganta*

21. Can you open your mouth?	21. ¿Puede Vd. abrir la boca?
22. Open your mouth, please.	22. Abra Vd. la boca, por favor.
23. Say "ah".	23. Diga "ah."
24. Close it, please.	24. Ciérrela Vd., por favor.

Breasts / *Los pechos*

25. I am going to examine your breasts.	25. Voy a examinarle los pechos.

Female Genitalia / *Los órganos genitales femininos*

26. I have to examine you internally.	26. Tengo que examinarle por dentro.
27. I am going to do a pelvic examination.	27. Voy a hacerle ahora un examen de la pelvis.
28. Put your feet in these stirrups.	28. Ponga Vd. los pies en estos estribos.
29. Spread your knees and legs apart.	29. Abra Vd. las rodillas y las piernas.
30. Stay quiet.	30. Esté Vd. tranquila.
31. You should not have sexual intercourse.	31. No debería Vd. tener relaciones sexuales.
32. Do not use any douche.	32. No se dé Vd. duchas vaginales.

Rectal Exam / *Reconocimiento rectal*

33. I am going to examine you rectally.	33. Voy a examinarle el recto.
34. Please kneel.	34. Póngase Vd. de rodillas, por favor.
35. Turn on your left side and draw your knees up to your chin.	35. Póngase Vd. del lado izquierdo y doble Vd. las rodillas hasta la barbilla.
36. Pull your legs toward you.	36. Encoja Vd. las piernas.

37. Stay on your back.

37. **Esté Vd. boca arriba.**
     Esté Vd. postrado (-ada).

Extremities and Orthopedic Exam

Las extremidades y el reconocimiento ortopédico

38. Please stand up.

38. **Levántese Vd., por favor.**

39. Please sit down.

39. **Siéntese Vd., por favor.**

40. Walk a little.

40. **Camine Vd. un poco.**

41. Come back, please.

41. **Vuelva Vd., por favor.**
     Regrese Vd.

42. Walk backwards.

42. **Camine Vd. hacia atrás.**

43. Walk on your toes.

43. **Camine Vd. sobre los dedos.**

44. Walk on your heels.

44. **Camine Vd. sobre los talones.**

45. Bend over.

45. **Dóblese Vd. hacia adelante.**

46. Bend backwards.

46. **Dóblese Vd. hacia atrás.**

47. Bend your trunk forward as far as you can.

47. **Doble Vd. el tronco hacia adelante tanto como pueda.**

48. Close your hand.

48. **Cierre Vd. la mano.**

49. Open it.

49. **Ábrala Vd., por favor.**

50. Close your fist.

50. **Cierre Vd. el puño.**

51. Open it.

51. **Ábralo Vd., por favor.**

52. Grip my hands tightly.

52. **Apriete Vd. mis manos con fuerza.**

53. Can't you do it better than that?

53. **¿No puede Vd. hacerlo más fuerte?**

54. Raise your arms.

54. **Suba Vd. los brazos.**
     Levante Vd. sus brazos.

55. Higher.

55. **Más alto.**

56. Raise your arms all the way up.

56. **Levante Vd. los brazos completamente.**
     Suba Vd. los brazos completamente.

57. Lower.

57. **Más bajo.**

58. Raise your left (right) leg.

58. **Levante Vd. la pierna izquierda (derecha).**
     Suba Vd. la pierna izquierda (derecha).

59. Can you move that arm?

59. **¿Puede Vd. mover ese brazo?**

60. Can you lift that arm?

61. Can you move that leg?

62. Can you lift that leg?

63. When did you sprain ___ ?

Neurological Exam

64. Cross the left leg over the right one.

65. Now cross the right leg over the left.

66. Bend your right (left) knee.

67. Bend your right (left) elbow.

68. Move a little over to the right.

69. Does it hurt?

70. Where?

71. Turn your ankle.

72. To the right.

73. To the left.

74. This way.

75. Stretch your fingers.

76. Grasp this object between your fingers.

77. Stretch your legs.

78. Flex your feet.

60. **¿Puede Vd. levantar ese brazo?**

61. **¿Puede Vd. mover esa pierna?**

62. **¿Puede Vd. levantar esa pierna?**

63. **¿Cuándo se torció ___ ?**

Reconocimiento neurológico

64. **Cruce Vd. la pierna izquierda sobre la derecha.**

65. **Ahora cruce Vd. la pierna derecha sobre la izquierda.**

66. **Doble Vd. la rodilla derecha (izquierda).**

67. **Doble Vd. el codo derecho (izquierdo).**

68. **Muévase Vd. un poco hacia la derecha.**

69. **¿Le duele?**

70. **¿Dónde?**

71. **Gire el tobillo.**

72. **A la derecha.**

73. **A la izquierda.**

74. **Hacia acá.**

75. **Estire Vd. los dedos.**

76. **Apriete Vd. este objeto entre los dedos.**

77. **Estire Vd. las piernas.**

78. **Flexione Vd. los pies.**

Exercise   *Ejercicio*

Statements 1–12 are polite commands (See Verb section, pp. 291–300). Several acceptable substitutes exist for the polite command. These involve using some form of *please* and the infinitive. In Spanish several forms of *please* may be used:

> **haga Vd. el favor de**
> **favor de**
> **tenga la bondad de**
> **sírvase**

Rewrite all polite commands in this section using the above ways to say *please*.

Example :

Bend your head to the right, please. Doble Vd. la cabeza a la derecha, por favor.

(Haga Vd. el favor de)_____

Haga Vd. el favor de doblar la cabeza a la derecha.
(Favor de) _____

Favor de doblar la cabeza a la derecha.
(Tenga la bondad de) _____

Tenga la bondad de doblar la cabeza a la derecha.
(Sírvase)_____

Sírvase doblar la cabeza a la derecha.

Continue in this fashion with all the commands listed.

TEMPERATURE

LA TEMPERATURA

1. I am going to take your temperature.
2. Let me take your temperature.
3. Moisten your lips, please.
4. Please keep the thermometer in your mouth, under the tongue.
5. Open your mouth.
6. Don't be afraid.
7. You have a high fever.
8. You have a slight fever.
9. How long have you had fever?
10. Did you have fever last night? Yesterday?
11. How much?[12]

1. **Voy a tomarle la temperatura.**
2. **Permítame tomarle la temperatura.**
3. **Por favor, humedezca sus labios.**
   Favor de humedecer los labios.
4. **Por favor, mantenga el termómetro en la boca, bajo la lengua.**
   Favor de mantener el termómetro en la boca, bajo la lengua.
5. **Abra Vd. la boca, por favor.**
6. **No tenga Vd. miedo.**
7. **Vd. tiene fiebre alta.**
8. **Vd. tiene un poco de fiebre.**
9. **¿Desde cuándo tiene Vd. fiebre?**
10. **¿Tuvo Vd. fiebre anoche? ¿ayer?**
11. **¿Cuánta?**

[12] Remember, many Spanish-speaking people use centigrade temperatures. See page 34 for a conversion table.

12. Did you take any medicine before coming to the hospital?

12. ¿Tomó Vd. alguna medicina antes de venir al hospital?

VITAL SIGNS

SIGNOS VITALES

1. I am going to take your blood pressure.

1. Voy a tomarle la presión.
Voy a tomar su presión de la sangre.

2. Roll up your sleeve.

2. Arremánguese las mangas, por favor.

3. Relax.

3. Afloje Vd. el cuerpo, por favor.

4. Bend your elbow.

4. Doble Vd. el codo, por favor.

5. Make a fist.

5. Haga Vd. el puño, por favor.
Cierre Vd. el puño, por favor.

6. Your blood pressure is normal.

6. Su presión arterial es normal.

7. Your pressure is too low.

7. Su presión está demasiado baja.

8. Your pressure is quite high.

8. Su presión arterial está bastante alta.

9. Your pressure is too high.

9. Su presión está demasiado alta.

10. Your pressure is higher than normal.

10. Su presión está más alta que lo normal.

11. We have to try to determine why you have high blood pressure, although sometimes this is not possible.

11. Debemos tratar de determinar por qué tiene Vd. la presión alta, aunque en muchos casos la causa no es conocida.

12. Here is a prescription to reduce your blood pressure.

12. Aquí tiene Vd. una receta para reducir la presión arterial.

13. Take one pill every day after breakfast.

13. Tome Vd. una píldora cada día después de desayunar.

14. Let me feel your pulse.

14. Déjeme tomarle el pulso.

15. Your pulse is too rapid.

15. El pulso está demasiado rápido.

16.	Please step on the scale.	16.	**Súbase Vd. en la báscula, por favor.** **Párese Vd. en la báscula, por favor.**
17.	I am going to listen to your chest.	17.	**Voy a escuchar al pecho.**
18.	Take a deep breath.	18.	**Respire Vd. profundo.**
19.	Breathe slowly.	19.	**Respire Vd. al paso.** (Coll.) **Respire Vd. lento.**
20.	Breathe rapidly.	20.	**Respire Vd. rápido.**
21.	Raise both arms over your head.	21.	**Levante Vd. los dos brazos sobre la cabeza.**
22.	Lower your arms.	22.	**Baje Vd. los brazos.**
23.	Breathe deeply in and out through your mouth.	23.	**Respire Vd. fuertemente hacia dentro y hacia fuera, por la boca.**
24.	Cough, please.	24.	**Tosa Vd. por favor.**
25.	Again.	25.	**Otra vez.**
26.	Once more.	26.	**Una vez más.**
27.	Please don't breathe for one minute.	27.	**Favor de no respirar por un minuto.**
28.	Hold your breath.	28.	**Mantenga Vd. la respiración.**
29.	Now you can breathe.	29.	**Ya Vd. puede respirar.**

ADMISSION OF THE PATIENT TO THE ROOM

ADMISION DEL PACIENTE AL CUARTO

1.	I am _____.	1.	**Soy _____.**
2.	I am the day nurse, night nurse, nurse on duty, nurse's aide, head nurse.	2.	**Soy la enfermera de día, la enfermera de noche, la enfermera de guardia, la ayudante de enfermera, la jefa de enfermeras.**
3.	I am the public health nurse, visiting nurse.	3.	**Soy la enfermera de salud pública, la enfermera ambulante.**
4.	Do you need a wheelchair?	4.	**¿Necesita Vd. una silla de ruedas?**

5. Your family may accompany you to the room.

6. You can accompany your wife (husband) to her (his) room.

7. When is your family coming? I want to talk to them.

8. I want to introduce you to_____ (other patient in the room).

9. Here is a hospital gown, please put it on. Do you need help?

10. Instruct your family (or a friend) to take your suitcase home.

11. I need a urine specimen.

12. When you urinate, fill up this bottle and give it to the nurse on duty.

13. Here is a booklet that deals with the rules of the hospital.

14. This is the buzzer (bell).

15. This is the call light.

16. If you need anything, press the button.

17. The light over your door will stay on until a member of the nursing staff answers your call.

18. This button raises the headboard.

19. This button lowers the headboard.

20. This button raises (lowers) the bed.

21. This button raises the foot of the bed.

5. **Su familia puede acompañarle al cuarto.**

6. **Vd. puede acompañar a su esposa (esposo) hasta el cuarto.**

7. **¿Cuándo viene su familia? Quiero hablarles.**

8. **Quiero presentarle a _____.**

9. **Aquí está una bata del hospital. Favor de ponérsela. ¿Necesita ayuda?**

10. **Pida Vd. que su familia (amigo) devuelva su maleta a casa.**

11. **Necesito una muestra de orina de Vd.**

12. **Cuando Vd. orine, llene este frasco y déselo a la enfermera de guardia.**

13. **Aquí está un librito que trata de las reglas del hospital.**

14. **Este es el timbre.**

15. **Esta es la luz para llamar a la enfermera.**

16. **Si Vd. necesita algo, oprima el botón.**

17. **La luz que está sobre la puerta se mantendrá prendida hasta que un miembro del personal de enfermeras conteste a su llamada.**

18. **Este botón levanta la cabecera de la cama.**

19. **Este botón baja la cabecera de la cama.**

20. **Este botón levanta (baja) la cama.**

21. **Este botón levanta el pie de la cama.**

22.	This button lowers the foot of the bed.	22.	**Este botón baja el pie de la cama.**
23.	Call someone to help you.	23.	**Llame a alguien para que le (la) ayude.**
24.	Do not turn without calling the nurse.	24.	**No se voltee sin llamar a la enfermera.**
25.	Do you want me to raise your headboard?	25.	**¿Quisiera la cabecera de la cama más alta? ¿Quiere Vd. que le levante un poco la cabecera de la cama?**
26.	Do you want me to lower your headboard?	26.	**¿Quiere Vd. que le baje un poco la cabecera de la cama?**
27.	Do you want me to raise the knee rest (your knees)?	27.	**¿Quiere Vd. que le { levante suba } un poco las rodillas?**
28.	Do you want me to lower your knees?	28.	**¿Quiere Vd. que le baje un poco las rodillas?**
29.	The side rails on your bed are for your protection.	29.	**Los rieles del costado están para su protección. Las barandas protectoras de la cama están para su protección.**
30.	Please do not try to lower or climb over the side rail.	30.	**No pretenda bajarlos (bajarlas) o treparse sobre ellos.**
31.	Please wear slippers or shoes and a robe at all times when you are out of bed.	31.	**Por favor, use Vd. pantuflas o zapatos y una bata en todo momento cuando no esté en la cama.**
32.	The bathroom is behind this door.	32.	**El inodoro está detrás de esta puerta.**
33.	The bathtub is along the hall to the right (to the left).	33.	**La bañera (la bañadera [Amer.]) está por el { pasillo corredor } a la derecha (a la izquierda).**
34.	This is a special denture cup to store your dentures in when you are not wearing them.	34.	**Este es un recipiente especial para guardar su dentadura postiza cuando no la esté usando.**

35. You must remove your dentures or any partial dentures before surgery or any procedure involving a general anesthetic.

35. **Vd. debe quitarse su dentadura postiza o cualquier diente postizo antes de la cirugía, o si Vd. está en la lista para algún tratamiento que envuelva anestesia general.**

36. To place a local telephone call, dial 9, wait for the dial tone, then dial the number you wish.

36. **Para hacer una llamada local, marque 9 [nueve] y espere el tono, luego marque el número que Vd. desee.**

37. For long distance or suburban calls, dial 0 and the operator will help you.

37. **Para llamadas de larga distancia o a los suburbios, marque 0 [cero] y la operadora lo (la) asistirá.**

38. Telephone calls can (not) be added to your hospital bill.

38. **Las llamadas telefónicas (no) pueden ser agregadas en su cuenta de hospital.**

39. Newspapers are sold each morning and evening throughout the hospital and are also available in the lobby.

39. **Se venden los periódicos todas las mañanas y todas las noches por todo el hospital y también están a disposición en el salón de entrada.**

40. Television sets can be rented here in the hospital at a nominal cost.

40. **Se puede alquilar televisores (aparatos de televisión) aquí en el hospital por un pago nominal.**

41. I will call the dietician to discuss your menu.

41. **Llamaré al dietista para que discutan su menu.**

42. You will be given a choice of foods for your meals according to the diet prescribed by your doctor.

42. **Se le dará a elegir los alimentos para sus comidas según la dieta que su médico le prescribe.**

43. Breakfast is served at 8 a.m.

43. **Se sirve el desayuno a las ocho de la mañana.**

44. Lunch is served at 11:30.

44. **Se sirve el almuerzo a las once y media.**

45. Dinner is at 5 p.m.

45. **Se sirve la cena a las cinco de la tarde.**

46. A snack is served at 8:45 p.m.

46. **Se sirve una merienda a las nueve menos cuarto de la noche.**

47. The patients' chapel is located on the main floor and is open to members of all faiths.

47. **La capilla de los pacientes se halla en el piso principal y está a disposición de los miembros de todos los credos.**

48. There are brief services there every Sunday at 10:30 a.m.

48. **Hay breves servicios allí todos los domingos a las diez y media de la mañana.**

49. If you wish, your own priest, minister, or rabbi, can come to visit you.

49. **Si Vd. desea, su propio sacerdote, ministro, o rabí puede venir a visitarle.**

50. The head nurse is _____.

50. **La jefa de enfermeras es _____.**

51. Your doctor usually visits at _____.

51. **Su médico suele visitar a las _____.**

52. Do you need more blankets or another pillow?

52. **¿Necesita Vd. más { frazadas cobijas u otra almohada?**

53. You may not smoke in the room.

53. **No se puede fumar en el cuarto.**

54. Is the room too hot?

54. **¿Hace demasiado calor en el cuarto?**

55. Do you want me to open (close) the window?

55. **¿Quiere que yo abra (cierre) la ventana?**

56. Do you want me to turn on (turn off) the lights?

56. **¿Quiere Vd. que encienda (apague) la luz?**

57. Are you hungry?

57. **¿Tiene Vd. hambre?**

58. Are you thirsty?

58. **¿Tiene Vd. sed?**

59. Are you allergic to any medication?

59. **¿Padece Vd. de alguna alergia? ¿Es Vd. alérgico (alérgica) a alguna medicina?**

60. Are you on a restricted diet?

60. **¿Sigue Vd. dieta rigurosa?**

61. I am the orderly.

61. **Soy el ayudante.**

62. I have come to take you for your tests.

62. **He venido para llevarle a que le hagan sus análisis.**

63. Please move over to the stretcher.

63. **Acuéstese en la camilla, por favor. Por favor, pásese a la camilla.**

64. Please sit down on the wheel-chair.

64. **Siéntese Vd. en la silla de ruedas, por favor.**

65. Wait here until you hear your name.

65. **Espere aquí hasta**
   { **oir su nombre.**
   { **que oiga su nombre.**
   { **que escuche su nombre.**

Exercise   *Ejercicio*

Answer the questions using the cue given in parenthesis.

¿Quién es Vd.? (la enfermera)
Soy la enfermera.

¿Quién es Vd.? (la enfermera de noche)
Soy la enfermera de noche.

¿Quién es Vd.? (la jefa de enfermeras)
Soy la jefa de enfermeras.

¿Quién es Vd.? (la ayudante de enfermera)
Soy la ayudante de enfermera.

¿Quién es Vd.? (la enfermera de guardia)
Soy la enfermera de guardia.

¿Quién es Vd.? (la enfermera de salud pública)

Soy la enfermera de salud pública.

¿Quién es Vd.? (la enfermera ambulante)
Soy la enfermera ambulante.

¿Quién es Vd.? (el enfermero)
Soy el enfermero.

¿Quién es Vd.? (el enfermero de salud pública)
Soy el enfermero de salud pública.

¿Quién es Vd.? (el enfermero ambulante)
Soy el enfermero ambulante.

¿Quién es Vd.? (el ayudante de hospital)
Soy el ayudante de hospital.

Exercise   *Ejercicio*

Make the appropriate substitutions:

Este botón levanta la cabecera de la cama.
(baja)_____
Este botón baja la cabecera de la cama.
(la cama) _____
Este botón baja la cama.
(levanta) _____

Este botón levanta la cama.
(el pie de la cama) _____
Este botón levanta el pie de la cama.
(baja)_____
Este botón baja el pie de la cama.

VISITING HOURS

LAS HORAS DE VISITAS

1. Visitors are allowed unless you or your physician request "no visitors."

1. **Se permiten visitas a no ser que Vd. o su médico dispongan lo contrario.**

2. Visitors are only allowed during visiting hours.

2. **Se admite visitantes solamente durante las horas de visita.**

3. The visiting hours are from _____ to _____.

3. **Las horas de visita son desde las _____ hasta las _____ de la tarde.**

4. Visitors must obtain a pass from the information desk in the lobby.

4. **Los visitantes deben obtener un pase en la mesa de información del salón de entrada.**

5. No more than two visitors at a time.

5. **No más de dos** $\left\{ \begin{array}{l} \textbf{visitas} \\ \textbf{visitantes} \end{array} \right.$ **al mismo tiempo.**

6. Only two visitors per patient are allowed.

6. **Solamente se permiten dos visitantes por paciente.**

7. Please return the passes when you leave.

7. **Por favor, no se olviden de devolver los pases cuando Vds. salgan.**

8. There are too many visitors in the room.

8. **Hay demasiado visitantes en el cuarto.**

9. Please do not smoke in the patient's room.

9. **Le(s) pedimos que siga(n) las reglas de no fumar en los cuartos de los pacientes.**

10. Smoking is allowed in the waiting room of each floor.

10. **Se permite fumar solamente en la sala de espera que está en cada piso.**

11. Children under 14 are not able to visit patients.

11. **Los niños que no tienen catorce años no pueden visitar a los pacientes.**

12. Children under 12 are not allowed to visit the patients.

12. **A los niños de menores de doce años, no se les permite visitar a los pacientes.**

13. Children from 12 to 16 must be accompanied by an adult.

13. **Los visitantes entre la edad de doce a dieciséis años tienen que ser acompañados por un adulto.**

14. Children accompanying visitors should not be left unattended in the lobby.

14. **No se debe dejar solos en el salón de entrada a los niños que acompañan a los visitantes.**

15. Visiting hours for the Intensive Care Unit are:

15. **Las horas de visita para la Unidad de Cuidados Intensivos son:**

16. Visiting hours for the Cardiac Care Unit are:

16. **Las horas de visita para la Unidad de Cuidados Coronarios son:**

17. One (two) visitors for 5 minutes every hour on the hour beginning at ____ and ending with ____.

18. One visitor for 5 minutes every hour on the half hour beginning at ____ and ending with____.

17. **Un (dos) visitante(s) por cinco minutos cada hora en la hora comenzando a la ____ y terminando con ____.**

18. **Un visitante por cinco minutos cada hora en la media hora comenzando a la ____ y terminando con ____.**

CONVERSATION WITH THE PATIENT

CONVERSACION CON EL PACIENTE

1. May I help you?
2. Did you call?

3. Did you sleep well?
4. Do you feel better today?
5. Do you still feel (very) weak?

6. Are you sleepy?
7. It is necessary to rest more.
8. Can I help you?
9. Can you help me?
10. The doctor wants to see that prescription.
11. The doctor will examine you now.
12. You will not be able to walk for ten days.
13. You must lie flat in bed until tomorrow.
14. You are to remain in bed today.

15. You may get up for about 15 minutes this afternoon.

1. **¿En qué puedo servirle?**
2. **¿Me llamó Vd.?**
   ¿Me ha llamado Vd.?
3. **¿Durmió Vd. bien?**
4. **¿Se siente mejor hoy?**
5. **¿Todavía se siente (muy) débil?**
6. **¿Tiene Vd. sueño?**
7. **Es necesario descansar más.**
8. **¿Puedo ayudarle en algo?**
9. **¿Puede ayudarme?**
10. **El médico quiere ver esa receta.**
11. **El doctor le (la) examinará ahora.**
12. **No podrá caminar por diez días.**
13. **Vd. debe permanecer acostado (-a) hasta mañana.**
14. **Vd. debe guardar cama hoy.**
    Vd. debe permanecer en cama hoy.
15. **Vd. puede levantarse por unos quince minutos esta tarde.**

16. You may get out of bed, but not by yourself.

16. **Vd. puede salir de la cama, pero no sin ayuda.**

17. You may be able to get (up) out of bed tomorrow.

17. **Vd. podrá levantarse de la cama mañana.**

18. You may take a bath.

18. **Vd. puede bañarse.**

19. You may take a shower.

19. **Vd. puede darse una ducha.
Vd. puede darse un regaderazo.** (Mex.)
Vd. puede ducharse.

20. You may take a sitzbath.

20. **Vd. puede darse
un baño de asiento.
un semicupio.**

21. Take a hot sitzbath every four hours.

21. **Tome Vd.** { **un baño de asiento
un semicupio**
caliente cada cuatro horas.

22. Do not lock the door, please.

22. **No cierre Vd. la puerta con llave, por favor.**

23. Call if you feel faint or in need of help.

23. **Llame si Vd. se siente débil, o si necesita ayuda.**

24. Can you wash yourself or do you need help?

24. **¿Puede Vd. lavarse, o necesita ayuda?**

25. Do you want me to wash you?

25. **¿Quiere Vd. que yo le (la) bañe?
¿Quiere Vd. que yo le (la) lave?**

26. We are going to give you a (sponge) bath.

26. **Nosotros vamos a darle un baño (de esponja).**

27. You may use the wash basin.

27. **Vd. puede usar la
basija.
jofaina.
ponchera.** (Cent. Am.)
palanga. (Mex.)

28. Wash your genitals.

28. **Lávese
los privados.
sus [órganos] genitales.**

29. Can you comb your hair without help?

29. **¿Puede peinarse sin ayuda?**

30. Can you shave yourself or do you want me to shave you?

30. **¿Puede afeitarse a sí mismo, o quiere que yo le afeite?**

31. Try to do it yourself.

31. **Trate de hacerlo por sí mismo (misma).**

32.	Call when you have to go to the toilet.	32.	**Llame cuando tenga que ir** { **al inodoro.** **a los servicios.** { **al [cuarto] de baño.**
33.	Do you need the bed pan, or do you want to go to the bathroom?	33.	**¿Necesita Vd.** { **la cuña** { **la silleta** **el cómodo** (Mex.) **o quiere ir al inodoro?**
34.	I am going to put the bed pan on the table.	34.	**Voy a dejar** { **la cuña** { **el cómodo** (Mex.) **sobre la mesa.**
35.	Flex your knees and raise your buttocks off the bed.	35.	**Flexione Vd. las rodillas y levante las nalgas de la cama.**
36.	Use the signal cord to call as soon as you have urinated.	36.	**Use Vd. el botón para llamar tan pronto como Vd. haya orinado.**
37.	Do you need tissues, toilet paper?	37.	**¿Necesita Vd. kleenex,** { **papel de baño?** { **pañuelo de papel?**
38.	Are you constipated?	38.	**¿Está Vd. estreñido (estreñida)?**
39.	I will give you an enema.	39.	**Le pondré una enema.**
40.	Turn on your left (right) side.	40.	**Acuéstese Vd. sobre el lado izquierdo (derecho).**
41.	Turn over.	41.	**Vólteese del otro lado, por favor.** **Vírese Vd. del otro lado.** **Vuélvase del otro lado, por favor.**

42.	Do you need a sleeping pill?	42.	**¿Necesita Vd.**
			{ **una pastilla para dormir?**
			  una píldora somnífera?
			{ **un somnífero?**
			{ **una soporífera?**
			  algo para ayudarle a dormir?

43.	Do you need a stool softener?	43.	**¿Necesita Vd. una cápsula para ablandar sus evacuaciones?**

44.   Do you need supplies?

44.   ¿Le faltan $\begin{cases} \text{artículos?} \\ \text{materiales?} \end{cases}$

SURGERY

CIRUGIA

1.   We will notify your family of the approximate time that your operation is scheduled.

1.   **Le avisaremos a su familia de la hora aproximada en que la operación está programada.**

2.   Your family may come to see you before the operation and accompany you to the surgical floor.

2.   **Su familia puede venir a verle antes de la operación y acompañarle al piso quirúrgico.**

3.   You have to sign the permission to operate.

3.   **Hay que firmar el permiso para operar.**

4.   I am going to prepare you for the operation.

4.   **Voy a prepararle (prepararla) para la operación.**

5.   I have to shave you.

5.   **Tengo que rasurarle. (rasurarla).**

6.   We are going to give you a sedative before taking you to the operating room.

6.   **Vamos a darle un calmante antes de llevarle a la sala de operaciones.**

7.   We are going to remove your appendix.

7.   **Vamos a sacarle el apéndice.**

8.   The anesthesiologist will be here soon to discuss what anesthesia he is going to give you.

8.   **El anestesiólogo estará aquí dentro de poco para discutir qué anestesia va a darle.**

9.   Perhaps he will use a local anesthetic.

9.   **Tal vez usará anestesia local.**

10.   Do you prefer sodium pentothal?

10.   **¿Prefiere Vd. el pentotal de sodio?**

11.   The surgery will be at 6 a.m. and you will be in the recovery room by 9 a.m.

11.   **La cirugía será a las seis de la mañana y Vd. estará en la sala de recuperación a eso de las nueve de la mañana.**

12.   Do not eat or drink anything after midnight.

12.   **No coma ni beba nada después de medianoche.**

13.   The surgeon has just arrived.

13.   **El cirujano acaba de llegar.**

14.   The patient is becoming sicker.

14.   **El (la) paciente se pone más enfermo (enferma).**

15. The patient is in a lot of pain.

16. The operation turned out all right.

17. The patient is out of danger.

18. The patient is not expected to live.

19. The patient is going to live.

20. The patient has been taken to the recovery room.

21. The patient has been taken to Intensive Care, or Cardiac Care.

22. He will leave Intensive Care tomorrow.

23. They are not going to operate on him (her) any more.

24. When the stitches are taken out, you may have a scar.

15. El (la) paciente tiene mucho dolor.

16. La operación salió bien.

17. El (la) paciente está fuera de peligro.

18. No se cree que el (la) paciente va a vivir.

19. El (la) paciente va a vivir.

20. El paciente ha sido llevado a la sala de recuperación.

21. La paciente ha sido llevada a Cuidado Intensivo, o a Cuidado Cardíaco.

22. Saldrá del Cuidado Intensivo mañana.

23. No le van a operar más.

24. Cuando le quitamos las puntadas, quizás tenga una cicatriz.

MEDICATION AND TREATMENT

MEDICACION Y TRATAMIENTO

1. Whose medicine is this?

2. Whose vaccine is that?

3. Give me the medicine, please.

4. Take the medicine today.

5. Don't take the medicine tomorrow.

6. I am going for the medicine.

7. Are you taking the medicine?

8. You have to take your medicine, Ma'am.

9. Take only what the nurse gives you.

1. ¿De quién es esta medicina?

2. ¿De quién es esa vacuna?

3. Favor de darme la medicina.

4. Tome Vd. la medicina hoy.

5. No tome Vd. la medicina mañana.

6. Voy por la medicina.

7. ¿Toma Vd. la medicina?

8. Vd. tiene que tomar su medicina, señora.

9. Tome Vd. solamente las (medicinas) que le da la enfermera.

10. Do not take any medicine from home.

11. Do not take any medicine before coming to the hospital.

12. The doctor will give you a prescription.

13. Who is taking your prescriptions to the pharmacy?

14. Take this medicine four times a day.

15. Take two pills twice a day.

16. Instead of taking two pills, you can take only one.

17. Three times a day.

18. Every four hours.

19. Take one capsule at breakfast.

20. Take one of these tablets before bedtime.

21. Do not drink alcohol with this.

22. Chew them.

23. Don't chew them.

24. Swallow without chewing.

25. Take this medicine before meals.

26. After meals.

27. Whenever it hurts you.

28. A glass of water, juice, milk.

29. Take a tablespoonful of this.

30. Take a teaspoonful of this.

31. Take this every time you feel pain.

32. Dissolve a teaspoonful of this in a glass of water.

33. Don't drive a car after taking this.

10. **No tome Vd. ninguna medicina traída de su casa.**

11. **No tome Vd. ninguna medicina antes de venir al hospital.**

12. **El doctor le dará una receta.**

13. **¿Quién lleva las recetas a la farmacía?**

14. **Tome esta medicina cuatro veces al día.**

15. **Tome Vd. dos píldoras dos veces al día.**

16. **En vez de tomar dos píldoras, puede tomar solamente una.**

17. **Tres veces al día.**

18. **Cada cuatro horas.**

19. **Tome Vd. una cápsula con el desayuno.**

20. **Tome Vd. una de estas pastillas antes de acostarse.**

21. **No tome Vd. alcohol con esto.**

22. **Mastíquelas Vd.**

23. **No las mastique Vd.**

24. **Trague Vd. esto sin masticar.**

25. **Tome Vd. esta medicina antes de las comidas.**

26. **Después de las comidas.**

27. **Cuando le duela.**

28. **Un vaso de agua, jugo, leche.**

29. **Tome una cucharada de esto.**

30. **Tome Vd. una cucharadita de esto.**

31. **Tome Vd. esto cada vez que sienta dolor.**

32. **Disuelva una cucharadita de esto en un vaso de agua.**

33. **No conduzca Vd. un coche después de tomar esto.**

34. Put two drops in each ear; in each eye; in each nostril.

35. Is there anyone in house who knows how to give an injection?

36. Use one of these suppositories every evening.

37. Insert one of these suppositories using this applicator.

38. Its sale requires a prescription.

39. Keep in a cool, dry place.

40. Keep out of children's reach.

41. Shake well before using.

42. Change the bandages every day.

43. Apply this to the affected area.

44. Apply the ointment without rubbing.

45. Put this over the rash, burn, wound.

46. Apply a wet bandage every two hours.

47. Paint the swelling with this.

48. Apply a hot water bag over the _____.

49. Put your _____ in warm water.

50. Bathe with warm (cold) water.

51. Rub yourself with alcohol.

52. You must wear an elastic bandage.

34. **Póngase dos gotas en cada oído; en cada ojo; en cada ventana de la nariz.**

35. **¿Hay alguien en su casa que sepa poner inyecciones?**

36. **Póngase uno de estos supositorios cada noche.**

37. **Introdúzcase uno de estos supositorios por medio de este aplicador.**

38. **Su venta requiere receta médica.**

39. **Consérvese en lugar fresco y seco.**

40. **No se deje al alcance de los niños.**

41. **Agite Vd. bien antes de usar.**

42. **Cambie Vd. los vendajes cada día.**

43. **Aplíquese esto en la parte afectada.**

44. **Aplíquese la pomada sin frotarse.**

45. **Póngase esto en el sarpullido, en la quemadura, en la herida.**

46. **Póngase una venda húmeda cada dos hora.**

47. **Es preciso que Vd. pinte el hinchazón con esto.**

48. **Aplique una bolsa de agua caliente sobre _____.**

49. **Ponga _____ en agua caliente.**

50. **Báñese con agua caliente (fría).**

51. **Frótese con alcohol.**

52. **Debe llevar una venda elástica.**

53.	Put on an elastic stocking.	53.	**Póngase Vd. una media elástica.**
54.	Your doctor is going to remove your stitches today.	54.	**Su doctor va a quitarle los puntos hoy.** **Su médico va a quitarle las puntadas hoy.**
55.	Tomorrow the doctor will probably change your dressing.	55.	**Mañana el doctor probablemente le cambiará el vendaje.**
56.	The doctor will put the broken arm in a cast.	56.	**El doctor le pondrá el brazo roto dentro de un yeso.**

Exercise   *Ejercicio*

Substitution Drill. Using the cue given in parenthesis, give the correct instructions for taking medication:

Tome Vd. la medicina.
(hoy)

Tome Vd. la medicina hoy.
(mañana)

Tome Vd. la medicina mañana.
(No)

No tome Vd. la medicina mañana.
(ninguna medicina)

No tome Vd. ninguna medicina mañana.
(alcohol)

No tome Vd. alcohol mañana.

Substitution Drill: More of the same

Tome Vd. esta medicina cuatro veces al día.
(dos píldoras)

Tome Vd. dos píldoras cuatro veces al día.
(tres veces)

Tome Vd. dos píldoras tres veces al día.
(cada cuatro horas)

Tome Vd. dos píldoras cada cuatro horas.
(cápsulas)

Tome Vd. dos cápsulas cada cuatro horas.
(estas pastillas)

Tome Vd. estas pastillas cada cuatro horas.
(antes de las comidas)

Tome Vd. estas pastillas antes de las comidas.
(esta medicina)

Tome Vd. esta medicina antes de las comidas.
(después de las comidas)

Tome Vd. esta medicina después de las comidas.
(cuando le duela)

Tome Vd. esta medicina cuando le duela.
(con un vaso de agua)

Tome Vd. esta medicina con un vaso de agua.
(un vaso de jugo)

Tome Vd. esta medicina con un vaso de jugo.
(un vaso de leche)

Tome Vd. esta medicina con un vaso de leche.

BLOOD TESTS, LABORATORY TESTS, AND INJECTIONS

ANALISIS DE SANGRE, PRUEBAS LABORATORIAS E INYECCIONES

1. Good morning (good afternoon), I am the technician.
2. You need some blood tests.
3. I am going to take a sample of your blood.
4. Don't be nervous.
5. Roll up your sleeve.
6. Make a fist, please.
7. Keep your hand closed.
8. It will not hurt.
9. I am sorry, but I have to stick you again.
10. I wasn't able to get enough blood the first time.
11. Don't move, please.
12. Open your hand.
13. Fold your arm.
14. Keep this bandaid on for a few minutes.
15. I am going to give you a shot.
16. Stretch out your arm.
17. Roll over on your side.
18. I am going to give you an intravenous feeding.
19. The IV will go into your veins through this needle.

1. **Buenos días (buenas tardes), yo soy el técnico.**
2. **Vd. necesita unos análisis de sangre.**
3. **Voy a tomar una muestra de su sangre.**
4. **No se ponga nervioso (nerviosa).**
5. **Suba la manga.**
6. **Cierre Vd. el puño, por favor.**
7. **Mantenga Vd. la mano cerrada.**
8. **No le dolerá.**
9. **Lo siento, pero tengo que picarle otra vez.**
10. **No pude obtener bastante sangre la primera vez.**
11. **No se mueva, por favor.**
12. **Abra Vd. la mano, por favor.**
13. **Doble Vd. el brazo, por favor.**
14. **Déjese Vd. esta curita por unos minutos.**
15. **Voy a ponerle una inyección.**
16. **Extienda Vd. el brazo, por favor.**
17. **Voltéese Vd. del lado, por favor.**
18. **Le voy a aplicar suero.**
19. **El alimento intravenoso pasará sus venas a través de esta aguja.**

20. It is not painful once it is in place.

20. **No duele**
   { **cuando está en su sitio.**
   { **una vez que está en su sitio.**

21. Do you feel dizzy?

21. **¿Se siente mareado (mareada)?**

22. Please, lean forward, and put your head down between your legs for a few minutes.

22. **Favor de inclinarse hacia adelante y poner la cabeza entre las piernas por unos minutos.**
   Por favor, inclínese Vd. hacia adelante y coloque Vd. su cabeza entre las piernas por unos minutos.

23. We have to do some tests.

23. **Tenemos que hacerle algunos análisis.**

24. I want to explain them to you.

24. **Quiero explicárselos.**

25. You have to go to the clinic (laboratory) for the tests.

25. **Vd. tiene que ir a la clínica (al laboratorio) para los análisis.**

26. Tomorrow they will give you a special test.

26. **Mañana le harán un análisis especial.**

27. You cannot eat or drink anything after midnight.

27. **Vd. no puede comer ni tomar nada después de medianoche.**

28. Don't eat or drink anything before the test.

28. **No coma ni beba nada antes del análisis.**

29. It is important to come to the laboratory without eating.

29. **Es importante venir al laboratorio sin comer.**

30. Don't eat anything.

30. **Venga en ayunas.**

31. Have you eaten or drunk since midnight?

31. **¿Ha comido o bebido desde la medianoche?**

32. We will bring you breakfast after the test.

32. **Le traeremos el desayuno después del análisis.**

33. Do you have the doctor's written orders?

33. **¿Tiene Vd. las instrucciones escritas del doctor?**

34. What type of test are you here for?

34. **¿Para qué clase de análisis vino Vd. aquí?**

35. Blood count?

35. **¿Biometría hemática?**

36. Blood chemistry (analysis of the blood)?

36. **¿Análisis de sangre?**

37. Serology test?

37. **¿Prueba serológica?**

38. Sputum test?

38. **¿Análisis de esputos?**

39.	Pap smear?	39.	**¿Los untos de Papanicolaou?**	
			¿Los frotis de Papanicolaou?	
40.	Stool specimen?	40.	**¿Análisis del excremento?**	
41.	An electrocardiogram?	41.	**¿Un electrocardiograma?**	
42.	I am going to do a urinalysis.	42.	**Voy a hacerle**	

39. Pap smear?

39. **¿Los untos de Papanicolaou?**
    ¿Los frotis de Papanicolaou?

40. Stool specimen?

40. **¿Análisis del excremento?**

41. An electrocardiogram?

41. **¿Un electrocardiograma?**

42. I am going to do a urinalysis.

42. **Voy a hacerle**
    { **un urinálisis.**
    { **un análisis de la orina.**

43. I need a urine specimen from you.

43. **Necesito una muestra de orina de Vd.**

44. You must drink lots of liquids.

44. **Vd. debe tomar muchos líquidos.**

45. When you urinate, fill up this bottle and give it to the nurse on duty.

45. **Cuando Vd. orine, llene este frasco y déselo a la enfermera de guardia.**

46. Collect and bring your urine of the previous 24 hours.

46. **Recoja y traiga la orina de todo el día.**

47. Call when you have to go to the toilet.

47. **Llame Vd. cuando tenga que ir**
    { **al inodoro.**
    { **a los servicios.**

48. Go to the bathroom.

48. **Vaya Vd.**
    { **al inodoro.**
    { **a los servicios.**
    { **al cuarto de baño.**

49. Did you urinate?

49. **¿Orinó Vd.?**

50. You need an x-ray.

50. **Vd. necesita**
    { **tomarse unas radiografías.**
    { **radiografías.**

51. Give yourself an enema before coming.

51. **Póngase una enema antes de venir.**

52. Take a laxative the night before.

52. **Tome Vd. un laxante la noche anterior.**

53. Bring me a (recent) specimen of your stools in this container.

53. **Tráigame una muestra (reciente) de**
    { **su excremento**
    { **sus evacuaciones**
    en este frasco.

54. I will give you an enema.

54. **Le pondré un enema.**

55. Turn on your left (right) side.

55. **Acuéstese Vd. sobre el lado izquierdo (derecho).**

56.	Turn over.	56.	**Voltéese Vd. del otro lado, por favor.**
57.	Lie down on the x-ray table.	57.	**Acuéstese Vd. sobre la mesa radiográfica.**
58.	It may be a little cold.	58.	**Pudiese estar un poco fría.**
59.	Let me put you in the right position.	59.	**Déjeme** $\begin{cases} \textbf{ponerle} \\ \textbf{colocarle} \end{cases}$ **en la postura correcta.**
60.	In order to take the x-ray you must swallow this mixture.	60.	**Para tomarle la radiografía, Vd. tiene que tomar esta mezcla.**
61.	Hold the cup up and every time that I say "Drink," take a sip.	61.	**Mantenga el vaso en alto, y cada vez que le diga «Beba,» tome Vd. un trago.**
62.	It may not taste good.	62.	**Quizás no tenga un buen sabor.**
63.	Don't drink all the mixture now. Drink only half.	63.	**No tome Vd. toda la mezcla ahora. Beba solamente la mitad.**
64.	Stand here and place your chest against this plate.	64.	**Párese Vd. aquí y apoye el pecho contra esta placa.**
65.	Let me put you in the right position.	65.	**Permítame colocarle en la postura correcta.**
66.	Move a little over to the right (left).	66.	**Muévese Vd. un poco hacia la derecha (izquierda).**
67.	Rest your chin here.	67.	**Apoye Vd.** $\begin{cases} \textbf{la barbilla} \\ \textbf{el mentón} \end{cases}$ **aquí**
68.	Put your hands on your hips with the palms facing out, like so.	68.	**Póngase Vd. las manos en las caderas con las palmas hacia afuera, así.**
69.	Take a deep breath and hold it.	69.	**Respire Vd. profundamente y sostenga la respiración.**
70.	Don't move, please.	70.	**No se mueva Vd., por favor.**
71.	Now you may breathe.	71.	**Ahora Vd. puede respirar.**
72.	Turn your body slowly to the left; to the right.	72.	**Gire Vd. el cuerpo lentamente hacia la izquierda; hacia la derecha.**

73. We have to take another film.

73. **Tenemos que tomar otra placa.**

74. Thank you for your cooperation.

74. **Gracias por su**
{ **cooperación.**
{ **colaboración.**

75. Your doctor will tell you the results.

75. **Su doctor le dira los resultados.**

76. Sit down on the wheelchair and wait for the orderly.

76. **Siéntese Vd. en la silla de ruedas y espere al ayudante.**

77. The orderly will take you back to your room.

77. **El ayudante le llevará a su cuarto.**

78. Come back Thursday at 9 a.m.

78. **Vuelva Vd. el jueves a las nueve de la mañana, por favor.**

79. You have an appointment for Monday.

79. **Vd. tiene una cita para el lunes.**

Exercise   *Ejercicio*

Rewrite all polite commands in this section using the acceptable substitutes of *please* plus the infinitive:

Please {
Haga Vd. el favor de
Favor de
Tenga la bondad de
Sírvase

No se ponga nervioso, por favor.
(Haga Vd. el favor de) _____

Haga Vd. el favor de no ponerse nervioso.
(Favor de) _____

Favor de no ponerse nervioso.
(Tenga la bondad de) _____

Tenga la bondad de no ponerse nervioso.
(Sírvase) _____

Sírvase no ponerse nervioso.

CHAPTER
SIX
CONVERSATIONS FOR ADMINISTRATIVE PERSONNEL
CONVERSACIONES PARA PERSONAL ADMINISTRATIVO

INFORMATION FOR ADMISSION

1. What is the patient's complete and correct name?[1]

2. What is the address and zip code of the patient?

3. What is the patient's telephone number?

4. What is the sex of the patient?

5. To what race does the patient belong?[2]

6. How old is the patient?

7. On what day, month, and year was the patient born?

8. Where was the patient born?

9. Tell me the name of the town, the state, and the country.

10. What is the patient's religion?[3]

INFORMACION PARA ADMISION

1. **Dígame el nombre completo y correcto del (de la) paciente. ¿Cómo se llama el (la) paciente?**

2. **¿Cuál es la dirección y la zona postal del (de la) paciente?**

3. **¿Cuál es el número de teléfono del (de la) paciente?**

4. **¿Cuál es el sexo del (de la) paciente?**

5. **¿A qué raza pertenece el (la) paciente?**

6. **¿Qué edad tiene el (la) paciente? ¿Cuántos años tiene el (la) paciente?**

7. **¿En qué día, mes y año nació el (la) paciente?**

8. **¿(En) dónde nació el (la) paciente?**

9. **Dígame el nombre del pueblo, del estado y del país.**

10. **¿Cuál es la religión del (de la) paciente?**

---

[1] See note 5, page 105.

[2] Racial problems in the Iberian Peninsula theoretically do not exist because all inhabitants are supposedly of Caucasian background. This is not the case in Latin America. Racial problems originated in the sixteenth century when the Conquistadors came to the New World for "Gold," "Glory," and the "Gospel." Women in the beginning did not come, for the men did not intend to stay permanently. Unions were formed with either native women or with Black slaves who were imported from Africa. New races resulted:

Mestizo—offspring of a White and an Indian.
Mulato—offspring of a White and a Black.
Zambo—offspring of a Black and an Indian.

In Latin America the indigenous and Black elements play important roles. As for racial identification, a person is frequently called White if he is not Black. (In the United States a person is classified as Black if he is not completely White.)

Race membership is often more closely linked to socio-economic status than to physical characteristics. The Mestizo inhabits all economic classes, and now occupies many positions which were formerly held by Whites alone. Racial characteristics are not important, nor do they deter the Mestizo. Education and economics provide for advancement. The Indian is generally a country dweller. He is often poorly educated if not illiterate, poor, and limited in opportunity for future advancement. The Mulato and the Black are found along the coastal regions of South America and in the Caribbean. While poor, and often poorly educated, hope exists for future advancement.

[3] See page 254.

11. What is the patient's marital status?

11. **¿Qué es su estado civil?**

12. If married, what is the spouse's name?

12. **Si es casado (casada), ¿cómo se llama la esposa (el esposo)?**

13. What kind of work does the patient do?[4]

13. **¿Qué clase de trabajo hace el (la) paciente?**
¿Cuál es su ocupación?
¿En qué se ocupa el (la) paciente?

14. What is the name of the patient's employer or the responsible party?

14. **¿Cómo se llama el patrón del (de la) paciente o el del responsable?**

15. What is the address of that employer?

15. **¿Cuál es la dirección de ese patrón?**

16. What is the telephone number there?

16. **¿Cuál es el número de teléfono allí?**

17. Of what country is the patient a citizen?

17. **¿De qué país es el (la) paciente ciudadano (ciudadana)?**
¿Cuál es su ciudadanía?

18. What is the name of the patient's nearest relative?

18. **¿Cómo se llama el pariente más cercano al (a la) paciente?**

19. What is his/her address?[5]

19. **¿Cuál es su dirección?**

20. What is his/her telephone number?[6]

20. **¿Cuál es su número de teléfono?**

21. What is the relationship with the patient?

21. **¿Qué parentesco tiene con el (la) paciente?**
¿Qué es la relación entre ellos?

22. What is the patient's social security number?[7]

22. **¿Cuál es el número de la tarjeta de seguro social del (de la) paciente?**

23. To whom shall the bill be sent?

23. **¿A quién debemos mandar la cuenta?**

24. What is the address and zip code of this person?

24. **¿Cuál es la dirección y zona postal de esta persona?**

---

[4] See pages 227ff.
[5] See above page 33.
[6] See above page 106.
[7] See above page 33.

25. When was the patient admitted to the hospital?

26. What was the time?
27. When was the patient discharged?
28. Is this his/her first time in the hospital.
29. Was the patient admitted to the hospital within the last six months?

30. Does the patient have Blue Cross/Blue Shield?
31. What is the certificate and group number of the patient's Blue Cross?

32. What is the name of the policyholder?
33. What is the sex of the policyholder?
34. What is the patient's relation to the policyholder?

35. What is the social security number of the policyholder?

36. Does the patient have other medical, hospitalization, or health insurance?
37. What is the name of his/her insurance company (companies)?

25. ¿Cuándo fue admitido el paciente (admitida la paciente) al hospital?
¿Cuándo ingresó el (la) paciente al hospital?

26. ¿Qué hora era?
27. ¿A qué hora se le dieron de alta al (a la) paciente?
28. ¿Es ésta la primera vez en el hospital?
29. ¿Tuvo el (la) paciente admisión previa al hospital dentro de los últimos seis meses?
¿Fue admitido el paciente (admitida la paciente) al hospital dentro de los últimos seis meses?

30. ¿Tiene el (la) paciente Blue Cross o Blue Shield?
31. ¿Cuál es el número del certificado y del grupo de la Blue Cross del (de la) paciente?

32. ¿Cómo se llama el tenedor de la póliza?
33. ¿Cuál es el sexo del poseedor de la póliza?
34. ¿Qué es la relación entre el (la) paciente y el asegurado (la asegurada)?

35. ¿Cuál es el número de la tarjeta de seguro social del tenedor de la póliza?

36. ¿Tiene el (la) paciente algún otro seguro médico, de hospital o de enfermedad?
37. ¿Cuál es el nombre de su(s) aseguranza(s)?
¿Cómo se llama(n) la(s) empresa(s) con que está asegurado (asegurada)?

38. What is the insurance policy number?	38. ¿Cuál es el número de su póliza de seguros?
39. What is the name of the policy-holder?	39. ¿Cómo se llama el tenedor de esta póliza?
40. What is the name of the policyholder's employer?	40. ¿Cómo se llama el patrón del tenedor de esta póliza?
41. What is the employer's address?	41. ¿Cuál es la dirección del patrón?
42. Was the patient admitted because of an accident?	42. ¿Se le admitieron al (a la) paciente a causa de un accidente?
43. When did the accident happen?	43. ¿Cuándo ocurió el accidente?
44. Where did the accident happen?	44. ¿Dónde ocurrió el accidente?
45. Was the patient admitted from a general hospital?	45. ¿Ingresó el (la) paciente de un hospital general?
46. From home?	46. ¿De casa?
47. From an extended care facility?	47. ¿De una institución de cuidado prolongado?
48. What was the admission diagnosis?	48. ¿Cuál fue el diagnóstico al ingresar?
49. Is the condition due to injury or sickness arising from the patient's employment?	49. ¿Es la condición debida a una herida o enfermedad que proviene del empleo del (de la) paciente?
50. If "yes," what is the name and address of the employer?	50. Si lo es, dígame el nombre y la dirección del patrono.
51. Does the patient want a private room?	51. ¿Desea el (la) paciente un cuarto privado (individual)?
52. A semiprivate room?	52. ¿Un cuarto semiprivado (doble)?
53. A ward?	53. ¿Una crujía (una sala de los enfermos)?
54. What is the name and address of the patient's physician?	54. Dígame el nombre y la dirección del médico del (de la) paciente.
55. Whom shall we notify in case of emergency?	55. ¿A quién se notifica en caso de emergencia? ¿A quién podemos notificar en caso de emergencia?

56. Does the patient authorize release of information requested on this form by the above-named hospital?

57. Does the patient authorize payment directly to the above-named hospital of any benefits payable in this case, realizing that the patient shall be responsible for the charges not covered?

58. Does the patient consent to and authorize all treatments, surgical procedures, and administration of all anesthetics which in the judgment of his/her physician may be considered necessary for the diagnosis or treatment of this case while a patient in _____ hospital?

56. **¿Autoriza el (la) paciente un descargo de la información contenida en este informe por el hospital ya nombrado?**

57. **¿Autoriza el (la) paciente el pago de todos los beneficios aplicables en este caso directamente al susodicho hospital, dándose cuenta de que hay que pagar lo que no paga el seguro?**

58. **¿Da el (la) paciente su consiento y autorización para todos los tratamientos, procedimientos quirúrgicos y administración de todas anestesias que crea necesarios su médico para el diagnóstico o tratamiento de este caso mientras estar paciente en _____ hospital?**

REPORT FOR BLUE CROSS/BLUE SHIELD

1. Admitting Date _____
2. Patient's Name _____
3. Blue Cross Certificate Number _____

The following questions must be answered for all claims which may be "work related" in order for Blue Cross to determine eligible benefits. Thank you for cooperating.

4. Was the condition which required hospital care caused by your employment? If yes, answer only questions 5 through 9.
5. Are you entitled to Workmen's Compensation benefits for this disability?

6. Give reason: _____
7. Briefly explain in what way condition was caused by employment.

8. If you are employed, give the following information:
    What is the name of your employer?_____
    What is his address? _____
    In what city and state is he? _____
    What is the zip code? _____
    What is the telephone number where you work?_____
9. Signature of informant _____
    Date_____Informant's telephone number _____
    If the response to Question 4 is no, answer only what follows. Skip questions 5–9.
10. Signature of informant.
    Date_____Informant's telephone number _____

Note carefully: If subsequent investigation reveals your condition is "work related," benefits paid for you by Blue Cross must be returned.

INFORME PARA BLUE CROSS/BLUE SHIELD

1. Fecha de admisión————————————————————————
2. Nombre del paciente ——————————————————————
3. Número del certificado de Blue Cross ————————————————

Hay que contestar a las preguntas que siguen para todas reclamaciones que sean "relacionadas al trabajo" para que Blue Cross determine los beneficios admisibles. Gracias para su cooperación.

4. ¿Fue la condición que necesitó hospitalización causada por su empleo?
   Si la respuesta es afirmativa, conteste a las preguntas 5 a 9 solamente.
5. ¿Tiene derecho a recibir algunos beneficios de la compensación obrera en cuanto a esta incapacidad?
6. Explíqueselo. ————————————————————————
7. Con brevedad explique la manera en que su empleo causó esta incapacidad.

8. Si tiene trabajo, dé la información siguiente:
   ¿Cómo se llama su patrón? ————————————————————
   ¿Cuál es su dirección? ——————————————————————
   ¿En qué ciudad y estado está?————————————————————
   ¿Cuál es la zona postal?——————————————————————
   ¿Cuál es el número de teléfono del lugar donde trabaja? ————————
9. Firma del informante————————————————————————
   Fecha———Número de teléfono del informante—————————————
   Si la respuesta es negativa, solamente conteste a lo que sigue y omita a las preguntas 5 a 9.
10. Firma del informante.
   Fecha ———Número de teléfono del informante—————————————

Fíjese bien: Si investigación subsecuente revela que su condición es «relacionada al trabajo,» será preciso devolver todos los beneficios pagados por Blue Cross.

EMERGENCY ROOM REPORT

INFORME DE LA SALA DE EMERGENCIA

1. Are you the patient?

1. **¿Es Vd. el paciente?**
   ¿Es Vd. la paciente?

2. What is your name?

2. **Cómo se llama Vd.?**
   Dígame su nombre completo y correcto.

3. What is your last (surname) name?[8]

3. **¿Cuál es su apellido?**

4. What is your first name?

4. **¿Cuál es su primer nombre?**
   ¿Cuál es su nombre de bautismo?

5. What is your middle initial?

5. **¿Cuál es su segunda inicial?**

6. What is your maiden name?

6. **¿Cuál es su nombre de soltera?**

7. What is your home telephone number?[9]

7. **¿Qué es el número de teléfono de su casa?**

8. What is your address?[10]

8. **¿Cuál es su dirección?**
   ¿Dónde vive Vd.?

9. What is your zip code?

9. **¿Cuál es su zona postal?**

10. What is the name of your nearest relative?

10. **¿Cómo se llama su pariente más cercano (cercana)?**

11. What is the relationship with you?

11. **¿Qué parentesco tiene con Vd.?**
    ¿Qué es la relación entre Vds.?

12. How is she/he related to you?

12. **¿Qué es de Vd.?**

13. Where does she/he live?

13. **¿Dónde vive?**

14. What is the zip code there?

14. **¿Cuál es la zona postal allí?**

15. What is her/his telephone number?

15. **¿Qué es su número de teléfono?**

16. How old are you?

16. **¿Qué edad tiene Vd.?**
    ¿Cuántos años tiene Vd.?

17. On what day, month, and year were you born?

17. **¿En qué día, mes y año nació Vd.?**

18. Where were you born?

18. **¿(En) dónde nació Vd.?**

[8] See note 5, page 105.
[9] See note 7, page 106.
[10] See page 33.

19. What is your race?[11]

20. What is your marital status?

21. Are you married?

22. Are you divorced?

23. Are you single?

24. Are you a widow(er)?

25. Are you separated?

26. When were you hurt?

27. What was the time?

28. When did the accident happen?

29. What kind of work do you do?[12]

30. What is the complete name of your employer?

31. What is the address of the place where you work?

32. What is the zip code?

33. What is the telephone number where you work?

34. Do you have Illinois Blue Cross and/or Blue Shield?

35. What is the number of your Blue Cross policy? of your Blue Shield policy?

36. What is the name of the group policyholder?

37. Do you have a Medicare card?

38. What is the number of your card? (You must include all the letters, also.)

19. **¿A qué raza pertenece Vd.?**

20. **¿Qué es su estado civil?**

21. **¿Es Vd. casado (casada)?**

22. **¿Es Vd. divorciado (divorciada)?**

23. **¿Es Vd. soltero (soltera)?**

24. **¿Es Vd. viudo (viuda)?**

25. **¿Es Vd. separado (separada)?**

26. **¿Cuándo se lastimó?**

27. **¿A qué hora?**

28. **¿Cuándo ocurrió el accidente?**

29. **¿Qué clase de trabajo hace Vd.?**
¿Cuál es su ocupación?
¿En qué se ocupa Vd.?

30. **Dígame el nombre completo del lugar donde trabaja.**

31. **¿Cuál es la dirección del lugar donde trabaja?**

32. **¿Cuál es la zona postal?**

33. **¿Cuál es el número de teléfono donde trabaja?**

34. **¿Tiene Vd. Blue Cross y/o Blue Shield de Illinois?**

35. **¿Cuál es el número de su certificado de Blue Cross? ¿de Blue Shield?**

36. **¿Cómo se llama el tenedor de la póliza del grupo?**
Dígame el nombre del asegurado (de la asegurada) del grupo.

37. **¿Tiene Vd. una tarjeta de Medicare?**

38. **¿Cuál es el número de su tarjeta? (Hay que incluir todas las letras también.)**

[11] See note 2 page 141.
[12] See pages 227ff.

39.	Do you receive public assistance?		39.	¿Recibe Vd. el bienestar público?
40.	What is the number of your green card?		40.	¿Cuál es el número de su tarjeta verde?
41.	When does the card expire?		41.	¿Cuándo expira la tarjeta?
42.	Do you have medical insurance?		42.	¿Tiene Vd. seguros médicos?
43.	Do you have hospitalization?		43.	¿Tiene Vd. seguros de hospital?
44.	What type of insurance do you have?		44.	¿Qué tipo de seguros tiene Vd.?
45.	What is the name of your insurance company?		45.	¿Cuál es el nombre de su aseguranza? ¿Cuál es el nombre de la empresa con que está asegurado (asegurada)?
46.	Where did the injury occur?		46.	¿En qué lugar ocurrió la herida?
47.	Where was the onset of the illness?		47.	¿En qué lugar empezó la enfermedad?
48.	Were the police notified?		48.	¿Fue notificada la policía?
49.	What was the police district number?		49.	¿De qué barrio fue la policía?
50.	The above instruction(s) have been explained to me as continued care following treatment in emergency room at _____ Hospital.		50.	Se me han explicado las antedichas instrucciones como cuidado continuo siguiente el tratamiento en la sala de emergencia a_____ Hospital.

INFORMATION FOR THE CERTIFICATE OF LIVE BIRTH

INFORMACION PARA LA PARTIDA DE NACIMIENTO VIVO

Child

Nene

1.	Tell me the complete and correct name of the child.		1.	Dígame el nombre completo y correcto del recién nacido.
2a.	On what day, month, and year was he/she born?		2a.	¿En qué día, mes y año nació?

2b. At what time was the child born?

2b. **¿A qué hora exacta nació?**

3. What is the sex?

3. **¿Cuál es su sexo?**

4a. Was this a single birth, twin, triplet, etc.?

4a. **¿Fue un parto único, doble, triple, etc.?**

4b. If this was not a single birth, was this child born first, second, third, etc.? (Specify)

4b. **Si éste no fue un parto único, ¿nació este hijo primero, segundo, tercero, etc.? (Especifique.)**

5a. In what county was the child born?

5a. **¿En qué partido nació el nene?**

5b. Tell me the name of the city, town, township.

5b. **Dígame el nombre de la ciudad, del pueblo, del municipio.**

5c. Was the child born inside the city?

5c. **¿Nació el nene dentro de la ciudad?**

5d. What is the name of the hospital? If the birth did not occur in the hospital, tell me the street and number.

5d. **¿Cómo se llama el hospital? Si el parto no ocurrió en el hospital, dígame el nombre de la calle y el número allí.**

Mother

Madre

6a. What is your complete and correct maiden name?

6a. **Dígame su nombre completo y correcto de soltera.**

6b. How old are you at the time of this birth?

6b. **¿Cuántos años tiene al parir?**

6c. Where were you born? Tell me the state or foreign country.

6c. **¿Cuál es su lugar de nacimiento? Dígame el nombre del estado o del país extranjero.**

7a. In what state is your permanent address?

7a. **¿En qué estado está su dirección permanente?**

7b. In what county is your permanent address?

7b. **¿En qué partido está su dirección permanente?**

7c. In what city, town or township do you live?

7c. **¿En qué ciudad, pueblo o municipio vive Vd.?**

7d. Do you live inside the city?

7d. **¿Vive Vd. dentro de la ciudad?**

7e. What is your exact address?

7e. **¿Cuál es su dirección exacta?**

7f.	What is your complete mailing address?	7f.	**¿Cuál es su dirección completa del correo?**
8a.	Is this your first pregnancy?	8a.	**¿Es ésta su primera preñez? ¿Es su primer embarazo?**
8b.	How many living children have you had?	8b.	**¿Cuántos hijos vivos ha tenido?**
8c.	How many miscarriages or abortions have you had?	8c.	**¿Cuántos malpartos o abortos ha tenido?**
8d.	How many still births have you had?	8d.	**¿Cuántos nati-muertos ha tenido?**
9a.	What is your blood type?	9a.	**¿Qué tipo de sangre tiene? ¿Tiene factor RH?**
9b.	Are you going to nurse the baby?	9b.	**¿Piensa darle el pecho al nene?**

Father

Padre

10a.	Tell me the complete and correct name of the father.	10a.	**Dígame el nombre completo y correcto del padre.**
10b.	How old was the father at the time of this birth?	10b.	**¿Qué edad tiene el padre al nacer su nene?**
10c.	Where was the father born? Tell me the state or foreign country.	10c.	**¿Dónde está el lugar de nacimiento del padre? Dígame el nombre del estado o del país extranjero.**
11a.	Signature of the informant.	11a.	**Firma de la informante.**
11b.	What is the relation to the child?	11b.	**¿Qué es la relación entre Vd. y el nene?**

SEVEN

AUTHORIZATIONS AND SIGNATURES

AUTORIZACIONES Y FIRMAS

This chapter contains sample hospital authorization and signature forms. At crucial times patients are shown these forms. Students should practice reading them for fluency and comprehension. Key words and idioms are boldface or underscored in the Spanish texts. The following vocabulary should be helpful.

KEY WORDS AND IDIOMS FOR CONSENT FORMS

PALABRAS Y MODISMOS PRINCIPALES PARA LAS AUTORIZACIONES

abortion
   induced abortion
   therapeutic abortion
above (written)
above named
administer, to
administration
advantage
adverse results
advisable
anesthetic
apply for admission, to
appropriate
assistant
assume, to
assurance
attending physician
authorization
authorize, to

be capable, to
be gowned, to
be guaranteed, to
be successful, to
become pregnant, to
blood
   blood components

   blood donors
   blood stock
   blood transfusion
   blood, whole
body

certify, to
commentary
complication
component
consent
consent, to
consider, to

aborto (m)
   inducción del aborto (f)
   aborto terapéutico (m)
arriba escrita (adv)
ya citado (adj)
administrar
administración (f)
ventaja (f)
resultados adversos (m)
aconsejable (adj)
anestético (m)
solicitar admisión a
apropiado (adj)
ayudante (m/f)
asumir
aseguramiento (m)
médico de atendencia (m)
permiso (m), **autorización** (f)
autorizar

ser capaz
vestirse de bata de hospital
ser garantizado
tener éxito
salir encinta (embarazada)
sangre (f)
   componentes de sangre (m)
   componentes sanguíneos (m)
   donantes de sangre (m/f)
   depósito de sangre (m)
   transfusión de sangre (f)
   sangre pura (f)
cuerpo (m)

certificar
comentario (m)
complicación (f)
parte constitutiva (f)
consentimiento (m)
consentir
considerar

155

cross-matching	**prueba cruzada** (f)
daily	**por día**
destroyed	**destruido** (adj)
detect, to	**detectar**
disposal	**eliminación** (f)
educational	**educacional** (adj)
effects, ill	**malos efectos** (m)
eight p.m.	**las ocho de la noche** (f)
element	**elemento** (m)
emergency	**emergencia** (f)
examination	**examinación** (f)
exception	**excepción** (f)
exempt, to (to release)	**eximir**
feeding hours	**horas de alimentación** (f)
fitness (good health)	**buena salud** (f)
free will	**libre voluntad** (f)
give up (a claim), to	**ceder**
guarantee, to	**hacer garantías**
gynecological floor	**piso ginecológico** (m)
have children, to	**tener niños**
hepatitis	**hepatitis** (f)
infectious hepatitis	**hepatitis infecciosa** (f)
viral hepatitis	**hepatitis viral**(f)
incompatible	**incompatible** (adj)
incompetent	**incompetente** (adj)
lack	**falta** (f)
law suit	**pleito** (m)
maternity floor	**piso de maternidad** (m)
medical purposes	**fines médicos** (m)
mentally	**mentalmente** (adv)
necessary	**necesario** (adj)
newborn	**recién nacido** (m/f)
no one	**nadie**
occasionally	**de vez en cuando**
operating room	**quirófano** (m)
operation	**operación** (f)
patient	**paciente** (m/f)
performance	**ejecución** (f)
permanent sterility	**esterilidad permanente** (f)
permit	**permiso** (m)

photography	**fotografía** (f)
physically	**físicamente**
plasma	**plasma** (f)
procedure	**procedimiento** (m)
produce, to	**producir**
reaction	**reacción** (f)
registered nurse	**enfermera registrada** (f)
release	**descargo** (m)
request	**petición** (f)
require, to	**requirir**
risk	**riesgo** (m)
scientific	**científico** (adj)
sixteen years old	**dieciséis años** (m)
sterilization	**esterilización** (f)
sterilized person	**persona estéril** (f)
surgical	**quirúrgico** (adj)
test	**prueba** (f)
there may be	**haya**
tissue	**tejido** (m)
transfusion	**transfusión** (f)
treatment	**tratamiento** (m)
two p.m.	**las dos de la tarde** (f)
undersigned	**abajo firmado** (adj)
understand, to	**comprender**
unexpected	**inesperado** (adj)
virus	**virus** (m)
visiting hours	**horas de visita** (f)
visitor	**visitante** (m/f)
waiver	**renuncia voluntaria** (f)
warrant, to	**hacer certificación**
wash one's hands, to	**lavarse las manos**
witness	**testigo** (m)

AUTHORIZATION FOR SURGICAL AND OTHER PROCEDURES

Date _____

Time _____

     I hereby authorize the following operation_____

          (State nature and extent of operations or procedures)

to be performed upon_____

           (myself, or name of patient)

under the direction of Dr. _____

            (surgeon)

and whomever may be designated as his assistants.

     I consent to the performance of all operations and procedures in addition to or different from those now contemplated, whether or not arising from presently unforeseen conditions, which the above named doctor or his assistants may consider necessary or advisable on the basis of findings during the course of the operation.

     I consent to all necessary, usual or convenient procedures in connection with the operation including blood transfusions, and I consent to the administration of such anesthetics as may be considered necessary or advisable by the physician responsible for this service. I make the following exceptions: None _____ or Other _____.

     I consent to the photography of the operation procedures to be performed including appropriate portions of my body for medical, scientific, or educational purposes provided identification is not revealed by the pictures or by descriptive texts accompanying them.

     I consent to the admittance of proper professional observers to the operating room.

     I consent to the examination of and disposal by hospital authorities of any tissue or part which may be removed during the operation.

     I hereby certify that I have read and fully understand the above authorization for surgical treatment and possible blood transfusion, the reasons why these procedures are considered necessary, and the advantages and possible complications, which have been explained to me by Dr. _____. I also certify that no guarantee or assurance has been made as to the results that may be obtained.

Witness:

Name_____

Address_____

           _____
           (Signature of patient)

           _____
           (Signature of person authorized to consent for patient)

           _____
           (Relationship to patient)

           _____
           (Address)

PERMISO PARA PROCEDIMIENTOS QUIRURGICOS Y OTROS PROCEDIMIENTOS

Fecha _____

Hora _____

Por este medio **autorizo** la siguiente **operación** _____

(Declare la naturaleza y extensión de operaciones o **procedimientos**)
que será ejecutada sobre_____

(mí mismo, o nombre de paciente)
bajo la dirección del doctor _____

(cirujano)
y quienquiera que denomine como sus **ayudantes**.

Consiento en la ejecución de todos los procedimientos y operaciones además de o diferente de los pensados, que pueda ocurir o no, de condiciones ya **inesperadas**, que el médico ya citado, o sus ayudantes consideren **necesarios** o **aconsejables** a base de descubrimientos durante la operación.

Consiento en todos los procedimientos necesarios, comunes o convenientes con respecto a la operación incluso **transfusiones de sangre**, y consiento en **la administración** de tales **anestéticos** que el médico responsable para este servicio considere necesarios o **aconsejables**. Hago las siguientes **excepciones**: Ninguna _____ u Otra _____.

Autorizo **la fotografía** de los procedimientos quirúrgicos que serán ejecutados incluso porciones **apropiadas** de mi **cuerpo** para **fines médicos, científicos** o **educacionales** con tal que la identificación no sea revelada por las fotos o por **comentarios** descriptivos que las acompañan.

Autorizo la admisión de decentes observadores profesionales al **quirófano**.

Autorizo **la examinación** de y **la eliminación** de cualquier **tejido** o parte que pueda ser **destruido** durante la operación por las autoridades del hospital.

Por este medio certifico que he leído y que comprendo completamente la **arriba escrita** autorización para **tratamiento quirúrgico** y para posible transfusión de sangre, las razones por qué estos procedimientos son considerados necesarios, **las ventajas** y **las complicaciones** posibles, que me han sido explicadas por el doctor _____. También certifico que ninguna garantía ni **aseguramiento** ha sido hecho en cuanto a los resultados que sean obtenidos.

Testigo:
Nombre_____

Dirección _____

_____
(Firma del paciente)

_____
(Firma de la persona autorizada a consentir en nombre del paciente)

_____
(Parentesco al paciente)

_____
(Dirección)

REQUEST FOR TRANSFUSION OF WHOLE BLOOD OR ANY OF ITS COMPONENTS

(Consent and Waiver Form)

I, _____, do hereby request Dr. _____ (Attending Physician) and any of his assistants or associates (hereinafter called physician) to administer to me such blood transfusions or any blood components including, but not limited to, plasma, as may be deemed advisable in the judgment of any such physician.

It has been explained to me that it is not always possible to detect the existence or nonexistence of some elements occasionally present in blood, such as the virus causing infectious hepatitis or other unusual blood components, and that there is a possibility of ill effects, such as infectious hepatitis resulting from the transmission of its virus or a transfusion reaction resulting from the transmission of unusual blood components. I also understand that there is the possibility of the transmission of the causative agent of other diseases.

It has also been explained to me that emergencies may arise when it is not possible to make adequate cross-matching or other tests and that immediate need may make it necessary to use existing stocks of blood, which may include some incompatible blood types or substances.

I fully understand that the blood supplied in accordance with this agreement is incidental to the rendition of services and that no requirements, guarantee or warranty of fitness, quality or absence of undetectable substances such as viruses shall apply.

After considering all of the items set forth above and the possibility of adverse results from the said blood transfusions, it is still my desire that one or more transfusions of blood or its components be administered to me, if in the opinion of my physician such transfusions are needed.

I hereby assume any and all risks in connection with any said blood transfusions and release physician and_____ Hospital, its personnel and employees, all blood donors and all other persons, firms and corporations which in any way handled or processed said blood, from any responsibility whatsoever for any resulting contraction of viral hepatitis or any reaction from any such transfusion. I further assume any and all risks in connection with said blood transfusions and agree that I will never bring suit in connection with said transfusions.

Date _____

Witness:

_____ R.N.

_____ M.D.

(Signature of Attending Physician)

_____

(Signature of patient or person authorized to consent for patient)

_____

(Relationship to patient)

PETICION PARA TRANSFUSION DE <u>SANGRE PURA</u> O DE CUALQUIER DE SUS <u>PARTES CONSTITUTIVAS</u>

(Consentimiento y renuncia voluntaria)

Por este medio yo——, **autorizo** al Dr.—— (**médico de atendencia**) y a alguno de sus **ayudantes** o asociados (más adelante llamados «médico») que me administre tales **transfusiones de sangre** o **componentes de sangre** incluso, pero no limitado a **plasma**, que según el juicio del médico sean aconsejables.

Se me explicaron que no es posible siempre **detectar** la existencia o la falta de existencia de algunos **elementos** presentes **de vez en cuando** en la sangre, como por ejemplo **el virus** que cause **la hepatitis infecciosa**, u otros **componentes sanguíneos** no muy comunes y que puede haber la posibilidad de **malos efectos**, tal como la hepatitis infecciosa que resulta de la transmisión de su virus o **una reacción** de transfusión que resulta de la transmisión de extraordinarios componentes sanguíneos. También **comprendo** que **haya** la posibilidad de la transmisión de agentes que causan otras enfermedades.

También se me han explicado que **emergencias** aparezcan cuando no sea posible hacer suficientes **pruebas cruzadas** u otras **pruebas** y que la necesidad inmediata pueda **requirir** la necesidad de usar **el depósito de sangre** que incluya algunos tipos o substancias de sangre que sean **incompatibles**.

Comprendo completamente que la sangre provista de acuerdo con este consentimiento es elemento incidental a la rendición de servicios y que nadie me **hace garantías** ni **certificación** de **buena salud**, cualidad ni falta de substancias ocultas como virus.

Después de **considerar** todo lo que se me ha explicado y la posibilidad **de resultados adversos** de las ya citadas **transfusiones de sangre**, todavía quiero que me sean administradas tantas transfusiones de sangre y sus componentes como mi médico juzgue necesarias.

Por este medio **asumo** cualquier y todos **los riesgos** con respecto a cualquier citada transfusión de sangre y les **eximo** al médico, a —— Hospital, y a su personal y empleados, a todos **los donantes de sangre** y a todas las personas, firmas y corporaciones que, de cualquier manera hayan manejado o preparado dicha sangre, de cualquier responsabilidad si contraigo **la hepatitis viral** o alguna **reacción** de semejante transfusión. Además asumo cualquier y todos los riesgos con respecto a las citadas transfusiones de sangre y cedo que nunca seguiré **un pleito** con respecto a tales transfusiones.

Fecha————

Testigo:

————————————
(Firma de la **enfermera registrada**)

————————————, Médico
(Firma del **médico de atendencia**)

(Firma de paciente o de la persona autorizada a dar permiso para paciente)

————————————
(Parentesco a paciente)

AUTHORITY TO PERFORM A THERAPEUTIC ABORTION

Date _____

    This is to certify that I, the undersigned, consent to the administration of whatever anesthetic may be necessary and the performing of a therapeutic abortion upon

Name _____

Address _____

Signature of Patient _____

Signature of Patient's Husband _____

Witness: _____

Name

_____

Address

_____

AUTORIZACION PARA <u>UN ABORTO TERAPEUTICO</u>

Fecha _____

    Esto es para certificar que yo, **la abajo firmada**, **consiento** en la **administración** de cualquier **anestético** que sea necesario y en **la ejecución** de un aborto terapéutico sobre

Nombre _____

Dirección _____

Firma de la paciente _____

Firma del esposo de la paciente _____

Testigo: _____

Nombre

_____

Dirección

_____

RELEASE FROM RESPONSIBILITY FOR ABORTION

Date _____ 19 ____ Time ____ a.m./p.m.

This is to certify that I,_____, a patient applying for admission to_____
Hospital believe that I am in a condition of abortion. I hereby declare that neither the
attending physician nor any person employed by or connected with the said hospital
has knowingly performed any act that may have contributed to the induction of the
abortion, and I do hereby absolve said persons from any responsibility or liability for
my conditon.

Witness_____   Signed _____
Witness_____   (Patient or nearest relative)

_____
(Relationship)

Authorization must be signed by the patient, or by the nearest relative when the
patient is physically or mentally incompetent.

DESCARGO DE LA RESPONSABILIDAD PARA UN ABORTO

Fecha _____ Hora _____

Esto es para **certificar** que yo,_____, una paciente **solicitando admisión**
a_____Hospital, creo estar en condiciones de aborto. Por la presente declaro que
ni el médico que me atiende ni ninguna persona empleada por o conectada con este
hospital ha realizado ningún acto que haya contribuido a **la inducción del aborto**,
y por medio de la presente descargo a estas personas de cualquier responsabilidad
por mi condición.

Testigo _____   Firma_____
Testigo _____   (Paciente o pariente más cercano)

_____
(parentesco)

Autorización debe ser firmada por la paciente o por su pariente más cercano cuando
la paciente es **incompetente física o mentalmente**.

STERILIZATION PERMIT

We, the undersigned, husband and wife, hereby authorize Dr. _____ to perform _____ (name of operation) the sole purpose of which is to produce permanent sterility, on _____ (name of patient) which in all likelihood will be the result, but in no case can it be guaranteed. The operation may not be a success.

We voluntarily request this operation and understand that it is intended to result in sterility although this result cannot be guaranteed. Sterilization has been explained to us, and we understand that a sterile person is not capable of becoming pregnant and bearing a child.

Signed _____
(Wife)

_____
(Husband)

Date _____

Witness: _____
Name

_____
Address

_____

Date _____

PERMISO PARA ESTERILIZACION

Nosotros, los **abajo firmados**, esposo y esposa, por este medio autorizamos al doctor _____ a hacer_____ (nombre de la operación) con el propósito único de **producir esterilidad permanente** sobre_____ (Esposa) o_____ (Esposo). Con toda probabilidad la operación **tendrá éxito**, pero puede haber la posibilidad de que la operación no tenga éxito.

Nosotros solicitamos esta operación por nuestra **libre voluntad** y **comprendemos** que el propósito de la operación es la esterilización, aunque este resultado no puede **ser garantizado**. Se nos explicó lo que es la esterilización, y entendemos que **una persona estéril** no **es capaz** de **salir encinta** (**embarazada**) y **tener niños**.

Firma_____
(esposa)

_____
(esposo)

Fecha_____

Testigo:_____
Nombre

_____
Dirección

_____
Fecha_____

VISITING POLICY FOR ALL MATERNITY AND GYNECOLOGY PATIENTS

Fathers and/or husbands are permitted to visit from 2 p.m. to 8 p.m. The father of the baby visiting during feeding hours must wash his hands and be gowned.

Other visitors to Maternity and Gynecology are permitted from 2 p.m. to 3 p.m. and 7 p.m. to 8 p.m.

Maternity and Gynecological patients are permitted two visitors per day, exclusive of the father and/or husband.

No persons under 16 years of age are permitted to visit a maternity or gynecological patient other than the father of the baby or husband of the patient.

HORAS DE VISITA PARA PACIENTES DEL PISO DE MATERNIDAD Y DEL PISO GINECOLOGICO

Se permiten visitas de los padres y/o los esposos desde **las dos de la tarde** hasta **las ocho de la noche**. Durante **las horas de alimentación**, el padre **del recién nacido** debe **lavarse las manos** y **vestirse de bata de hospital** si está presente.

Se permiten otros **visitantes** al piso de maternidad y al piso ginecológico desde las dos hasta las tres de la tarde y desde las siete hasta las ocho de la noche.

Además del padre y/o esposo, se permiten dos visitantes a cada paciente de maternidad o de ginecología **por día**.

Nadie de menos de **dieciséis años** pueda visitar a ninguna paciente de maternidad o de ginecología a menos que sea el padre del recién nacido o el esposo de la paciente.

CHAPTER

EIGHT

CRUCIAL VOCABULARY
FOR MEDICAL PERSONNEL

VOCABULARIO CRUCIAL
PARA PERSONAL MEDICO

CONTENTS

INDICES

CRUCIAL VOCABULARY FOR MEDICAL PERSONNEL

MAJOR CLINICS	CLINICAS PRINCIPALES
Acute care	**primeros auxilios** (m, pl)
Admitting	**ingresos** (m, pl)
Allergy	**alergia** (f)
Audiology	**audiología** (f)
Bronchology	**broncología** (f)
Cafeteria	**cafetería** (f)
Central Testing Laboratory	**laboratorio central** (m)
Chest	**pulmonar** (adj)
Cardiology	**cardiología** (f)
Congenital cardiology	**cardiología congénita** (f)
Rheumatic cardiology	**cardiología reumática** (f)
Dental	**dental** (adj)
Dermatology	**dermatología** (f)
Diabetic	**diabética** (adj)
ECG-Electrocardiogram	**electrocardiograma** (m)
EEG-Brain Wave Test	**laboratorio para encefalogramas** (m)
Emergency Room	**sala de urgencia** (f)
Employees' Health Service	**dispensario de empleados** (m)
ENT–Ear, Nose and Throat	**GNO–garganta, nariz, oídos**
Eyes	**ojos** (m)
Genetics	**genética** (f)
Gynecology	**ginecología** (f)
Hematology	**hematología** (f)
Immunology	**inmunología** (f)
Kidneys-nephritic	**riñones-nefrítica**
Maternity	**maternidad** (f)
Medicine	**medicina** (f); **médica** (adj)
Neurology	**neurología** (f)
Obstetrics	**obstétrica** (f)
Occupational therapy	**terapia ocupacional** (f)
Operating room	**sala de operaciones** (f); **quirófano** (m)
Optics	**óptica** (f)

Orthopedics	**ortopedia** (f)
Special Orthopedics	**ortopedia especial** (f)
Pharmacy	**farmacia** (f)
Physical Therapy	**fisioterapia** (f)
Snack Shop	**tienda de refrescos** (f)
Social Service	**servicio social** (m)
Special seizure	**convulsiones** (f)
Speech	**del habla** (m)
Voice, Articulation	**voz, articulación** (f)
Surgery	**cirugía** (f)
Plastic Surgery	**cirugía plástica** (f)
Special Surgery	**cirugía especial** (f)
Urology	**urología** (f)
X-rays	**rayos x (equis)** (m)

KEY DISEASES AND INJURIES

ENFERMEDADES Y HERIDAS PRINCIPALES

accident	**accidente** (m)
acne	**acné** (f)
addicted	**adicto** (adj)
ailment	**dolencia** (f)
alcoholism	**alcoholismo** (m)
allergy	**alergia** (f)
amebic dysentery	**disentería amibiana** (f)
anemia	**anemia** (f)
aneurysm	**aneurisma** (f)
angina	**angina** (f)
angina pectoris	**angina del pecho** (f)
anxiety	**ansiedad** (f)
aortic insufficiency	**insuficiencia aórtica** (f)
aphasia	**afasia** (f)
appendicitis	**apendicitis** (f)
arteriosclerosis	**arteriosclerosis** (f)
arthritis	**artritis** (f)
Asiatic flu	**influenza asiática** (f)

asthma	**asma** (f); **fatiga** (f, slang)
astigmatism	**astigmatismo** (m)
athlete's foot	**pie de atleta** (m); **infección de serpigo** (f)
atrial fibrillation	**fibrilación auricular** (f)
atrophy	**atrofia** (f)
attack	**ataque** (m)
bedsore	**úlcera por decúbito** (f)
Bell's palsy	**parálisis facial** (f)
bite	**mordedura** (f); **mordida** (f); **picadura** (f)
blemish	**lunar** (m); **mancha** (f)
blind	**ciego** (adj)
blind in one eye	**tuerto** (adj)
blindness	**ceguera** (f); **ceguedad** (f)
blisters	**ampolla** (f); **vesícula** (f)
blood clot	**coágulo de sangre** (m)
blood poisoning	**envenenamiento de la sangre** (m); **toxemia** (f); **septicemia** (f); **sepsis** (f)
boil	**furúnculo** (m)
bronchial asthma	**asma bronquial** (f)
bronchitis	**bronquitis** (f)
bruise	**contusión** (f); **magulladura** (f)
bubonic plague	**peste bubónica** (f)
bunion	**juanete** (m)
burn	**quemadura** (f); **quemazón** (m)
bursitis	**bursitis** (f)
cancer	**cáncer** (m)
cancerous	**canceroso** (adj)
canker	**úlcera** (f); **llaga ulcerosa** (f); **ulceración** (f)
carcinoma	**carcinoma** (f)
cardiac arrest	**fallo cardíaco** (m); **paro cardíaco** (m)
caries	**caries** (f)
case	**caso** (m)

cat bite	**mordida de gato** (f)
cataract	**catarata** (f)
celiac disease	**celíaca** (f)
cerebrospinal meningitis	**meningitis cerebroespinal** (f)
chancre	**chancro** (m)
chicken pox	**varicela** (f); **viruelas locas** (f, slang)
chigger flea	**nigua** (f)
chills	**escalofríos** (m)
cholera	**cólera** (f)
chorea	**corea** (f); **mal** o **baile de San Guido** o **de San Vito** (m)
chronic	**crónico** (adj)
cirrhosis of the liver	**cirrosis del hígado** (f); **cirrosis hepática** (f)
cold	**catarro** (m); **resfriado** (m)
colic	**cólico** (m)
colitis	**colitis** (f)
color blindness	**daltonismo** (m); **acromatopsia** (f); **ceguera para los colores** (f)
coma	**coma** (f)
complication	**complicación** (f)
concussion	**concusión** (f); **golpe** (m)
congenital	**congénito** (adj)
conjunctivitis	**conjuntivitis** (f)
constipation	**constipación** (f); **estreñimiento** (m)
contagious	**contagioso** (adj)
contusion	**contusión** (f)
convalescence	**convalecencia** (f)
convulsion	**convulsión** (f)
corn	**callo** (m)
coronary thrombosis	**trombosis coronaria** (f)
corpse	**cadáver** (m)
cough	**tos** (f)
cramps	**calambres** (m)
charley horse	**rampa** (f)
menstrual	**dolores del período** (m)
postpartum	**entuertos** (m)
stomach	**retortijón de tripas** (m)

cripple	**tullido** (adj, m); **inválido** (adj, m)
crippled hand	**manco** (adj)
cross-eyed	**bizco** (adj)
cyst	**quiste** (m)
cystitis	**cistitis** (f); **infección de la vejiga** (f)
dandruff	**caspa** (f)
dead	**muerto** (adj, m)
deaf	**sordo** (adj)
deafness	**sordera** (f); **ensordecimiento** (m)
deafmute	**sordomudo** (m)
death	**muerte** (f); **fallecimiento** (m)
death rattle	**estertor agónico** (m)
defect	**defecto** (m)
deformity	**deformidad** (f)
dehydration	**deshidratación** (f); **desecación** (f)
delirium	**delirio** (m)
dementia	**demencia** (f)
depressed	**deprimido** (adj)
depression	**depresión** (f); **abatimiento** (m)
dermatitis	**dermatitis** (f)
diabetes	**diabetes** (f)
diabetes insipidus	**diabetes insípida** (f)
diabetes mellitus	**diabetes mellitus** (f); **diabetes sacarina** (f)
diabetic	**diabético** (adj)
diagnosis	**diagnóstico** (m); **diagnosis** (f)
diarrhea	**diarrea** (f); **cursera** (f, slang)
diphtheria	**difteria** (f); **garrotillo** (m)
disability	**inhabilidad** (f); **incapacidad** (f); **invalidez** (f)
discharge (bloody)	**derrame** (m)
discharge	**secreción** (f); **flujo** (m); **supuración** (f)
discomfort	**malestar** (m)
disease	**enfermedad** (f); **mal** (m); **dolencia** (f)
dislocation	**dislocación** (f)

diverticulitis	**diverticulitis** (f); **colitis ulcerosa** (f)
dog bite	**mordida de perro** (f)
drainage	**supuración** (f); **drenaje** (m)
dropsy	**ahogamiento** (m); **hidropesía** (f)
drug addict	**drogadicto** (m, f); **adicto a las drogas** (m, f)
dwarf	**enano** (m, f)
dysentery	**disentería** (f)
earache	**dolor de oído** (m)
eczema	**eczema** (f)
edema	**edema** (m)
emaciation	**enflaquecimiento** (m); **demacración** (f)
embolism	**embolismo** (m); **embolia** (f)
emergency	**emergencia** (f); **urgencia** (f)
emphysema	**enfisema** (m)
encephalitis	**encefalitis** (f)
enlargement	**ensanchamiento** (m); **ampliación** (f), **agrandamiento** (m)
epidemic	**epidémico** (adj); **epidemia** (f)
epilepsy	**epilepsia** (f)
epileptic attack	**ataque epilético** (m); **convulsión** (f)
eruption	**erupsión** (f)
fainting spell	**desmayo** (m); **mareo** (m, colloq); **vértigo** (m); **desvanecimiento** (m); **desfallecimiento** (m)
farsighted	**présbita** (adj)
farsightedness	**presbicia** (f); **hipermetropía** (f), **presbiopía** (f)
fatigue	**fatiga** (f)
fever	**fiebre** (f)
fibroma	**fibroma** (f)
fissure	**fisura** (f); **grieta** (f); **partidura** (f)
fistula	**fístula** (f)
fit	**convulsión** (f); **arrebato** (m); **paroxismo** (m)

flat foot	**pie plano** (m)
flatus	**flato** (m); **ventosidad** (f); **pedo** (m, slang)
flu	**influenza** (f); **gripe** (f)
food poisoning	**envenenamiento por comestibles** (m)
fracture	**fractura** (f); **quebradura de huesos** (f)
compound fracture	**fractura compuesta** (f)
complicated fracture	**fractura complicada** (f)
Green Stick Fracture	**fractura en tallo verde** (f)
multiple fracture	**fractura múltiple** (f)
simple fracture	**fractura simple** (f)
serious fracture	**fractura mayor** (f)
freckle	**peca** (f)
frigidity	**frigidez** (f)
frost bite	**congelación** (f); **daño sufrido por causa de la helada** (m)
furuncle	**furúnculo** (m)
gallbladder attack	**ataque vesicular** (m); **dolor de la vesícula** (m)
gall stone	**cálculo en la vejiga** (m); **cálculo biliar** (m) **piedra en la vejiga** (f)
gangrene	**gangrena** (f)
gash	**cuchillada** (f)
gastric ulcer	**úlcera gástrica** (f)
gastritis	**gastritis** (f)
germ	**germen** (m); **microbio** (m)
German measles	**rubéola** (f); **sarampión alemán** (m); **fiebre de tres días** (f)
glandular fever	**fiebre glandular** (f)
glaucoma	**glaucoma** (f)
goiter	**bocio** (m); **buche** (m, slang)
gonorrhea	**gonorrea** (f); **purgación** (f, slang); **blenorragia** (f)
gout	**gota** (f)
hallucination	**alucinación** (f)
handicap	**impedimento** (m)

hard of hearing	**duro de oído** (m); **corto de oído** (m)
harelip (cleft palate)	**labio leporino** (m); **paladar hendido** (m); **grietas en el paladar** (f); **cheuto** (adj, Chile)
hay fever	**fiebre de heno** (f)
headache	**dolor de cabeza** (m); **jaqueca** (f)
heart attack	**ataque al corazón** (m); **ataque cardíaco** (m); **ataque del corazón** (m); **infarto** (m)
heartbeat	**latido (cardíaco)** (m); **palpitación** (f)
irregular heartbeat	**latido irregular** (m); **palpitación irregular** (f)
rhythmical heartbeat	**palpitación rítmica** (f)
slow heartbeat	**palpitación lenta** (f)
tachycardia (rapid heartbeat)	**taquicardia** (f); **palpitación rápida** (f)
heartburn	**acedía** (f); **agriera** (f, SpAm); **agruras** (f); **cardialgia** (f); **pirosis** (f); **ardor de estómago** (m)
heart disease	**enfermedad del corazón** (f); **enfermedad cardíaca** (f); **cardiopatías** (f)
heart failure	**insuficiencia cardíaca** (f); **fallo del corazón** (m); **paro del corazón** (m)
heart murmur	**soplo** (m); **murmullo** (m)
hemophilia	**hemofilia** (f)
hemorrhage	**hemorragia** (f)
hemorrhoids	**almorranas** (f); **hemorroides** (f, pl)
hepatitis	**hepatitis** (f); **inflamación del hígado** (f)
hernia	**hernia** (f); **quebradura** (f)
inguinal hernia	**hernia inguinal** (f); **quebradura en la ingle** (f)
herpes	**herpes** (m)
high blood pressure	**presión arterial alta** (f); **hipertensión arterial** (f)
hives	**urticaria** (f)

hoarseness	**ronquera** (f); **carraspera** (f, coll)
hornet sting	**picadura de avispa** (f)
human bite	**mordedura humana** (f)
hunchback	**jorobado** (m, f, adj)
hypertension	**hipertensión** (f)
hypochondria	**hipocondría** (m & f)
hypotension	**hipotensión** (f)
hysteria	**histeria** (f)
ill	**malo** (adj); **enfermo** (adj)
illness	**mal** (m); **enfermedad** (f); **padeci-miento** (m)
immune	**inmune** (adj)
immunization	**inmunización** (f)
impetigo	**impetigo** (m); **erupción cutánea** (f)
impotence	**impotencia** (f)
indigestion	**indigestión** (f)
infantile paralysis	**parálisis infantil** (f)
infarct	**infarto** (m)
infection	**infección** (f)
infectious	**infeccioso** (adj)
inflammation	**inflamación** (f)
inflammation of the throat	**garrotillo** (m)
influenza	**influenza** (f); **gripe** (f)
injured	**herido** (adj); **lisiado** (adj)
injury	**herida** (f); **lesión** (f)
insanity	**locura** (f); **demencia** (f)
insomnia	**insomnio** (m)
intermittent fever	**fiebre intermitente** (f)
irritation	**irritación** (f)
itch	**picazón** (f); **comezón** (f); **sarna** (f)
jaundice	**derrame biliar** (m); **ictericia** (f); **piel amarilla** (f, coll)
kidney stone	**cálculo en el riñón** (m); **ataque ve-sicular** (m); **dolor de la vesícula** (m); **cálculo renal** (m); **piedra en los riñones** (f)

laceration	**laceración** (f); **desgarradura** (f)
lame	**lisiado** (adj); **cojo** (adj)
laryngitis	**laringitis** (f)
lead poisoning	**envenenamiento del plomo** (m); **saturnismo** (m); **envenenamiento plúmbico** (m)
leprosy	**lepra** (f)
lesion	**lesión** (f)
leukemia	**leucemia** (f); **cáncer de la sangre** (m)
lisp (studder)	**tartamudeo** (m); **ceceo** (m)
lockjaw	**tétanos** (m); **trismo** (m)
louse	**piojo** (m)
crab louse	**ladrilla** (f)
nit	**liendra** (f)
low blood pressure	**hipotensión arterial** (f); **presión arterial baja** (f)
lump	**dureza** (f); **protuberancia** (f); **hinchazón** (f); **borujo** (m)
large lump	**borujón** (m)
lump or bump on head	**chichón** (m)
mad (insane)	**loco** (adj)
madness	**locura** (f); **manía** (f)
malaise	**malestar** (m)
malaria	**malaria** (f); **paludismo** (m)
malarial fever	**fiebre palúdica** (f); **chucho** (m, Chile, Arg)
malignancy	**malignidad** (f)
malignant	**maligno** (adj)
malnutrition	**malnutrición** (f); **desnutrición** (f)
malta fever	**fiebre de Malta** (f); **fiebre ondulante** (f)
mania	**manía** (f)
maniac	**maníaco** (adj)
manic-depressive insanity	**locura de doble forma** (f); **mania-melancolía** (f) ; **sicosis maníacodepresiva** (f)
measles	**sarampión** (m)

melancholia	**melancolía** (f)
meningitis	**meningitis** (f)
menopause	**menopausia** (f); **cambio de vida** (m)
mental illness	**enfermedad mental** (f)
metastasis	**metástasis** (f)
migraine	**migraña** (f); **jaqueca** (f)
mite	**ácaro** (m)
mononucleosis	**mononucleosis infecciosa** (f)
multiple sclerosis	**esclerosis múltiple** (f); **esclerosis en placa** (f)
mumps	**paperas** (f); **farfallota** (f, P.R.); **parótidas** (f, pl); **bolas** (f, Chicano)
muscular dystrophy	**distrofia muscular progresiva** (f)
mute	**mudo** (adj)
myocardial infarct	**infarto miocardiaco** (m)
myopia	**miopía** (f)
myopic	**miope** (adj)
nausea	**náusea** (f)
morning nausea	**malestares de la mañana** (m); **asqueo** (m); **enfermedad matutina** (f)
nearsighted	**miope** (adj); **corto de vista** (adj)
nearsightedness	**miopía** (f)
nephritis	**nefritis** (f)
nervous breakdown	**desarreglo nervioso** (m); **colapso** (m); **neurastenia** (f)
nervous disorder	**desorden nervioso** (m)
nervousness	**nerviosidad** (f)
neuralgia	**neuralgia** (f)
neurasthenia	**neurastenia** (f)
neurasthenic	**neurasténico** (adj)
neuritis	**neuritis** (f)
neurosis	**neurosis** (f)
neurotic	**neurótico** (adj)
night blindness (nyctalopia)	**nictalopía** (f)

obese	**obeso** (adj); **gordo** (adj)
obeseness	**obesidad** (f); **gordura** (f)
obstruction	**obstrucción** (f); **impedimento** (m)
old age	**senectud** (f); **vejez** (f)
one-eyed	**tuerto** (adj)
ophthalmia (inflammation of the eye)	**oftalmía** (f); **inflamación de los ojos** (f)
osteomyelitis	**osteomielitis** (f); **inflamación de la médula del hueso** (f)
otitis	**otitis** (f)
overdose	**dosis excesiva** (f)
overweight (adj)	**excesivamente gordo** (adj); **excesivamente grueso** (adj)
overweight	**sobrepeso** (m); **exceso de peso** (m)
pain, ache	**dolor** (m)
growing	**dolor de crecimiento** (m)
labor	**dolor de parto** (m)
phantom limb	**dolor de miembro fantasma** (m)
referred	**dolor referido** (m)
root	**dolor radicular** (m)
sharp	**punzada** (f)
shooting	**dolor fulgurante** (m)
thoracic	**dolor torácico** (m)
palpitation	**palpitación** (f)
palsy	**parálisis** (f); **paralización** (f)
Bell's palsy	**parálisis facial** (f)
cerebral palsy	**parálisis cerebral** (f)
shaking palsy (Parkinson's disease)	**enfermedad de Parkinson** (f); **parálisis agitante** (f)
pancreatitis	**pancreatitis** (f)
paralysis	**parálisis** (f); **paralización** (f)
paranoia	**paranoia** (f)
paraplegia	**paraplejía** (f); **parálisis de la mitad inferior del cuerpo** (f)
paratyphoid fever	**fiebre paratífica** (f); **fiebre paratifoidea** (f)
pellagra	**pelagra** (f)
peptic ulcer	**úlcera péptica** (f)
perforated eardrum	**tímpano perforado** (m)

pericarditis	**pericarditis** (f)
peritonitis	**peritonitis** (f)
pernicious anemia	**anemia perniciosa** (f)
pertussis	**tos convulsiva** (f); **tosferina** (f); **coqueluche** (f); **tos ferina** (f)
pharyngitis	**faringitis** (f)
phlebitis	**flebitis** (f); **tromboflebitis** (f)
phthisis	**tisis** (f); **consunción** (f)
pigeon-toed	**patizambo** (adj)
pile	**almorrana** (f); **hemorroides** (f, pl)
pimple	**grano de la cara, barrillo** (m); **butón** (m); **pústula** (f); **buba** (f)
blackhead pimple	**espinilla** (f)
pinkeye	**oftalmía contagiosa** (f); **conjuntivitis catarral aguda** (f)
plague	**peste** (f); **plaga** (f)
bubonic plague	**peste bubónica** (f)
pleurisy	**pleuresía** (f)
pneumonia	**pulmonía** (f); **neumonía** (f)
pock	**viruela** (f); **postilla** (f) **cacaraña** (f, Guat, Mex)
poison ivy	**hiedra venenosa** (f); **chechén** (m); **zumaque venenoso** (m)
polio(myelitis)	**poliomielitis** (f); **parálisis infantil** (f)
polyp	**pólipo** (m)
presbyopia	**presbiopía** (f); **presbicia** (f); **hipermetropía** (f)
prickly heat	**salpullido** (m); **picazón** (f); **erupción debido al calor** (f)
proctitis	**proctitis** (f)
prostration	**postración** (f)
heat prostration	**postración del calor** (f)
psoriasis	**soríasis** (f)
psychosis	**sicosis** (f)
psychosomatic	**sicosomático** (adj)
psychotic	**sicótico** (adj)
pus	**pus** (m)

pustule	**pústula** (f); **grano** (m)
pyorrhea	**piorrea** (f)
quinsy (sore throat)	**esquinancia** (f); **amigdalitis supurativa** (f)
rabies	**rabia** (f); **hidrofobia** (f)
rash	**salpullido** (m); **erupción** (f); **alfombra** (f, P.R., Cuba)
ratbite fever	**fiebre por mordedura de rata** (f)
relapse	**recidiva** (f); **recaída** (f)
renal	**renal** (adj)
rheum	**reuma** (m)
rheumatic fever	**fiebre reumática** (f)
rheumatism	**reumatismo** (m); **reumas** (f)
rheumatoid arthritis	**artritis reumatoidea** (f)
rickets	**raquitis** (m); **raquitismo** (m)
ringworm	**culebrilla** (f); **tiña** (f); **empeine** (m); **serpigo** (m)
Rocky mountain fever	**fiebre de las montañas rocosas** (f)
roseola	**roséola** (f); **rubéola** (f)
rubella	**sarampión alemán** (m); **rubéola** (f); **roséola epidémica** (f); **fiebre de tres días** (f)
rupture (hernia)	**hernia** (f); **ruptura** (f); **relajación** (f); **rotura** (f); **reventón** (m); **quebradura** (f)
sarcoma	**sarcoma** (f)
scab	**postilla** (f); **costra** (f)
scabies	**sarna** (f)
scar	**cicatriz** (f)
scarlet fever	**fiebre escarlatina** (f)
schizophrenia	**esquizofrenia** (f)
schizophrenic	**esquisofrénico** (adj)
sciatica	**ciática**
scratch	**rasguño** (m)
scurvy	**escorbuto** (m)
seasickness	**mareo** (m); **mal de mar** (m)
seborrhea	**seborrea** (f)

senile	**senil** (adj)
senility	**senilidad** (f); **senectud** (f); **caduquez** (f)
septicemia	**septicemia** (f); **bacteriemia** (f); **toxemia** (f); **piemia** (f)
severe	**agudo** (adj); **severo** (adj)
shock	**choque** (m); **sobresalto** (m); **conmoción nerviosa** (f)
short-sighted	**miope** (adj); **cegato** (adj, coll)
sick	**enfermo** (adj); **malo** (adj)
sickliness	**achaque** (m)
sickly	**enfermizo** (adj); **pálido** (adj); **demacrado** (adj)
sickness	**enfermedad** (f); **padecimiento** (m); **mal** (m); **dolencia** (f)
simulation	**fingimiento** (m)
sinus congestion	**congestión nasal** (f)
sleeping sickness	**enfermedad del sueño** (f)
slipped disc	**disco desplazado** (m); **disco intervertebral luxado** (m)
small pox	**viruela** (f)
snakebite	**mordedura de serpiente** (f)
sore (wound)	**llaga** (f); **úlcera** (f)
sore	**pena** (f); **dolor** (m); **aflicción** (f)
sore ears	**mal** o **dolor de oídos** (m)
sore eyes	**dolor de ojos** (m)
sore throat	**mal** o **dolor de garganta** (m)
spasm	**espasmo** (m); **contracción muscular** (f)
spasmodic	**espasmódico** (adj); **itermitente** (adj); **irregular** (adj)
spastic	**espástico** (adj); **espasmódico** (adj)
spider bite	**picadura de araña** (f)
spotted fever	**fiebre purpúrea (de las Montañas Rocosas)** (f); **tifus exantemático** (m); **fiebre manchada** (f)
sprain	**torcedura** (f); **dislocación** (f); **esguince** (f)

squint-eyed	**ojituerto** (adj); **bizco** (adj); **bisojo** (adj)
stammering	**tartamudeo** (m); **balbucencia** (f)
stiff neck	**tortícolis** (m); **torticolis** (m)
stomachache	**dolor de estómago** (m)
stomach ulcer	**úlcera del estómago** (f)
strabismus	**estrabismo** (m); **bizco** (Cent Am)
strain	**tensión** (f); **torcedura** (f)
stricture	**constricción** (f); **estrictura** (f); **estenosis** (f); **estrechez** (f)
stroke	**derrame cerebral** (m); **embolia cerebral** (f); **parálisis** (f); **hemorragia vascular** (f); **ataque fulminante** (m); **apoplejía** (f)
stuttering	**tartamudez** (f); **balbucencia** (f)
sty	**orzuelo** (m)
suffocation	**sofocación** (f); **asfixia** (f)
suicide	**suicidio** (m)
sunburn	**quemazón** (f); **solanera** (f); **eritema solar** (m)
sunstroke	**insolación** (f); **soleada** (f, SpAm)
suntanned	**bronceado** (adj); **tostado** (adj)
suppuration	**supuración** (f)
swelling	**hinchazón** (f); **tumor** (m); **tumefacción** (f)
on the head	**chichón** (m)
symptom	**síntoma** (m)
syndrome	**síndrome** (m)
syphilis	**sífilis** (f); **sangre mala** (f, slang); **mal francés** (m, slang); **mal de bubas** (m, slang)
tachycardia	**taquicardia** (f)
tantrum	**berrinche** (m, coll)
temper tantrum	**pataletas** (f)
tapeworm	**solitaria** (f); **lombriz solitaria** (f); **tenia** (f)
tartar, dental	**sarro** (m); **saburra** (f); **tártaro** (m)
tetanus	**tétanos** (m); **mal de arco** (m, slang)

threadworms	**tricocéfalos** (f); **tricocefalosis** (f)
thrombophlebitis	**tromboflebitis** (f); **flebitis** (f)
thrombosis	**trombosis** (f)
coronary thrombosis	**trombosis coronaria** (f)
thrush	**afta** (f)
tic	**tic** (m); **tirón** (m); **sacudida** (f)
tic douloureux	**tic doloroso de la cara** (m)
tonsillitis	**amigdalitis** (f); **tonsilitis** (f)
toothache	**dolor de muelas** (m); **dolor de dientes** (m); **odontalgia** (f)
tooth decay	**caries** (f)
toxemia	**toxemia** (f)
trauma	**traumatismo** (m); **trauma** (m)
tremor	**tremor** (m); **tremblor** (m)
tuberculosis	**tuberculosis** (f); **tisis** (f)
tumor	**tumor** (m); **neoplasma** (f); **neoformación** (f)
tumor on the head	**chiporra** (f, Guat, Hond)
typhoid fever	**fiebre tifoidea** (f); **tifus abdominal** (m)
typhus	**tifus** (m); **tifo** (m)
ulcer	**úlcera** (f)
unconsciousness	**insensibilidad** (f); **inconsciencia** (f)
underweight	**peso escaso** (m); **falta de peso** (f)
undulant fever	**fiebre ondulante** (f)
uremia	**uremia** (f)
urticaria	**urticaria** (f)
uterus prolapse	**prolapso de la matriz** (m); **caída de la matriz** (f); **prolapso del útero** (m)
valley fever (coccidioidomycosis)	**fiebre del valle** (f)
varicose vein	**várice** (f); **vena varicosa** (f); **variz** (m)
venereal disease	**enfermedad venérea** (f); **secreta** (f, slang)
canker sore	**postemilla** (f); **úlcera gangrenosa** (f)

chancre	**chancro** (m); **grano** (m)
noninfecting	**chancro simple** (m); **chancro blando** (m)
hard	**chancro duro** (m); **chancro sifilítico** (m)
chlamidia	**clamidia** (f)
cold sore	**fuegos en la boca** o **los labios** (m); **herpes labial** (m)
condyloma	**condiloma** (m)
genital wart	**verruga genital** (f); **verruga venérea** (f)
gonorrhea	**gonorrea** (f); **blenorragia** (f); **purgaciones** (f, pl, slang)
herpes	**herpe(s)** (m)
genitalis	**herpes genital** (m)
menstrualis	**herpes menstrual** (m)
moniliasis	**moniliasis** (f)
nongonoccocal urethritis	**uretritis no gonocal** (f)
nonspecific urethritis	**uretritis no específica** (f); **uretritis inespecífica** (f)
sexually transmitted diseases	**enfermedades pasadas sexualmente** (f)
syphilis	**sífilis** (f); **sangre mala** (f, slang)
trichomonas	**tricomonas** (f)
venereal lesion	**úlcera** (f); **chancro** (m); **grano** (m)
victim	**víctima** (f)
virus	**virus** (m)
vomit	**vómito** (m)
wart	**verruga** (f)
weak	**débil** (adj)
weakness	**debilidad** (f)
weal (large welt)	**verdugón** (m); **cardenal** (m)
wen	**lobanillo** (m); **lupia** (f)
wheal	**roncha** (f); **pápula** (f)
whooping cough	**tos convulsiva** (f); **tos ferina** (f); **coqueluche** (f); **tosferina** (f)
worm	**gusano** (m)
wound	**herida** (f); **llaga** (f)
yellow fever	**fiebre amarilla** (f); **tifus icterodes** (m); **fiebre tropical** (f)

COMMON MEDICATIONS

MEDICINAS COMUNES

absorbent cotton	**algodón absorbente** (m)
activated charcoal	**carbón activado** (m)
adhesive plaster	**emplasto adhesivo** (m)
adhesive tape	**esparadrapo** (m); **tela adhesiva** (f); **cinta adhesiva** (f)
alcohol	**alcohol** (m)
ammonia	**amoníaco** (m)
amphetamine	**anfetamina** (f)
analgesic	**analgésico** (m)
anesthesia	**anestesia** (f)
anesthetic	**anestético** (m, adj)
ankle support	**tobillera** (f)
antacid	**antiácido** (m, adj)
antibiotic	**antibiótico** (m, adj)
antibody	**anticuerpo** (m)
anticoagulant	**anticoagulante** (m, adj)
antidote	**antídoto** (m)
antigen	**antígeno** (m)
antihemorrhagic	**antihemorrágico** (adj)
antihistamine	**antihistamínico** (m, adj); **droga antihistamínica** (f)
antipyretic	**febrífugo** (m); **antipirético** (m)
antiseptic	**antiséptico** (m, adj)
antispasmodic	**antiespasmódico** (m, adj)
antitetanic; anti-tetanus	**antitetánico** (adj)
application	**aplicación** (f)
arch supports	**soportes para el arco del pie** (m)
arsenic	**arsénico** (m)
artificial	**artificial** (adj); **postizo** (adj)
artificial limb	**miembro artificial** (m)
artificial respiration	**respiración artificial** (f)
ascorbic acid	**ácido ascórbico** (m)
aspirin	**aspirina** (f)
children's aspirin	**aspirina para niños** (f)
astringent	**astringente** (m, adj)

atropine	**atropina** (f)
balsam	**bálsamo** (m); **ungüento** (m)
band	**cinta** (f); **faja** (f)
bandage	**vendaje** (m); **venda** (f)
band aid	**curita** (f); **venda** (f); **parchecito** (m)
barbiturate	**barbiturato** (m)
belladonna	**belladona** (f)
benzedrine	**bencedrina** (f)
benzoin	**benjuí** (m); **benzoína** (f)
bicarbonate of soda	**bicarbonato de soda** (m)
binder	**vendaje abdominal** (m); **cintura** (f); **faja** (f)
bleach	**cloro** (m); **blanqueo** (m)
blood plasma	**plasma sanguíneo** (m)
blood transfusion	**transfusión de sangre** (f)
booster shot	**inyección secundaria** (f); **búster** (m); **inyección de refuerzo** (f); **reactivación** (f)
borax	**bórax** (m)
brace	**braguero** (m)
bromide	**bromuro** (m)
calamine	**calamina** (f)
calcium	**calcio** (m)
cane	**bastón** (m); **báculo** (m)
capsule	**cápsula** (f)
carbon tetrachloride	**tetracloruro de carbono** (m)
castor oil	**aceite de ricino** (m)
cataplasm	**cataplasma** (f)
cathartic	**purgante** (m)
cauterization	**cauterización** (f)
chloride	**cloruro** (m)
chlorine	**cloro** (m)
chlorophyll	**clorofila** (f)
coagulant	**coagulante** (m, adj)
cocaine	**cocaína** (f); **nieve** (f, slang)
cod liver oil	**aceite de hígado de bacalao** (m)
codeine	**codeína** (f)

cold pack	**emplasto frío** (m); **compresa fría** (f)
compress	**compresa** (f); **cabezal** (m)
contact lens	**lente de contacto** (m)
contraceptive	**contraceptivo** (m); **anticonceptivo** (m)
contraceptive pills	**pastillas anticonceptivas** (f)
Coramine	**coramina** (f)
corn plaster	**emplasto para callos** (m)
cortisone	**cortisona** (f)
cotton	**algodón** (m)
cotton, sterile	**algodón estéril** (m)
cotton swab	**hisopillo** (m); **escobillón** (m)
cough drops	**gotas para la tos** (f); **pastillas para la tos** (f)
cough lozenges	**pastillas para la tos** (f)
cough syrup	**jarabe para la tos** (m)
crutch	**muleta** (f)
cure	**cura** (f); **método curativo** (m)
curettage	**curetaje** (m); **raspado** (m)
dental floss	**hilo dental** (m); **cordón dental** (m); **seda encerada** (f)
dentifrice	**dentífrico** (m, adj)
deodorant	**desodorante** (m, adj)
depilatory	**depilatorio** (m, adj)
dextrose	**dextrosa** (f); **azúcar de uva** (m)
diaphragm	**diafragma** (m); **diafragma anti- conceptivo** (m)
digitalin	**digitalina** (f)
disinfectant	**desinfestante** (m)
disposable syringe	**jeringuilla descartable** (f)
diuretic	**diurético** (m, adj); **píldora diurética** (f)
dose	**dosis** (f)
douche	**ducha** (f); **ducha interna** (f); **lavado vaginal** (m); **lavado interno** (m); **ducha vaginal** (f); **irrigación** (f)

DPT	**vacuna triple** (f)
drainage (surgical)	**drenaje** (m)
drainage	**desagüe** (m)
dram	**dracma** (m)
dressing	**cura** (f); **curación** (f); **apósito** (m); **emplaste** (m); **parche** (m); **vendaje** (m)
drops	**gotas** (f)
drug	**droga** (f); **medicina** (f)
drug store	**farmacia** (f, Spain); **droguería** (f, Sp Am); **botica** (f)
elastic bandage	**venda elástica** (f)
emetic	**vomitivo** (m, adj)
emulsion	**emulsión** (f)
enema	**enema** (f); **lavativa** (f); **ayuda** (f); **lavado** (m)
enema bag	**bolsa para enema** (f)
ephedrine	**efedrina** (f)
Epsom salt	**sal de higuera** (f); **sal de Epsom** (f)
expectorant	**expectorante** (m, adj)
external	**externo** (adj)
extract	**extracto** (m)
eye cup	**copa ocular** (f); **ojera** (f); **lavaojos** (m)
eye dropper	**gotero (para los ojos)** (m, SpAm); **cuentagotas** (f)
eye glasses	**anteojos** (m, pl); **lentes** (m, pl); **gafas** (f, pl); **espejuelos** (m, pl); **quevedos** (m, pl)
eye salve	**ungüento para los ojos** (m)
first aid	**primeros auxilios** (m, pl); **primera ayuda** (f)
flask	**frasco** (m)
foam	**espuma** (f)
gargle	**gárgara** (f)
gargle, to	**hacer gárgaras**
gauze	**gasa** (f)
germicide	**germicida** (f)

glass eye	**ojo de vidrio** (m)
glucose	**glucosa** (f)
glue	**goma** (f); **cola** (f)
glycerine	**glicerina** (f)
guaiacol	**guayacol** (m)
hallucinogenic drug	**droga alucinadora** (f); **alucinógeno** (m)
hearing aid	**aparato para la sordera** (m); **prótesis auditiva** (f); **prótesis acústica** (f); **audífono** (m); **aparato auditivo** (m); **audiófono** (m)
heat therapy	**termoterapia** (f); **tratamiento térmico** (m)
herbicides	**herbicidas** (f); **matayerbas** (f)
heroin	**heroína** (f)
hormone	**hormón** (m); **hormona** (f)
hot water bag	**bolsa de agua caliente** (f)
hydrogen peroxide	**agua oxigenada** (f); **peróxido de hidrógeno** (m)
hypodermic injection	**inyección hipodérmica** (f)
hypodermic needle	**aguja hipodérmica** (f)
hypodermic syringe	**jeringuilla hipodérmica** (f)
ice	**hielo** (m)
ice(bag) pack	**bolsa de hielo** (f); **bolsa de caucho para hielo** (f)
ichthyol	**ictiol** (m)
immunization (vaccine)	**inmunización** (f); **vacuna** (f)
ingredient	**ingrediente** (m)
injection	**inyección** (f)
intramuscular injection	**inyección intramuscular** (f)
intravenous injection	**inyección intravenosa** (f)
subcutaneous injection	**inyección subcutánea** (f)
inoculation	**inoculación** (f)
insect repellent	**repelente de insectos** (m)
insecticide	**insecticida** (f)
intrauterine device	**dispositivo intrauterino** (m); **aparato intrauterino** (m)

intrauterine loop	**espiral intrauterina** (f)
insulin	**insulina** (f)
internally	**internamente** (adv)
iodine	**yodo** (m)
iron	**hierro** (m)
isolation	**aislamiento por cuarentena** (m)
jelly	**jalea** (f)
kilogram	**kilogramo** (m)
kit	**estuche** (m); **botiquín** (m)
emergency kit	**botiquín de emergencia** (m)
first aid kit	**botiquín de primeros auxilios** (m); **equipo de urgencia** (m)
knife	**cuchillo** (m)
knot	**nudo** (m)
label	**etiqueta** (f)
laboratory	**laboratorio** (m)
lavage	**lavado** (m)
lavatory	**lavamanos** (m, sg)
laxative	**laxativo** (m); **laxante** (m); **purgante** (m)
lens	**lente** (m)
liniment	**linimento** (m)
liquid	**líquido** (m)
liter	**litro** (m)
lotion	**loción** (f)
loop (IUD)	**lazo** (m)
lozenge	**pastilla** (f); **trocisco** (m); **pastilla de chupar** (f)
LSD	**drogas alucinantes** (f); **DAL** (f)
lubricant	**lubricante** (m); **lubricativo** (adj)
lukewarm	**templado** (adj); **tibio** (adj)
lye	**lejía** (f)
magnesia	**magnesia** (f)
milk of magnesia	**leche de magnesia** (f)
marijuana	**mariguana** (f); **yerba** (f); **grifa** (f)
massage	**masaje** (m)
measure	**medida** (f)
measuring cup	**taza de medir** (f)

medicine	**medicina** (f); **medicamento** (m); **droga** (f)
medicine cabinet, medicine chest	**botiquín** (m)
menthol	**mentol** (m)
Mercurochrome®	**mercurocromo** (m)
Merthiolate	**mertiolato** (m)
methadone	**metadona** (f)
milligram	**miligramo** (m)
milliliter	**mililtro** (m)
mineral	**mineral** (m)
mineral oil	**aceite mineral** (m)
mineral water	**agua mineral** (f)
mixture	**mezcla** (f)
moderate	**moderado** (adj)
moist	**húmedo** (adj)
morphine	**morfina** (f)
mouth-to-mouth resuscitation	**resucitación boca a boca**
mouth wash	**lavado bucal** (m); **enjuagatorio** (m)
mustard	**mostaza** (f)
mustard bath	**baño de mostaza** (m)
mustard plaster	**cataplasma de mostaza** (f); **sinapismo** (m)
narcotic	**narcótico** (m); **droga somnífera** (f)
needle	**aguja** (f)
niacin	**niacina** (f)
nitro(glycerin)	**nitro(glicerina)** (f)
novocaine	**novocaína** (f)
ointment	**ungüento** (m); **crema** (f); **pomada** (f)
operation	**operación** (f)
opium	**opio** (m); **chinaloa** (f, slang)
oxygen	**oxígeno** (m)
pacemaker	**aparato cardiocinético** (m), **marcador de paso** (m); **marcapaso** (m)
pain killer	**calmante** (m)
palliative	**paliativo** (m, adj)

paregoric	**paregórico** (m)
patent medicine	**medicina patentada; medicina registrada** (f)
penicillin	**pencilina** (f)
peroxide	**peróxido,** (m); **agua oxigenada** (f)
pesticide	**pesticida** (f); **plaguicida** (f)
pharmacy	**farmacia** (f); **botica** (f)
phenobarbital	**fenobarbital** (m)
pill	**píldora** (f); **pastilla** (f)
birth control pill	**píldoras para control de embarazo** (f); **pastillas para no tener niños** (f); **píldora anticonceptiva** (f)
sleeping pill	**píldora para dormir** (f); **sedativo** (m)
thyroid pill	**medicación tiroides** (f)
plasma	**plasma** (f)
poison	**veneno** (m); **ponzoña** (f)
poisonous	**venenoso** (adj); **ponzoñoso** (adj)
pomade	**pomada** (f)
potion	**poción** (f); **dosis** (f)
poultice	**cataplasma** (f); **emplasto** (m)
powder	**polvo** (m)
powdered	**en polvo** (adj)
powdery	**polvoriento** (adj); **polvoroso** (adj); **empolvado** (adj)
prescribe, to	**recetar; prescribir un remedio**
prescription	**receta** (f); **prescripción** (f)
prick	**pinchazo** (m); **punzada** (f)
prick, to	**pinchar**
prophylactic	**profiláctico** (m, adj)
prosthesis	**prótesis** (f); **miembro artificial** (m)
purgation	**purgación** (f)
purgative	**purgante** (m); **catártico** (m, adj)
purge	**purga** (f); **purgante** (m)
quart	**cuarto** (m)
quinine	**quinina** (f)
radiation shield	**blindaje contra la radiación** (m)

radiation therapy	**radioterapia** (f)
radiation treatment	**radiaciones** (f)
relief	**alivio** (m)
relieve, to	**aliviar**
remedy	**remedio** (m); **medicamento** (m)
restroom	**baño** (m); **cuarto de baño** (m); **servicios** (m); **inodoro** (m); **retrete** (m, Spain)
rhythm method	**método del ritmo** (m); **ritmo** (m)
ring, IUD	**anillo** (m)
rub	**fricción** (f); **frotación** (f)
rub, to	**frotar; restregar**
rubber (condom)	**goma** (f); **condón** (m)
rubber gloves	**guantes de goma** (m, pl)
saccharine	**sacarina** (f)
saline solution	**agua con sal** (f); **agua salina** (f)
salt water	**agua salada** (f)
salve	**pomada** (f); **ungüento** (m)
sanitary napkin	**kotex** (m); **servilleta sanitaria** (f); **almohadilla higiénica** (f); **absorbente higiénico** (m)
sedative	**sedante** (m); **sedativo** (m); **calmante** (m)
serum	**suero** (m)
shield (IUD)	**escudo** (m)
shot	**inyección** (f)
sling	**cabestrillo** (m)
smelling salts	**sales aromáticas** (f, pl); **sales perfumadas** (f, pl)
soap	**jabón** (m)
sodium pentothal	**pentotal de sodio** (m); **pentotal sódico** (m)
sodium peroxide	**agua oxigenada** (f); **peróxido de sodio** (m)
solution	**solución** (f)
soporific	**soporífico** (m); **narcótico** (m)

spectacles	**anteojos** (m, pl, general term); **lentes** (m, pl, Mex.); **espejuelos** (m, pl, Cuba); **gafas** (f, pl); **quevedos** (m, pl, wire-rimmed)
spermaticide, vaginal	**espermaticida vaginal** (f)
spiral (IUD)	**espiral** (m)
splint	**tablilla** (f)
in a splint	**entablillado** (adj)
spoonful	**cucharada** (f)
spray	**rociador** (m); **pulverizador** (m); **pulverización** (f)
steam	**vapor** (m)
sterile	**estéril** (adj); **infecundo** (adj)
sterility	**esterilidad** (f); **infecundidad** (f)
sterilization	**esterilización** (f)
sterilized	**esterilizado** (adj)
sterilizer	**esterilizador** (m)
stimulant	**estimulante** (m)
stitch	**sutura** (f); **punto** (m); **puntada** (f)
substitute	**substituto** (m)
sugar	**azúcar** (m)
sulfathiazole	**sulfatiazol** (m)
sulphur	**azufre** (m)
sunglasses	**gafas de sol** (f, pl); **anteojos oscuros** (m, pl)
suntan lotion	**loción para el sol** (f); **loción bronceadora** (f)
support	**apoyo** (m); **soporte** (m); **sostén** (m)
supporter, athletic	**suspensorio** (m)
suture	**sutura** (f); **puntada** (f)
sweetner	**dulcificante** (m)
sweets	**dulces** (m, pl); **golosinas** (f, pl)
syringe	**jeringa** (f); **jeringuilla** (f)
disposable	**disponible** (adj)
syrup of ipecac	**jarabe de ipeca** (m)
tablespoonful	**cucharada** (f)
tablet	**comprimido** (m); **tableta** (f); **pastilla** (f)

tampon	**tampón** (m); **tapón** (m)
teaspoonful	**cucharadita** (f)
tepid	**tibio** (adj)
Terramycin	**terramicina** (f)
tetanus	**tétano(s)** (m); **mal de arco** (m)
therapeutic	**terapéutico** (adj)
thermometer	**termómetro** (m)
oral	**oral** (adj)
rectal	**rectal** (adj)
tongue depressor	**pisa-lengua** (f); **abate lengua** (f); **depresor de la lengua** (m)
tonic	**tónico** (m)
tourniquet	**torniquete** (m)
traction	**tracción** (f)
tranquilizer	**tranquilizante** (m); **calmante** (m); **apaciguador** (m)
transfusion	**transfusión** (f)
treatment	**tratamiento** (m)
turpentine	**trementina** (f)
ultraviolet lamp	**lámpara de rayos ultravioletas** (f)
unguent	**pomada** (f); **ungüento** (m)
vaccination	**vacunación** (f); **inoculación**
vaccine, immunization	**vacuna** (f); **inmunización** (f)
Vaseline	**vaselina** (f)
vial	**vial** (m); **botella** (f); **frasco** (m); **ampolla** (f)
vinegar	**vinagre** (m)
vitamin	**vitamina** (f)
vomitive	**vomitivo** (m, adj); **emético** (m, adj)
walker	**andador** (m)
walking cane	**bastón de paseo** (m)
warm	**tibio** (adj)
warmer	**más caliente** (adj); **calentador** (m)
weight	**peso** (m)
wheelchair	**silla de ruedas** (f)
X-ray	**radiografía** (f); **rayo equis** (m)
X-ray therapy	**radioterapia** (f)

COMMON POISONS	VENENOS COMUNES
Inhaled Poisons	*Venenos aspirados*
Gas	**gas** (m)
Smoke	**humo** (m)
Vapor	**vapor** (m)
Injected Poisons	*Venenos inyectados*
Rat bites	**picadas de ratones** (f)
Scorpion bites	**picadas de escorpión** (f)
Snake bites	**picadas de culebra** (f)
Oral Poisons	*Venenos tomados por la boca*
Acetic acid	**ácido acético (puro)** (m)
Ammonia	**amoníaco** (m)
Arsenic acid	**ácido arsénico** (m)
Ascorbic acid	**ácido ascórbico** (m)
Bichloride of mercury	**cloruro mercúrico** (m)
Camphor	**alcanfor** (m)
Carbolic acid	**ácido carbólico** (m)
Carbon tetrachloride	**tetracloruro de carbono** (m)
Cyanic acid	**ácido cianótico** (m)
Detergents	**detergentes** (m)
Disinfectant	**desinfectante** (m)
Furniture polish	**pulimento para muebles** (m)
Hydrochloric acid	**ácido clorhídrico** (m)
Hydrofluoric acid	**ácido fluorhídrico** (m)
Iodine	**yodo** (m)
Kerosene	**keroseno** (m)
Lye	**lejía** (f)
Mushrooms	**hongos** (m)
Nitric acid	**ácido nítrico** (m)
Oil of wintergreen	**aceite de gaulteria** (m)

Oxalic acid	**ácido oxálico** (m)
Phosphoric acid	**ácido fosfórico** (m)
Pine oil	**aceite de pino** (m)
Rubbing alcohol	**alcohol para fricciones** (m)
Silver nitrate	**nitrato de plata** (m)
Sodium carbonate	**carbonato de sodio** (m)
Sodium hydroxide	**hidróxido de sodio** (m)
Sodium hypochlorite (bleach)	**hipoclorito de sodio** (m) **(blanqueador de ropa)**
Sodium sulfate (in toilet cleaners)	**sulfato de sodio** (m) **(en limpiadores de inodoros)**
Strychnine	**estricnina** (f)
Sulfuric acid	**ácido sulfúrico** (f)
Turpentine	**esencia de trementina** (f)

PREGNANCY, CHILDBIRTH, CONTRACEPTION, POSTNATAL CARE OF THE MOTHER

EMBARAZO, PARTO, CONTRACEPCIÓN, CUIDADO POSNATAL DE LA MADRE

abortion	**aborto** (m)
induced abortion	**aborto inducido** (m); **aborto provocado** (m)
spontaneous abortion	**aborto espontáneo** (m)
therapeutic abortion	**aborto terapéutico** (m)
threatened abortion	**amenaza de aborto** (f)
abscess	**absceso** (m)
abscessed (adj)	**apostemado** (adj)
abstain from sexual relations, to	**abstenerse de las relaciones sexuales**
add, to	**añadir**
afterbirth	**secundinas** (f, pl, Mex.); **placenta** (f)
amnionic sac	**saco amniótico** (m)
anesthesia	**anestesia** (f)
block	**anestesia de bloque** (f)
caudal	**anestesia caudal** (f)

epidural	**anestesia epidural** (f)
general	**anestesia total** (f)
inhalation	**anestesia por inhalación** (f)
local	**anestesia local** (f)
regional	**anestesia regional** (f)
saddle block	**anestesia en silla de montar** (f)
spinal	**anestesia espinal** (f); **anestesia raquídea** (f)
twilight sleep	**sueño crepuscular** (m)
bag of waters	**fuente** (f, coll); **bolsa de las aguas** (f)
bear down, to	**pujar; hacer bajar por fuerza**
bilirubin	**bilirrubina** (f)
bind, to	**atar; amarrar**
binder	**cintura** (f); **faja** (f)
birth	**nacimiento** (m)
childbirth	**parto** (m)
birth certificate	**certificado de nacimiento** (m); **partida de nacimiento** (f)
post-term	**nacimiento tardío** (m)
premature	**nacimiento prematuro** (m)
birth control	**control de la natalidad** (m)
cervical cap	**gorro cervical** (m)
coitus interruptus	**interrupción de coito** (f)
condom	**condón** (m); **hule** (m, slang); **forro** (m, Arg, vulg)
diaphragm	**diafragma (anticonceptivo)** (m)
IUD	**DIU** (m); **dispositivo intrauterino** (m); **aparato intrauterino** (m)
pill	**píldora** (f)
rubber	**goma** (f); **forro** (m, Arg, vulg); **hule** (m, slang)
rhythm	**ritmo; método de ritmo** (m)
tubal ligation	**ligadura de trompas** (f)
vaginal cream	**crema vaginal** (f)
vaginal foam	**espuma vaginal** (f)
vaginal jelly	**jalea vaginal** (f)
vasectomy	**vasectomía** (f)
birth, to give	**dar a luz; parir; alumbrar**
birth weight	**peso del nacimiento** (m)
bladder	**vejiga** (f)
bleeding	**flujo de sangre** (m); **hemorragia** (f)

bleeding (adj)	**sangrante** (adj)
bleeding to excess	**desangramiento** (m)
bleeding, breakthrough	**hemorragia inesperada** (f); **flujo de sangre por la vagina inesperadamente** (f)
bloated	**aventado** (adj); **hinchado** (adj)
blood	**sangre** (f)
blood clot	**coágulo sanguíneo** (m)
blood count	**hematimetría** (f); **recuento sanguíneo** (m)
blood donor	**donante de sangre** (m, f)
blood group	**grupo sanguíneo** (m)
blood plasma	**plasma sanguíneo** (m)
blood stain	**mancha de sangre** (f)
blood stained	**manchado de sangre** (adj)
blood transfusion	**transfusión de sangre** (f)
blood, whole	**sangre entera** (f)
bloody	**cruento** (adj)
bloody show	**muestra de sangre** (f)
blotches, skin	**manchas oscuras en la piel** (f)
boil the bottles, to	**hervir las botellas**
breast	**seno** (m); **pecho** (m); **teta** (f); **chichi** (f, Mex); **chichas** (f, pl, C Rica)
breast of a wet nurse	**chiche** (m, Mex, Guat)
caked breast	**mastitis por estasis** (f)
painful breasts	**senos dolorosos** (m)
breastfeed, to	**dar el pecho; dar de mamar**
breastfeeding	**lactancia maternal** (f)
breast pump	**mamadera** (f); **bomba de ordeñar** (f); **tiraleches** (f)
breechbirth (frank breech)	**presentación trasera** (f); **presentación de nalgas** (f)
burp	**eructo** (m); **regüeldo** (m)
burp, to	**eructar**
buttock	**nalga** (f); **culo** (m, Arg, coll); **salvohonor** (m, coll); **bombo** (m, Ur)
caesarean delivery	**parto cesáreo** (m); **parto por operación** (m)
caesarean section	**operación cesárea** (f); **sección cesárea** (f)

catheter	**catéter** (m); **sonda** (f)
catheterize	**cateterizar**
cervix	**cerviz** (f); **cuello de la matriz** (m); **cuello del útero** (m)
childbirth	**parto** (m); **alumbramiento** (m)
chloasma (facial discoloration) (mask of pregnancy)	**paño** (m); **mancha del embarazo** (f); **mancha de la preñez** (f); **cloasma** (m)
circumcise, to	**circuncidar**
circumcision	**circuncisión** (f)
clitoris	**clítoris** (f); **bolita** (f, slang); **pelotita** (f, slang)
coitus	**coito** (m)
colic	**cólico** (adj)
colostrum	**calostro** (m)
conceive, to	**concebir**
conception	**concepción** (f); **fecundación del huevo** (f)
confinement	**puerperio** (m); **cuarentena** (f); **riesgo** (m); **alumbramiento** (m)
congenital malformations	**malformaciones congénitas** (f)
constipation	**estreñimiento** (m)
continue working, to	**seguir trabajando**
contraceptive	**anticonceptivo** (m, adj); **contraceptivo** (m, adj)
contractions	**contracciones de la matriz** (f); **dolores de parto** (m)
crib	**camilla de niño** (f); **cuna** (f)
warming crib	**camilla calentadora de niño** (f); **incubadora** (f); **estufa** (f); **armazón de calentamiento** (f)
crack, to	**agrietar**; **rajar**
cramps (menstrual)	**calambres** (m); **dolores del período** (m)
cramps (muscular)	**calambres** (m)
cramps (postpartum pains)	**entuertos** (m)
crown, to	**coronar**; **estar coronando**
crowning	**coronamiento** (m)
curettage	**curetage** (m); **raspado** (m)

dangle one's legs, to	**colgar las piernas**
deliver, to	**dar a luz; parir; tener el niño**
delivery	**parto** (m)
abdominal	**parto abdominal** (m)
breech	**extracción de nalgas** (f)
delivery room	**sala de partos** (f)
forceps	**extracción con fórceps** (f)
premature	**parto prematuro** (m)
diaper	**pañal** (m); **braga** (f)
diaper, to	**cambiar el pañal; renovar el pañal de; proveer con pañal**
diaper rash	**salpullido** (m); **escaldadura (en los bebés)** (f)
dilation (of cervix)	**dilatación del cuello de la matriz** (f)
diet	**dieta** (f); **régimen** (m)
be on a diet, to	**estar a dieta**
put on a diet, to	**poner a dieta**
discharge	**flujo** (m); **secreción** (f); **supuración** (f)
discharge (bloody)	**derrame** (m)
discharge (from the hospital), to	**dar de alta**
douche	**lavado vaginal** (m); **ducha** (f)
dry, to	**secar**
duct	**conducto** (m)
edema	**edema** (m); **hinchazón** (m)
ejaculate, to	**eyacular; venirse** (slang)
embryo	**embrión** (m)
enema	**enema** (f)
soapsuds	**enema jabonosa** (f)
engorgement	**estancamiento** (m)
episiotomy	**corte de las partes** (m); **episiotomía** (f); **tajo** (m, slang)
estrogen	**estrógeno** (m)
exercise moderately, to	**hacer ejercicios moderado**
eyepads	**paños en los ojos** (m); **toallas en los ojos** (f)
eye shield	**escudo ocular** (m)

fainting spell	**desvanecimiento** (m)
during pregnancy	**achaque** (m, C Rica)
family	**familia** (f)
family planning	**planificación de la familia** (f)
fetal heart tone	**latido del corazón fetal** (m)
fetoscope	**estetescopio fetal** (m); **fetoscopio** (m)
fetus	**feto** (m)
fissure	**fisura** (f); **cisura** (f)
fontanel	**fontanela** (f); **mollera** (f)
forceps (obs.)	**fórceps** (m)
formula	**fórmula** (f)
fundus	**fondo del útero** (m)
glucose water	**agua con azúcar** (f)
gynecologist	**ginecólogo** (m)
hair	**pelo** (m); **cabello(s)** (m)
pubic hair	**vello púbico** (m); **pelo púbico** (m); **pendejos** (m, Arg, slang)
heartbeat	**latido cardíaco** (m)
heartburn	**acedía** (f); **agriera** (f, Sp Am) **agruras** (f); **pirosis** (f); **acidez** (f)
heatingpad, electric	**almohadilla caliente eléctrica** (f)
hemorrhoids	**hemorroides** (f); **almorranas** (f)
hormone	**hormona** (f); **hormón** (m)
hymen	**himen** (m)
ice bag	**bolsa de hielo** (f)
ice pack	**aplicación de hielo empaquetado** (f)
incision	**incisión** (f)
incubator	**incubadora** (f); **estufa** (f)
infant	**infante** (m/f); **nene** (m); **nena** (f)
infection	**infección** (f)
intercourse	**relación sexual** (f)
labor	**parto** (m); **trabajo de parto** (m)
artificial	**parto artificial** (m)
be in labor, to	**estar de parto**
complicated	**parto complicado** (m)

dry	**parto seco** (m)
false	**parto falso** (m)
first stage of	**primer período del parto** (m)
immature	**parto inmaturo** (m)
induced	**parto inducido** (m)
instrumental	**parto instrumental** (m)
multiple	**parto multiple** (m)
pains	**dolores de parto** (m)
premature	**parto prematuro** (m)
prolonged	**parto prolongado** (m)
room, labor	**sala de partos** (f); **sala prenatal** (f)
second stage of	**segundo período del parto** (m)
spontaneous	**parto espontáneo** (m)
third stage of	**tercer período del parto** (m)
lactation	**lactancia** (f)
lump	**tumorcito** (m); **bola** (f); **bulto** (m); **protuberancia** (f)
massage	**masaje** (m)
massage, to	**masar; masajar**
maternity	**maternidad** (f); **de maternidad** (adj)
maternity clothes	**ropa de maternidad** (f)
maternity floor	**piso de maternidad** (m)
maternity hospital	**casa de maternidad** (f)
mental retardation	**retardo mental** (m)
mentally retarded	**retardado** (adj)
midwife (untrained)	**comadrona** (f)
midwife (trained)	**partera** (f)
miscarriage	**malparto** (m); **parto malogrado** (m)
morning sickness	**vómitos del embarazo** (m); **enfermedad matutina** (f)
nipple (breast)	**pezón** (m); **chichi** (f, Arg)
nipple, cracked	**grieta del pezón** (f)
nipple (of a baby nursing bottle)	**tetilla** (f); **chupón** (m); **mamadera** (f); **tetina** (f)
nipple shield	**escudo para el pezón** (m); **pezonera** (f)
nurse	**enfermera** (f)
baby nurse	**nodriza** (f); **ama de cría** (f); **niñera** (f)
nursemaid	**niñera** (f)

wet nurse	**nodriza** (f); **chichi** (f, Guat, Mex, coll); **chichigua** (f, Sp Am, vulg)
nurse, to	**amamantar; dar el pecho al niño; criar a los pechos; dar de mamar**
nursing	**amamantamiento** (m)
nursing bottle	**biberón** (m); **mamadera** (f); **tetera** (f)
nursing bra	**sostén de maternidad** (m)
nursing pad	**almohadita** (f)
nursery	**cuarto de los niños** (m)
newborn nursery	**sala de los recién nacidos** (f)
obstetric	**obstétrico** (adj)
obstetrical	**obstétrico** (adj)
obstetrician	**obstétrico** (m/f); **médico partero** (m/f); **tocólogo** (m/f)
obstetrics	**obstetricia** (f, sg); **tocología** (f)
ointment	**ungüento** (m); **pomada** (f)
orgasm	**orgasmo** (m)
ounce	**onza** (f)
outpatient	**paciente externo** (m/f); **paciente ambulatorio** (m/f)
ovary	**ovario** (m)
overdue	**atrasado** (adj)
ovum	**óvulo** (m); **huevo** (m)
ovulate, to	**ovar**
ovulation	**ovulación** (f)
pacifier	**chupete** (m)
pain	**dolor** (m)
bearing-down	**sensación de pesantez en el perineo** (f)
expulsive	**dolores expulsivos** (m)
false	**dolores falsos** (m)
hunger	**dolores de hambre** (m)
intermenstrual	**dolores intermenstruales** (m)
labor	**dolores de parto** (m)
premonitory	**dolores premonitorios** (m)
shooting	**dolor fulgurante** (m)
wandering	**dolor errante** (m)

pant, to	**jadear**
panting	**jadeante** (adj)
pediatric	**pediátrico** (adj)
pediatrician	**pedíatra** (m/f)
pediatrics	**pediatría** (f, sg)
pelvic	**pelviano** (adj); **pélvico** (adj)
pelvimeter	**pelvímetro** (m)
pelvis	**pelvis** (f)
perineal	**perineal** (adj)
perineum	**perineo** (m)
physician	**médico** (m); **doctor (doctora)** (m,
attending physician	f); **médico de cabecera** (m); **médico a cargo** (m); **médico asistente** (m)
consulting physician	**médico consultor** (m); **medico de apelación** (m)
resident physician	**médico residente** (m)
PKU (phenylketonuria)	**prueba del pañal** (f); **fenilcetonuria** (f)
placenta	**placenta** (f); **secudinas** (f)
placenta previa	**placenta previa** (f)
placental	**placentario** (adj)
planned parenthood	**procreación planeada** (f); **natalidad dirigida** (f)
postnatal care	**cuidado postnatal** (m)
pounds	**libras** (f)
pregnancy	**preñez** (f); **embarazo** (m)
ectopic pregnancy	**embarazo ectópico** (m)
false	**embarazo falso** (m)
hysteria	**embarazo histérico** (m)
incomplete	**embarazo incompleto** (m)
tubal pregnancy	**embarazo tubárico** (m); **embarazo en los tubos** (m)
pregnant	**preñada** (adj); **gruesa** (adj, coll); **embarazada** (adj)
premature	**prematuro** (adj); **sietemesino** (literally "seven months")
prenatal	**prenatal** (adj)
prenatal care	**cuidado prenatal** (m)

prescribe, to	**recetar; prescribir**
prescription	**receta médica** (f); **prescripción** (f)
presentation	**presentación** (f)
procreate	**procrear**
progeny	**prole** (f); **progenie** (f)
progesterone	**progesterona** (f)
prolapse	**prolapso** (m); **caída de la matriz** (f)
prophylactic	**profiláctico** (adj)
puerile	**pueril** (adj)
puerperal	**puerperal** (adj)
puerperal fever	**fiebre puerperal** (f)
puerperium	**puerperio** (m); **riesgo** (m)
pump, to	**sacar (leche) por medio de una bomba**
quadruplet	**cuatrillizo** (m); **cuadrúpleto** (m)
quintuplet	**quintillizo** (m); **quíntuplo** (m)
rabbit test	**examen de conejo** (m)
recessive	**recesivo** (adj)
recessive character	**carácter recesivo** (m)
rectal	**rectal** (adj)
rectocele	**rectocele** (m)
rectum	**recto** (m)
reddish	**rojizo** (adj); **bermejizo** (adj, hair)
red-haired	**pelirrojo** (adj)
reduce, to	**reducir(se)**
reducing exercises	**ejercicios físicos para adelgazar; ejercicios físicos para deducir peso**
relation	**pariente** (f); **parentesco** (m) **relación** (f)
relations, to have sexual	**tener relaciones sexuales; dormir con alguien; estar con alguien; chingar** (vulg); **cojer** (Arg, PR, Mex, vulg); **conocer**
relationship	**relación** (f); **parentesco** (m)
relax, to	**relajar; aflojarse**
relaxation	**relajación** (f); **descanso** (m)
relaxation of tension	**disminución de la tirantez** (f)

Rh factor	**factor Rh** (m); **factor Rhesus** (m)
Rh negative	**Rh-negativo** (adj)
Rh positive	**Rh-positivo** (adj)
rinse, to	**enjuagar**
rub, to	**frotarse; pasar la mano sobre la superficie de**
rubbing alcohol	**alcohol para fricciones** (m)
sanitary pad	**kotex** (m); **servilleta sanitaria** (f)
shave, to	**rasurar; afeitar**
sitzbath	**baño de asiento** (m); **semicupio** (m)
speculum	**espejo vaginal** (m); **espéculo** (m)
sperm	**semen** (m); **espermatozoide** (m); **semilla** (f, Mex slang)
spotting	**manchado** (m); **manchas de sangre** (f)
squat, to	**acuclillarse**
sterilize, to	**castrar; esterilizar**
sterilize the bottles, to	**esterilizar las botellas**
sterilizer	**esterilizador** (m)
stillbirth	**parto muerto** (m); **nati-muerto** (m)
stillborn	**nacido muerto** (adj); **mortinato** (adj)
stretch marks (strias)	**estrias** (f)
subtract, to	**sustraer; deducir**
suck, to	**mamar; chupar**
supplementary feedings	**alimentación suplementaria** (f)
swallow, to	**tragar**
tampex	**tampex** (m)
tie the tubes, to	**ligar trompas; ligar los tubos de Falopio; ligar los tubos uterinos**
tampon	**ta(m)pón** (m)
toxemia	**toxemia** (f)
of pregnancy	**toxemia del embarazo** (f)
tube	**tubo** (m)
Fallopian tube	**trompa de Falopio** (f); **tubo de Falopio** (m)
tube (for feeding)	**sonda** (f)

umbilical cord	**cordón umbilical** (m); **cordón del ombligo** (m)
umbilicus	**ombligo** (m)
urine specimen	**muestra de la orina** (f)
uterus	**útero** (m); **matriz** (f)
vagina	**vagina** (f)
vaginal	**vaginal** (adj)
vaginitis	**vaginitis** (f)
varicose	**varicoso** (adj)
varicose vein	**várice** (f); **variz** (m); **vena varicosa** (f)
varicosity	**varicosidad** (f)
vulva	**vulva** (f)
wash, to	**lavar**
weigh, to	**pesar**
womb	**matriz** (f); **útero** (m)

MEDICAL SPECIALISTS

ESPECIALISTAS MEDICAS

anesthesiologist	**anestesiólogo**
attending physician	**médico de cabecera; médico a cargo; médico de atendencia**
bacteriologist	**bacteriólogo**
biologist	**biólogo**
cardiologist	**cardiólogo**
charge nurse	**enfermera de cargo**
chiropodist	**quiropodista; pedicuro; callista**
chiropractor	**quiropráctico; quiropractor**
consulting physician	**médico consultor; médico de apelación**
cytologist	**citólogo**
day nurse	**enfermera de día**
dentist	**dentista**
dermatologist	**dermatólogo**

CRUCIAL VOCABULARY FOR MEDICAL PERSONNEL

dietician	**dietista**
doctor	**médico, doctor**
druggist	**farmacéutico; boticario**
ear, nose & throat (otorhinolaryngo-logist)	**otorrinolaringólogo**
embryologist	**embriólogo**
endocrinologist	**endocrinólogo**
endodontist	**endodontista**
general duty nurse	**enfermera general**
general practitioner	**médico general**
gynecologist	**ginecólogo**
head nurse	**jefa de enfermeras**
hematologist	**hematólogo**
histiologist	**histólogo**
homeopathist	**homeópata**
hygienist	**higienista**
intern	**interno; médico practicante**
internist	**internista**
midwife (untrained)	**comadrona**
midwife (trained)	**partera**
neurologist	**neurólogo**
neuropsychiatrist	**neuropsiquiatra**
neurosurgeon	**neurocirujano**
night nurse	**enfermera de noche**
nurse	**enfermero, enfermera**
nurse's aide	**ayudante de enfermera**
nurse on duty	**enfermera de guardia**
obstetrician	**obstétrico, médico partero, tocólogo**
occulist	**oculista**
ophthalmologist	**oftalmólogo**
optician	**óptico**
optometrist	**optometrista**
oral surgeon	**cirujano oral**
orderly	**ayudante (de hospital)**
orthodontist	**ortodontista**

orthopedist	**ortopedista**
orthoptist	**ortóptico**
osteopath	**osteópata**
otolaryngologist	**otolaringólogo**
otologist	**otólogo**
pathologist	**patólogo**
pediatrician	**pediatra ; pedíatra**
pedodentist	**pedodontista**
periodontist	**periodontista**
pharmacist	**farmacéutico; boticario**
pharmacologist	**farmacólogo**
physician	**médico; doctor**
physiotherapist	**fisioterapeuta**
plastic surgeon	**cirujano plástico**
podiatrist	**podiatra**
practical nurse	**enfermera no diplomada; enfermera práctica**
private nurse	**enfermera privada**
psychiatrist	**psiquiatra**
psychologist	**psicólogo**
psychoanalyst	**psicoanalista**
public health nurse	**enfermera de salud pública**
radiologist	**radiólogo**
registered nurse	**enfermera registrada; enfermera diplomada**
stretcher bearer	**camillero**
surgeon	**cirujano, quirurgo**
therapist	**terapeuta**
tocologist	**tocólogo**
traumatologist	**traumatólogo**
urologist	**urólogo**
venereologist	**especialista en enfermedades venéreas**
visiting nurse	**enfermera ambulante**

BATHROOM, TOILET ARTICLES AND PERSONAL EFFECTS

ARTICULOS PARA EL BAÑO Y EL TOCADOR Y OBJETOS PERSONALES

ashtray	**cenicero** (m)
bag	**bolsa** (f); **cartera** (f); **saco** (m)
bathbrush	**cepillo de baño** (m)
bath powder	**polvos de baño** (m, pl)
beautify oneself, to	**embellecerse**
bedpan	**bacín** (m); **bidet** (m); **cuña** (f); **chata** (f); **cómodo** (m, Mex); **paleta** (f); **pato** (m); **silleta** (f); **taza** (f)
billfold	**cartera** (f); **billetera** (f)
bleach, to	**blanquear**
bobby pin	**horquilla** (f); **clip** (m)
book	**libro** (m)
bracelet	**brazalete** (m); **pulsera** (f)
briefcase	**cartera** (f); **portapapeles** (m)
brooch	**prendedor** (m); **broche** (m); **prendero** (m)
brush one's teeth, to	**cepillarse los dientes**
checkbook	**talonario (de cheques)** (m)
cigar	**cigarro** (m); **puro** (m); **tabaco** (m); **habano** (m)
cigarette	**cigarrillo** (m); **pitillo** (m, Spain); **cigarro** (m, Sp Am)
cigar(ette) case	**petaca** (f); **pitillera** (f)
cigarette lighter	**encendedor** (m); **mechero** (m)
cigarettes, carton of	**cartón de cigarillos** (m)
cleansing cream	**crema limpiadora** (f)
cleansing tissue	**pañuelo de papel** (m)
clippers	**maquinilla para cortar** (f)
coat hanger	**percha** (f)
cold cream	**crema facial** (f)
cologne	**agua de colonia** (f); **colonia** (f)
comb	**peine** (m)
comb, to	**peinar(se)**

compact	**polvera** (f)
contact lenses	**lentes de contacto** (m)
contact lens case	**estuche** (m)
cosmetic	**cosmético** (adj)
cosmetics	**cosméticos** (m, pl); **productos de belleza** (m, pl)
cream	**crema** (f)
cuff links	**gemelos** (m, pl, Spain); **mancuernas** (f, pl, Mex); **mancuerillas** (f, pl, Sp Am); **colleras** (f, pl, Chile); **mancornas** (f, pl, Colombia)
curlers	**rizadores** (m); **rollos** (m); **rulos** (m)
curlers, to roll on	**poner los rulos,** etc.
curlers, to take off	**sacar los rulos,** etc.
cut hair, to	**cortar el pelo**
dental floss	**hilo dental** (m)
denture cup	**recipiente para guardar la dentadura** (m)
deodorant	**desodorante** (m)
depilatory	**depilatorio** (m)
drug	**droga** (f)
drugstore	**farmacia** (f, Spain); **droguería** (f, Sp Am); **botica** (f)
dry, to	**secar**
dye	**tintura** (f); **tinte** (m)
dye, to	**teñir**
earring	**arete** (m); **zarcillo** (m); **pantalla** (f, P.R.)
earring, drop	**pendiente** (m); **arracada** (f)
emery board	**lima para las uñas** (f)
emesis bowl	**riñonera** (f); **vasija para vomitar** (f)
envelope	**sobre** (m)
eyebrow brush	**cepillo para las cejas** (m)
eyebrow pencil	**lápiz para las cejas** (m)
eyelash curler	**rizador de pestañas** (m)
eye shadow	**sombra para los ojos** (f)
face powder	**polvo facial** (m)

facial tissues	**servilletas faciales** (f); **pañuelos faciales** (m); **kleenex** (m)
flowers	**flores** (f)
foot powder	**polvos para los pies** (m)
glasses	**anteojos** (m, pl); **gafas** (f, pl); **lentes** (m, pl, Mex.); **espejuelos** (m, pl, Cuba)
sun glasses	**gafas de sol** (f, pl)
glass case	**estuche** (m); **funda de gafas** (f)
hair brush	**cepillo para el pelo** (m); **cepillo de cabeza** (m)
hair cut	**corte de pelo** (m)
hairdresser	**peluquero (-a)** (m/f)
beautician	**peluquero (-a)** (m/f)
barber	**barbero (-a)** (m/f)
hair dryer	**secador del pelo** (m)
hair dye	**tinte para el pelo** (m)
hair net	**redecilla** (f)
hair pin	**horquilla** (f); **gancho para el pelo** (m); **sujetador** (m)
hair spray	**fijador para el pelo** (m)
hair tonic	**tónico para el pelo** (m)
handbag	**saquito de mano** (m)
hand cream	**crema para las manos** (f)
hand lotion	**loción para las manos** (f)
hankie, handkerchief	**pañuelo** (m)
jewelry	**joyas** (f, pl)
key	**llave** (f)
key ring	**llavero** (m)
kleenex	**kleenex** (m); **pañuelo de papel** (m)
lather	**espuma** (f)
lather the face, to	**enjabonar la cara; dar jabón en la cara**
letter	**carta** (f)
lipstick	**lápiz labial** (m); **pintura de labios** (f); **lápiz para los labios** (m)
lotion	**loción** (f)

magazine	**revista** (f)
makeup	**maquillaje** (m)
makeup, to put on	**maquillarse**
manicure	**manicura** (f); **arreglo de uñas** (m)
manicure, to	**hacer la manicura**
mascara	**máscara** (f)
match	**fósforo** (m); **cerilla** (f, Spain); **cerillo** (m, Mex)
medicated soap	**jabón medicinal** (m)
medicine	**medicina** (f)
mirror	**espejo** (m)
mouth wash	**lavado bucal** (m); **enjuague** (m)
nail brush	**cepillo para las uñas** (m)
nail clipper	**cortaúñas** (m, sg)
nail file	**lima para las uñas** (f)
nail hardener	**endurecedor de uñas** (m)
nail polish	**esmalte de uñas** (m); **pintura de uñas** (f); **barniz** (m); **laca de uñas** (f)
nail polish remover	**quitador de esmalte de uñas** (m)
necklace	**collar** (m); **gargantilla** (f)
needle	**aguja** (f)
newspaper	**periódico** (m); **diario** (m)
package	**paquete** (m); **cajetilla** (f)
perfume	**perfume** (m)
permanent wave	**ondulación permanente** (f); **ondulado permanente** (m)
pin	**alfiler** (m); **prendedero** (m)
pipe	**pipa** (f); **cachimba** (f, Sp Am)
pitcher	**jarra** (f)
pocketbook	**cartera** (f); **portamonedas** (f, sg); **bolsa** (f); **bolso** (m)
postcard	**tarjeta postal** (f)
powder	**polvo** (m)
powder box	**polvera** (f)
powder puff	**mota para empolvarse** (f); **borla** (f); **bellota** (f)

purse	**monedero** (m); **bolso** (m); **bolsa** (f)
put up one's hair, to	**ponerse los rulos**
razor	**navaja de afeitar** (f); **cuchilla de afeitar** (f)
razor, electric	**máquina de afeitar eléctrica** (f)
razor, safety	**máquina de afeitar** (f); **maquinilla de afeitar** (f); **maquinilla de seguridad** (f)
razor, straight, barber's razor	**navaja de afeitar** (f)
razor blade	**hoja de afeitar** (f); **navajita** (f); **gillette** (m, Cent Am)
razor strap	**correa** (f); **ascentador** (m)
ring	**anillo** (m); **sortija** (f); **argolla** (f, parts of Sp Am)
engagement ring	**anillo de prometida** (m); **anillo de compromiso** (m, Mex)
wedding ring	**alianza** (f); **anillo** (o **sortija**) **de matrimonio, de boda, de casamiento** (m)
rinse	**enjuagador** (m)
rinse, to	**enjuagar; aclarar**
rouge	**colorete** (m)
rubber gloves	**guantes de goma** (m)
safety pin	**imperdible** (m); **alfiler de seguridad** (m)
sanitary napkin	**servilleta sanitaria** (f); **kotex** (m); **almohadilla higiénica** (f); **absorbente higiénico** (m)
scissors	**tijeras** (f, pl)
set, to	**marcar**
set, setting	**peinado** (m)
shampoo	**champú** (m); **shampoo** (m)
shave	**afeitada** (f); **rasuración** (f)
shave (oneself), to	**afeitar(se); rasurar(se)**
shaving cream	**crema de afeitar** (f)
shaving lotion	**loción de afeitar** (f)
shaving soap	**jabón de afeitar** (m)
shoehorn	**calzador** (m)

shower	**ducha** (f); **regadera** (f, Mex); **baño de China** (m, Arg)
shower, to	**ducharse**
smoke, to	**fumar; pitar** (Arg & Chile)
smoke a pipe, to	**fumar en pipa**; **pipar**
soap	**jabón** (m)
soap, bar of	**pastilla de jabón** (f)
stamp (postage)	**timbre** (m, Mex); **estampilla** (f, Sp Am); **sello** (m, Spain)
stationery	**papel de escribir** (m)
suitcase	**maleta** (f)
suntan lotion	**loción para el sol** (f); **loción bronceadora** (f)
talcum powder	**polvo de talco** (m)
tampon	**tampón** (m); **tapón** (m)
thread	**hilo** (m)
tie clasp	**alfiler de corbata** (m)
toilet paper	**papel sanitario** (m); **papel de baño** (m); **papel de inodoro** (m); **papel higiénico** (m)
toilet soap	**jabón de tocador** (m)
toilet water	**agua de tocador** (f)
tooth brush	**cepillo de dientes** (m)
tooth paste	**pasta dental** (f); **dentífrico** (m); **pasta dentífrica** (f)
tooth powder	**polvo dental** (m)
towel	**toalla** (f)
towel, clean	**toalla limpia** (f)
towel, dirty	**toalla sucia** (f)
towel, Turkish	**toalla afelpada** (f)
truss	**braguero** (m)
tube	**tubo** (m)
tweezer	**pinzas** (f)
urinal	**orinal** (m)
vaseline	**vaselina** (f)
wallet	**cartera** (f); **billetera** (f); **portamonedas** (m, pl)

wash, to	**lavar(se)**
washbasin	**basija** (f); **jofaina** (f); **ponchera** (f, Cent Am); **palanga** (f, Mex)
washcloth	**paño de lavarse** (m); **toallita** (f)
waste basket	**papelera** (f)
watch	**reloj** (m)
wristwatch	**reloj de pulsera** (m)
wig	**peluca** (f)

BEDDING

ROPA DE CAMA

air cushion	**colchón de aire** (m)
bed	**cama** (f)
bedboard	**tabla para la cama** (f)
bed pad	**colchoncillo para la cama** (m)
bedspread	**colcha de cama** (f); **sobrecama** (f); **cubrecama** (f)
blanket	**frazada** (f); **manta** (f)
electric blanket	**frazada eléctrica** (f)
comforter	**sobrecama** (f)
cot	**catre** (m)
cover	**cubierta** (f)
headboard cover	**cubierta para la cabecera de la cama** (f)
mattress cover	**cubierta de colchón** (f)
pillowcase cover	**funda de almohada** (f)
covered with a bedspread	**encobertado** (adj)
covers	**cobertores** (m, pl); **cobijas** (f, pl, Mex and elsewhere)
crib	**cuna** (f); **camita de niño** (f)
hammock	**hamaca** (f)
headboard	**cabecera de cama** (f)
mattress	**colchón** (m)
air mattress	**colchón de aire** (m); **colchón de viento** (m)

feather mattress	**colchón de plumas** (m)
(inner)spring mattress	**colchón de muelles** (m)
mosquito net	**mosquitero** (m)
pad	**cojincillo** (m); **almohadilla** (f)
pillow	**almohada** (f)
feather pillow	**edredón** (m)
pillow case	**funda (de almohada)** (f) **almohada** (f)
quilt	**colcha** (f); **sobrecama acolchada** (f); **edredón** (m)
sheepskin	**zalea** (f)
sheet	**sábana** (f)
plastic sheet	**sábana de plástico** (f)
side rail	**riel del costado** (m); **baranda protectora** (f)

CLOTHING

ROPA

apron	**delantal** (m)
bathing suit	**traje de baño** (m); **bañador** (m, Spain)
bathing trunks (male)	**trusas** (f, pl, Cuba); **calzón de baño** (m); **calzoneta** (f, Guat)
bathrobe	**bata (de baño)** (f); **salida** (f, Arg)
bathrobe (terrycloth)	**albornoz** (m)
bedclothes	**ropa de cama** (f); **tendido** (m, Col, Ecuad, Mex)
belt	**cinto** (m); **cinturón** (m)
bikini	**bikini** (m)
blouse	**blusa** (f); **camiseta** (f)
blue jeans	**pantalones vaqueros** (m, pl.); **mezclillas** (f, Mex)
boot	**bota** (f); **botín** (m, Arg)
bow tie	**lazo** (m); **corbata de lazo** (f)

bra, brassiere	**sostén** (m); **sostenedor** (m); **porta-bustos** (m); **corpiño** (m, Arg); **ajustador** (m); **justillo** (m)
buckle	**hebilla** (f)
button	**botón** (m)
button, to	**abotonar; abrochar**
buttonhole	**ojal** (f)
cap	**gorra** (f); **montera** (f)
change clothes, to	**mudarse de ropa; cambiarse la ropa**
cloth	**tela** (f); **paño** (m); **tejido** (m)
batiste	**batista** (f)
calfskin	**becerro** (m)
checked	**a cuadros** (adj)
corduroy	**pana** (f)
cotton	**algodón** (m)
dark	**oscuro** (adj)
dotted	**moteado** (adj)
heavyweight	**grueso** (adj)
kid (leather)	**cabritilla** (f)
lace	**encaje** (m)
light	**claro** (adj)
lightweight	**delgado** (adj)
linen	**lienzo** (m); **lino** (m); **hilo** (m)
lining	**forro** (m)
little pattern	**algo de estampada** (adj)
satin	**raso** (m)
silk	**seda** (f)
solid color	**liso** (adj)
striped	**rayado** (adj); **a rayas**
taffeta	**tafetán** (m)
velvet	**terciopelo** (m)
wool	**lana** (f)
woolen	**de lana** (adj)
clothes, apparel	**ropa** (f, sg.); **vestimenta** (f)
coat	**abrigo** (m)

coat, fur	**abrigo de piel** (m)
coat, jacket	**chaqueta** (f)
coat, lightweight	**abrigo de entretiempo** (m)
coat, overcoat	**abrigo** (m); **sobretodo** (m)
coat, rain	**impermeable** (m)
coat, sportcoat	**americana** (f, Spain); **saco** (m, Sp Am)
coat, top	**gabán** (m)
collar	**cuello** (m)
corset	**corsé** (m)
cuff (shirt)	**puño** (m)
cuff (trousers)	**vuelta** (f)
diaper	**pañal** (m)
dress	**vestido** (m); **traje** (m, Peru, Panama)
dress, evening	**vestido de noche** (m)
dress, house	**vestido para la casa** (m)
dress, low-necked	**vestido de escote bajo** (m)
dress, maternity	**vestido de maternidad** (m)
dress, wash	**vestido que puede lavarse** (m)
dress, to	**vestir(se)**
dry clean, to	**limpiar en seco**
fade, to	**desteñir**
fur	**piel** (f)
galoshes	**galochas** (f); **chanclo** (m, Spain)
garter	**liga** (f)
garter belt	**portaligas** (m)
girdle	**ceñidor** (m); **cinturón** (m); **faja** (f)
gloves	**guantes** (m)
half slip	**saya interior** (f)
handkerchief	**pañuelo** (m)
hat	**sombrero** (m)
derby	**hongo** (m)
hat, felt	**sombrero de fieltro** (m); **sombrero flexible** (m)
hat, sport	**sombrero de deporte** (m)
hat, straw	**sombrero de paja** (m)

hat, top	**sombrero de copa** (m)
heel	**tacón** (m); **taco** (m, Arg, Mex)
high-heeled shoes	**zapatos de tacones altos** (m, pl.)
low-heeled shoes	**zapatos de tacones bajos** (m, pl.)
hem	**bastilla** (f); **ruedo** (m, Guatemala)
hook	**gancho** (m)
hooks and eyes	**corchetes** (m, pl.)
hose	**medias** (f, pl.)
pantyhose	**medias** (f, pl.); **medias pantalón** (f); **pantimedias** (f, pl.)
jacket	**chaqueta** (f); **saco** (m); **americana** (f)
jacket, dinner	**smoking** (m); **americana negra** (f)
jacket, ski	**gamberro** (m); **anorak** (m)
jeans	**pantalones vaqueros** (m, pl); **mezclilla** (f, Mex)
lapel	**solapa** (f)
leather	**cuero** (m)
light (color)	**claro** (adj)
light (weight)	**ligero** (adj)
lingerie	**ropa interior de mujer** (f)
low-cut	**escotado** (adj); **descotado** (adj)
mink	**visón** (m)
necktie	**corbata** (f)
bow-tie	**corbata de lazo** (f)
four-in-hand tie	**corbata de nudo** (f)
nightgown	**camisón de dormir** (m); **camisa de noche** (f); **bata** (f)
nylon	**nilón** (m)
oxfords	**zapatos bajos** (m, pl); **zapatos de estilo Oxford** (m)
pair	**par** (m)
pajama	**pijama** (f/m); **piyama** (f/m)
panties	**bragas** (f); **calzones** (m, pl); **pantalones interiores de mujer** (m); **pantaleta** (f)

pants (men's)	**pantalones** (m)
peignoir	**peinador** (m); **bata de señora** (f)
petticoat	**enaguas** (f)
pleat	**pliegue** (m)
pleated	**plisado** (adj)
pocket	**bolsillo** (m, Spain); **bolsa** (f, Sp Am)
pocket, hip	**bolsillo trasero** (m)
pocket, side	**bolsillo del costado** (m)
rubber pants	**pantalones plásticos** (m, pl)
rubber heel	**tacón de goma** (m)
rubber overshoe	**chanclo** (m, Spain); **zapato de goma** (m, SpAm), **zapato de hule** (m, Mex)
sandals	**sandalia** (f); **guaraches** (m, Mex); **caites** (m, Cent Am) **ojotas** (f, Chile, Ec, Peru, Bol)
sash	**faja** (f)
scarf	**bufanda** (f)
seam	**costura** (f)
shawl	**chal** (m); **rebozo** (m, Mex)
shirt	**camisa** (f)
shirt, sport	**camisa sport** (f)
shirt, sweat	**camisa enguatada** (f)
shirt, under	**camiseta** (f)
shirt, under (T-shirt)	**polera** (f, Sp Am)
shoe	**zapato** (m)
shoelace	**cordón de zapato** (m); **agujeta,** (f); **cinta** (f)
shorts	**calzones cortos** (m)
shorts, under	**calzoncillos** (m)
skirt	**falda** (f); **saya** (f); **sayuela** (f); **pollera** (f, Arg and Chile)
skirt, sport	**falda de deporte** (f)
sleeve	**manga** (f)
sleeve, long	**manga larga** (f); **manga larguita** (f)
sleeve, short	**manga corta** (f)

slip	**combinación** (f); **enagua** (f); **refajo** (m)
slipper	**zapatilla** (f); **chinela** (f); **chancleta** (f)
snaps	**botones automáticos** (m); **cierre de resorte** (m)
sneaker	**zapato de goma** (m); **zapato de gimnasio** (m)
sock	**calcetín** (m); **media** (f, Arg)
sole (of shoe)	**suela** (f)
sportswear	**ropa deportiva** (f)
stockings	**medias** (f)
suit	**traje** (m); **vestido** (m, Peru, Panama)
business	**traje de calle** (m); **traje civil** (m)
close-fitting	**entallado** (adj)
double-breasted	**cruzado** (adj)
dress	**traje de etiqueta** (m)
made-to-measure	**hecho a la medida** (adj)
pants suit	**traje pantalón** (m)
ready-made	**hecho** (adj)
single-breasted	**sin cruzar** (adj)
three-piece	**terno** (m); **flux** o **flus** (m, Sp Am)
tuxedo	**americana negra** (f)
suspenders	**tirantes (del pantalón)** (m, pl)
sweater	**sweater** (m); **suéter** (m); **jersey** (m)
tie	**corbata** (f)
trousers	**pantalones** (m)
trunks	**calzones de baño** (m); **shorts** (m)
unbutton, to	**desabotonar; desabrochar**
underpants	**calzoncillos** (m)
undershirt	**camiseta** (f)
underwear	**ropa interior** (f)
uniform	**uniforme** (m)
veil	**velo** (m)
vest	**chaleco** (m)
wash, to	**lavar**

wrinkle	**arruga** (f)
zipper	**cierre automático** (m); **cierre relámpago** (m)

COLORS

beige	**beige**
black	**negro**
blonde	**rubio; chelo** (Mex)
blue	**azul**
brown	**moreno; pardo; carmelita**
brunette	**moreno; trigueño**
chestnut	**castaño; pardo**
clear	**incoloro**
color	**color** (m)
cranberry	**arándano**
dark	**oscuro**
gold	**dorado**
gray	**gris**
green	**verde**

COLORES

light (color)	**claro**
maroon	**rojo obscuro; marrón**
opaque	**opaco**
orange	**anaranjado**
pale	**pálido**
pink	**rosado**
purple	**púrpura; purpúreo**
red	**rojo**
ruby	**rubí**
silver	**plateado**
transparent	**transparente**
violet	**violeta; morado**
white	**blanco**
yellow	**amarillo**

OCCUPATIONS[1]

actor	**actor**
actress	**actriz**
actuary	**actuario de seguros**
adjutant general	**ayudante general**
administrator	**administrador, gobernante**
admiral	**almirante**
advertiser	**anunciador, anunciante**
adviser, advisor	**consejero, consultor**

OCUPACIONES

[1] There is a general tendency to differentiate gender of nouns of occupation. New feminine forms are rapidly coming into the Spanish language, e.g., **abogada, arquitecta, presidenta.** See page 284.

CRUCIAL VOCABULARY FOR MEDICAL PERSONNEL

advocate	**abogado, defensor**
aerodynamic	**aerodinámico** (adj)
aerographer	**meteorologista naval**
aeromechanic	**mecánico de aviación**
aeronautic(al)	**aeronáutico** (adj)
aerospace	**aeroespacial** (adj)
agent	**agente, represente**
agent officer	**oficial pagador**
agricultural engineer	**ingeniero agrónomo**
agriculturist	**agricultor, agrícola, labrador, agrónomo**
agronomist	**agrónomo**
aide de camp	**ayudante de campo**
air hostess	**azafata**
alderman	**concejal, regidor**
ambassador	**embajador, enviado**
ambassadress	**embajadora, esposa de embajador**
ambulance driver	**conductor de ambulancia**
announcer	**anunciador(a), locutor(a)**
antique dealer	**anticuario**
apiculturist (beekeeper)	**apicultor**
apothecary	**boticario, farmacéutico**
applicant	**solicitante, candidato**
appointee	**electo, persona designada**
appraiser	**evaluador, tasador**
apprentice	**aprendiz, novicio, principiante**
aquanaut	**acuanauta**
arbitrator	**arbitrador, árbitro**
arboriculturist	**arboricultor**
archeologist	**arqueólogo**
archbishop	**arzobispo**
archdeacon	**arcediano**
archer	**arquero**
architect	**arquitecto**
archivist	**archivero**
arithmetician	**aritmético**

army chaplain	**capellán castrense**
artilleryman	**artillero**
artist	**artista**
assembler	**coordinador**
assemblyman	**asambleísta**
assistant	**asistente, ayudante**
assistant manager	**sub-gerente**
assistant professor	**profesor auxiliar**
associate professor	**profesor adjunto**
astrologer	**astrólogo**
astronaut	**astronauto, cosmonauta**
atronomer	**astrónomo**
astrophysicist	**astrofísico**
athlete	**atleta**
attaché	**agregado**
attendant	**ayudante, asistente**
attorney	**abogado, procurador**
attorney general	**procurador (fiscal) general**
auctioneer	**subastador, martillero**
author	**autor**
automotive engineer	**ingeniero de automación**
aviator	**aviador, piloto de avión**
babysitter	**niñera por horas**
baggagemaster	**jefe de equipajes**
bailiff	**alguacil**
bailsman	**fiador**
baker	**panadero, hornero**
balladeer	**trovador, romancero**
ballerina	**bailarina**
ballet dancer	**bailarín**
ballplayer	**pelotero, beisbolista**
band leader	**director de una orquesta popular**
bandmaster	**director de una banda**
bandsman	**miembro de una banda u orquesta**
bank employee	**bancario, empleado de banco**
banker	**banquero**

CRUCIAL VOCABULARY FOR MEDICAL PERSONNEL

barber	**barbero, peluquero**
barkeeper	**tabernero, cantinero**
barmaid	**moza de bar, tabernera, cantinera**
barman	**camarero, mozo de bar, cantinero**
bartender	**cantinero, tabernero**
beautician	**cosmetólogo (a)**
beggar	**mendigo, pordiosero, indigente**
bellboy	**botones, paje de hotel**
belly dancer	**bailarina de danzas sensuales del Oriente Medio**
bibliographer	**bibliógrafo**
bicyclist	**ciclista**
billposter	**cartelero**
binder	**atador**
biochemist	**bioquímico**
biographer	**biógrafo**
biologist	**biólogo**
biomechanic	**biomecánico**
biophysicist	**biofísico**
boatman	**barquero, botero**
boilermaker	**calderero**
bookbinder	**encuadernador de libros**
bookie	**corredor de apuestas**
booking clerk	**vendedor de billetes (de viajes o de teatro)**
bookkeeper	**tenedor de libros, contable**
bookseller	**librero, vendedor de libros**
bottle-washer	**criado de todo servicio**
boxer	**boxeador, púgil**
breeder	**criador**
broadcaster	**locutor radiodifusor**
broker	**cambista, intermediario**
builder	**constructor, arquitecto**
bullfighter	**torero, matador**
bum	**vagabundo, holgazán**
bureaucrat	**burócrata**

businessman	**hombre de negocios, comerciante, negociante**
businesswoman	**mujer de negocios, mujer de empresa**
busdriver	**conductor de ómnibus**
butcher	**carnicero**
butler	**mayordomo, despensero**
buyer	**comprador, agente comprador**
cabdriver	**taxista, cochero**
cabin boy	**camarero de abordo, grumete**
cabinetmaker	**ebanista**
caddie	**ayudante, portador de palos**
call girl	**prostituta**
cameraman (tel, cinem)	**camarógrafo**
campaigner	**propagandista, luchador**
camper	**acampador**
candidate	**candidato, pretendiente**
candlemaker	**candelero, velero**
canoeist	**canoero, piragüero**
captain	**capitán**
cardsharp	**fullero, tahúr**
career	**carrera, profesión**
caretaker	**guardián, cuidador, vigilante**
caricaturist	**caricaturista**
carpenter	**carpintero**
cartographer	**cartógrafo**
cartoonist	**caricaturista**
caseworker	**investigador**
cashier	**cajero**
cataloger	**catalogador**
catcher	**catcher o receptor en béisbol**
cattleman	**ganadero**
censor	**censor, criticón**
census taker	**empadronador, enumerador censal**
ceramist, ceramicist	**ceramista**

certified public accountant	**contador público titulado**
chainman	**cadenero, portacadena**
chairman	**presidente**
chairwoman	**presidenta**
chamberlain	**chambelán, gentilhombre de cámera**
chambermaid	**camarera, doncella, sirvienta**
chancellor	**canciller**
chargé d'affaires	**encargado de negocios**
charwoman	**criada por día u hora**
chauffeur	**chófer, chofer** (Sp Am)
check girl	**encargado de la guardarropía**
chef	**cocinero, jefe de cocina**
chemical engineer	**ingeniero química o industrial**
chemist	**químico, farmacéutico**
chess player	**jugador de ajedrez**
chief	**jefe, caudillo**
choirboy	**niño cantor**
choirmaster	**director de coro**
choreographer	**coreógrafo**
chorus girl	**corista**
chronicler	**cronista, historiador**
circumnavigator	**circunnavegante**
city editor	**redactor de noticias locales**
city manager	**administrador municipal**
city planner	**proyectista municipal**
civil engineer	**ingeniero civil**
civil servant	**funcionario público, empleado del estado**
claim agent	**agente de reclamación**
classical scholar	**erudito en lenguas clásicas**
cleaner	**tintorero, lavandero**
cleaning woman	**criada que limpia la casa**
clergyman	**clérigo, sacerdote, ministro, pastor, rabí**

clerk	**oficinista, empleado de oficina, secretario** (offices)
	dependiente, empleado de tienda, vendedor (stores)
	escribano (law)
clinician	**médico clínico**
clown	**payaso, bufón, hazmerreír**
coach	**maestro particular** (tutor), **entrenador** (sports)
coal miner	**minero de carbón**
coastguardsman	**guardacostas**
collector	**colector, coleccionista**
comedian	**comediante, cómico**
comedienne	**comedianta, cómica**
commanding officer	**comandante en jefe**
commentator	**comentarista, comentador**
commercial artist	**artista comercial**
commercial traveler	**agente viajero**
committeeman	**miembro de comité**
compiler	**compilador, recopilador**
composer	**compositor**
comptroller	**jefe de contaduría**
computer analyst	**analista de calculadores (computadores)**
conductor	**conductor, guía, director** (mus.); **recogedor de billetes** (train)
confectioner	**confitero, dulcero**
congressman	**congresista**
construction worker	**trabajador de edificacíon**
cook	**cocinero (-a)**
coordinator	**coordinador**
correspondent	**correspondiente, corresponsal**
councilman	**concejal**
counselor	**consejero, abogado consultor**
craftsman	**artesano**
creditor	**acreedor**
customhouse official	**aduanero**

dancer	**bailador(a), danzante**
day laborer	**jornalero, bracero**
deacon	**diácono**
dealer	**negociante, comerciante; tallador** (cards)
debater	**polemista, controversista**
deliveryman	**entregador, recadero, mozo de reparto**
dental technician	**técnico dental**
dentist	**dentista**
deputy governor	**teniente gobernador**
desk clerk	**recepcionista**
detail man	**propagandista de artículos médicos y medicinas**
detective	**detective, investigador**
diagnostician	**experto en hacer diagnósticos**
dietician	**dietista**
diplomat	**diplomático**
director	**director, administrador, dirigente**
disc jockey	**animador, montadiscos**
discoverer	**descubridor, explorador; inventor**
dishwasher	**lavaplatos, lavador(a) de platos**
dispatcher	**despachador**
distributor	**distribuidor, repartidor, dispensador**
district attorney	**fiscal de un distrito judicial**
ditch digger	**acequiador**
dockhand	**estibador, cargador**
doctor	**doctor**
domestic	**doméstico, criado, sirviente**
doorkeeper, doorman	**portero**
draftsman	**dibujante, diseñador, bosquejador**
dramatist	**dramaturgo, escritor**
dressmaker	**modista, costurera**
driver	**piloto, conductor, cochero, maquinista**
druggist	**farmacéutico, boticario**

dry cleaner	**tintorero, lavandero**
dry nurse	**ama seca, niñera**
editor	**redactor titular** (newspaper), **editor** (literary)
educator	**educador, maestro, pedagogo, instructor**
efficiency engineer	**ingeniero coordinador**
electrical engineer	**ingeniero electrotécnico**
electrician	**electricista**
embalmer	**embalsamador**
embroiderer	**bordador, recamador**
employment agent	**agente de colocaciones**
enameler	**esmaltador**
engineer	**ingeniero**
engineman	**maquinista**
engraver	**grabador**
enterpriser	**empresario, hombre de empresa**
entertainer	**artista**
entrepreneur	**empresario, contratista**
equestrian	**jinete**
errand-boy	**mandadero, recadero; mensajero**
escort	**acompañante**
essayist	**escritor de ensayos, ensayista**
ethnographer	**etnógrafo**
etymologist	**etimólogo**
examiner	**examinador**
exchanger	**cambista**
exchange student	**estudiante de intercambio**
executioner	**verdugo**
executive	**funcionario**
exhibitor	**exhibidor, expositor**
expediter	**coordinator; despachador**
experimenter	**experimentador**
explorer	**explorador**
exporter	**exportador**
farmer	**agricultor, hacendado**

farmhand	**labrador, campesino, labriego**
fellowship holder	**becario, becado**
fencer	**esgrimidor**
ferryman	**barquero**
film star	**estrella de cine**
financier	**financiero, financista**
finisher	**acabador** (same for both sexes)
fireman	**bombero**
fisherman	**pescador**
flight engineer	**mecánico de a bordo**
florist	**florista**
folk singer	**cantante de música folklórica**
foreman	**capataz, encargado, caporal**
forest ranger	**guardabosque**
forewoman	**oficiala, supervisora**
freight agent	**agente de carga**
funeral home director	**director de funeraria**
furrier	**comerciante en pieles de vestir**
gambler	**tahúr, jugador**
garageman	**trabajador de garaje, mecánico**
garbage collector	**basurero**
gardener	**jardinero**
gas station attendant	**trabajador de gasolinera**
geographer	**geógrafo**
geologist	**geólogo**
geophysicist	**geofísico**
glass blower	**vidriero**
go-go dancer	**chica go-go**
golfer	**golfista, jugador de golf**
governess	**institutriz, aya**
governor	**gobernador**
graduate student	**estudiante de escuela universitaria de graduados**
grease monkey	**mecánico de automóviles**
grocer	**tendero, abacero, bodeguero** (Am)
guard	**guardia, guardián, centinela**

guide	**guía**
guitarist	**guitarrista**
gunsmith	**armero, escopetero**
gymnast	**gimnasta**
hairdresser	**peinador, peluquero**
handicraftsman	**artesano**
handmaiden	**sirvienta, doncella, asistenta**
handyman	**hacelotodo, factótum**
harbor master	**capitán de puerto**
hard-hat	**operario de construcciones**
hardware dealer	**ferretero, quincallero**
harness maker	**guarnicionero**
harvester	**cosechero, segador**
headmaster	**director, rector**
headwaiter	**jefe de camareros, jefe de mozos**
healer	**sanador, curador**
health officer	**inspector de sanidad**
helper	**ayudante, asistente**
herdsman	**vaquero, ganadero**
hired hand	**mozo de campo**
historian	**historiador, cronista**
horseman	**caballista**
hotelier	**hotelero**
housekeeper	**ama de llaves, ama de gobierno; casera**
housemother	**directora en una residencia de jóvenes**
house painter	**pintor de brocha gorda**
housewife	**ama de casa, madre de familia**
houseworker	**doméstico, criado, sirviente**
humorist	**humorista, bromista**
huntsman	**cazador**
husband	**esposo, marido**
hydromechanic	**hidromecánico**
hymnologist	**himnólogo**
hypnotist	**hipnotizador, hipnotista**

ice cream vendor	**heladero**
illustrator	**ilustrador**
impressionist	**impresionista**
indexer	**conficcionador de índices**
industrialist	**industrialista**
informer	**informante**
innkeeper	**mesonero, posadero, hospedero, hostelero**
inspector	**inspector, supervisor**
installer	**instalador, montador**
instructor	**instructor, profesor, maestro**
insurance agent	**agente de seguros**
insurance broker	**corredor de seguros**
interior decorator	**decorador de interiores**
internal revenue agent	**agente de rentas internas**
interpreter	**intérprete**
interviewer	**entrevistador**
inventor	**inventor, creador**
investigator	**investigador, indagador**
ironer	**planchador**
ironworker	**herrero**
jack-of-all-trades	**factótum, hacelotodo**
jailer	**carcelero**
janitor	**portero, conserje**
jeweler	**joyero**
jobber	**corredor, trabajador a destajo**
jockey	**jinete**
journalist	**periodista, cronista**
journeyman	**oficial**
judge	**juez**
juggler	**malabarista**
junk dealer	**chatarrero**
jurist	**jurista**
keeper	**guardián, custodio, carcelero**
kitchen boy	**mozo de cocina**
kitchenmaid	**fregona**

knitter	**calcetero, tejedor de punto**
laboratory technician	**técnico de laboratorio**
laborer	**obrero, trabajador, jornalero, bracero**
labor leader	**dirigente laborista**
lamplighter	**foralero**
land agent	**corredor de fincas**
landholder	**terrateniente, hacendado**
landlady	**arrendadora, propietaria, casera**
landlord	**arrendador, propietario, casero**
landscape architect	**arquitecto que diseña jardines**
landscape artist	**paisajista**
landscape gardener	**experto en jardinería ornamental**
land surveyor	**agrimensor**
lathe operator	**tornero**
laundress	**lavandera**
lawmaker	**legislador**
lawman	**agente de policía, alguacil**
law student	**estudiante de derecho**
lawyer	**abogado, letrado, licenciado**
lay reader	**lego**
leader	**guía, conductor, jefe**
leaseholder	**arrendatario**
lecturer	**conferencista**
legal adviser	**abogado consultor, asesor legal**
legislator	**legislador**
librarian	**bibliotecario**
lifeguard	**salvavidas**
linesman	**guardalínea; juez de línea**
linguist	**lingüista**
linotypist	**linotipista**
liquor dealer	**vendedor de licores**
lithographer	**litógrafo**
locksmith	**cerrajero**
locomotive engineer	**maquinista**
longshoreman	**estibador, cargador**

lumberjack	**leñador, hachero**
machinist	**mecánico, maquinista**
magician	**mago, mágico**
magistrate	**magistrado**
maid	**criada, sirvienta**
mail carrier	**cartero**
major-domo	**mayordomo**
manager	**gerente, director, administrador, superintendente**
manageress	**administradora, directora**
manicurist	**manicuro, manicura**
manual laborer	**obrero de mano**
manufacturer	**fabricante, industrial**
map maker	**cartógrafo**
market researcher	**estudiante de los mercados**
mason	**albañil**
masseur	**masajista**
master mechanic	**jefe mecánico**
master of ceremonies	**maestro de ceremonias**
matchmaker	**fabricante de fósferos, casamentero, casamentera**
mathematician	**matemático**
mayor	**alcalde**
mechanic	**mecánico**
mechanical engineer	**ingeniero mecánico**
mediator	**mediador, intercesor**
medical examiner	**médico forense**
member	**miembro, socio**
mentor	**consejero, mentor**
mercantilist	**mercantilista**
mercenary	**mercenario**
merchant	**mercader, comerciante, negociante**
messenger	**mensajero, mandadero, recadero**
metallurgist	**metalúrgico**
metalworker	**metalario, metalista**
metaphysician	**metafísico**

meteorologist	**meteorólogo, meteorologista**
meter maid	**policía femenina que cuida de los reglamentos de estacionamiento**
microanalyst	**microanalista**
microbiologist	**microbiólogo**
milkmaid	**ordeñadora, lechera**
milkman	**lechero, repartidor de leche a domicilio**
miller	**molinero**
mind reader	**adivinador del pensamiento**
mineralogist	**mineralogista**
mining engineer	**ingeniero de minas**
minister	**ministro, clérigo, pastor, sacerdote, cura, rabí** (religion)
	ministro, enviado (diplomat)
model	**modelo**
money changer	**cambista**
money-lender	**prestamista**
morphologist	**experto en morfología**
mortgage banker	**banquero hipotecario**
mortician	**funerario**
motorcyclist	**motociclista**
motorman	**motorista, conductor**
mountain climber	**andinista, alpinista**
mover	**empleado de una casa de mudanzas**
musician	**músico**
naval attaché	**agregado naval**
naval engineer	**ingeniero naval**
navigator	**navegador, navegante**
necrologist	**escritor de necrologías**
needlewoman	**costurera**
negotiator	**negociador**
newsboy	**vendedor de periódicos, diariero**
newscaster	**cronista de noticiarios; comentarista radiofónico**

news dealer	**vendedor de periódicos y revistas**
newsman	**repórter, periodista**
night watchman	**sereno, guarda nocturno**
notary (public)	**escribano (público), notario (público)**
novelist	**novelista**
nuclear physicist	**físico nuclear**
nun	**monja, religiosa**
nursemaid	**niñera, aya, ama**
oarsman	**remero, remador**
observer	**observador**
occupational therapist	**terapeuta ocupacional, ergoterapeuta**
oceanographer	**oceanógrafo**
office boy	**mandadero, mensajero**
office clerk	**oficinista, escribano**
office manager	**jefe de oficina**
officer	**funcionario, oficial, policía, agente**
offset lithographer	**fotolitógrafo**
oil field worker	**obrero petrolero**
oilman	**petrolero**
olive dealer	**aceitunero**
olive presser	**lagarero**
ombudsman	**mediador en asuntos de interés público**
operator	**operador, telefonista**
orator	**orador**
orchardman	**horticultor, hortelano**
organ-grinder	**organillero**
owner	**propietario, dueño**
page	**botones** (hotel); **acomodador** (theater); **paje** (Congress)
painter	**pintor**
paleographer	**paleógrafo**
paleontologist	**paleontólogo**
pamphleteer	**folletista, panfletista**

paper hanger	**empapelador, papelista**
parachutist	**paracaidista**
partner	**socio, accionista**
pastrycook	**pastelero, repostero**
patrolman	**policía, guardia**
patternmaker	**carpintero modelador, modelista**
pawnbroker	**prestamista**
pay clerk	**pagador**
peddler	**buhonero, mercachifle**
penologist	**criminalista, penalista**
pharmacist	**farmacéutico, boticario, farmaceuta** (Sp Am)
philosopher	**filósofo**
phonologist	**fonólogo**
photoengraver	**fotograbador**
photographer	**fotógrafo, fotógrafa**
physical therapist	**fisioterapeuta**
physicist	**físico**
pieceworker	**destajero, trabajador a destajo**
pilot	**piloto, guía**
pipe cutter	**cortatubos**
pipe fitter	**cañero, montador de tuberías**
planner	**diseñador, proyectista, calculista**
plasterer	**enlucidor, revocador**
plowman	**arador, labrador, yuguero**
plumber	**plomero, cañero**
poet	**poeta, poetisa**
polemicist	**polemista**
policeman	**policía** (m), **vigilante** (Ven, Col), **guardia, gendarme** (Mex)
police reporter	**reportero de asuntos policiales**
policewoman	**mujer policía**
political economist	**experto en economía política**
political scientist	**experto en ciencia política**
politician	**político, estadista**
polling clerk	**escrutador**

porter	**portero, conserje**
postmaster	**administrador de correos**
potter	**alfarero, ceramista**
poultry dealer	**gallinero, pollero, recovero**
preacher	**predicador**
president	**presidente**
press agent	**agente de propaganda, agente de publicidad**
presser	**planchador**
priest	**sacerdote, presbítero, clérigo, cura**
principal	**director, rector; principal**
printer	**impresor; tipógrafo**
prizefighter	**boxeador profesional**
probation officer	**agente judicial de vigilancia**
producer	**fabricante, productor; director de escena** (theater)
professor	**profesor**
program director	**programador**
prompter	**apuntador**
proofreader	**corrector de pruebas**
propagandist	**propagandista**
prosecuting attorney	**fiscal, abogado acusador**
prostitute	**prostituta, ramera, puta**
psychoanalyst	**psicoanalista**
public accountant	**contador público**
public defender	**abogado de oficio**
public official	**funcionario público**
public prosecutor	**fiscal**
public servant	**empleado del gobierno**
publisher	**editor, publicador**
puppeteer	**titiritero**
purveyor	**proveedor, provisor**
quarryman	**picapedrero**
rabbi	**rabí**
racketeer	**estafador**

radioman	**radiotécnico, radiotelegrafista**
radio operator	**operador de radio**
ragman	**trapero**
ranchman	**hacendado; ganadero**
ranger	**vigilante**
reader	**lector**
realtor	**corredor de bienes raíces**
reamer	**escariador**
reaper	**segador**
receptionist	**recibidor(a), recepcionista**
recorder	**registrador, archivero**
recording secretary	**escribiente, secretario de actas**
recruiter	**reclutador**
refiner	**refinador**
reformer	**reformador**
registrar	**registrador; archivista; jefe de registros civiles**
repairman	**reparador, mecánico de reparaciones**
reporter	**repórter, reportero, noticiero**
representative	**representante**
researcher	**investigador**
retailer	**comerciante al por menor**
retired	**jubilado** (adj)
revenue officer	**aduanero, agente fiscal**
reviewer	**inspector, crítico**
rider	**ciclista; jinete**
riot policeman	**guardia de asalto**
riveter	**roblonador**
road worker	**peón caminero**
rocketeer	**cohetero**
ropemaker	**cordelero, soguero**
routeman	**vendedor viajero**
sailor	**marinero**
salesclerk	**vendedor(a), dependiente, dependienta**

saloonkeeper	**tabernero, cantinero**
sanitary engineer	**ingeniero sanitario**
scavenger	**basurero**
sceneshifter	**tramoyista**
schoolteacher	**maestro (-a) de escuela**
scientist	**científico**
scorekeeper	**tanteador**
scoutmaster	**jefe de tropa de niños exploradores**
scrapmerchant	**chatarrero**
screenwriter	**libretista**
scrubwoman	**fregona**
sculptor	**escultor**
seamstress	**costurera, modistilla**
secretary	**secretario (-a)**
section hand	**peón ferrocarrilero**
seismographer	**sismólogo**
seller	**vendedor (-a)**
senator	**senador**
serviceman	**mecánico, reparador; militar**
sheepman	**ganadero**
sheriff	**alguacil de policía**
shipping agent	**embarcador, transportista**
shipping clerk	**dependiente encargado del envío de mercaderías**
shirtmaker	**camisero**
shoemaker	**zapatero**
shoeshine boy	**limpiabotas**
shopkeeper	**tendero; almacenista**
shop steward	**dirigente obrero**
show girl	**corista**
signalman	**guardabarreras** (R.R.)
silversmith	**platero**
singer	**cantante, cantatriz**
social worker	**asistente social, trabajador social**
sociologist	**sociólogo**
soldier	**soldado**

solicitor	**solicitador**
spinner	**hilador (-a)**
spokesman	**portavoz**
stableman	**caballerizo, mozo de cuadra**
staffer	**funcionario**
stamp collector	**coleccionista de sellos de correo**
statesman	**estadista**
steelworker	**obrero en una fábrica de acero**
stenographer	**estenógrafo, taquígrafo**
stevedore	**estibador**
steward	**mayordomo, administrador**
stewardess	**azafata**
stockbreeder	**criador de ganado**
stockbroker	**bolsista, corredor de bolsa**
storyteller	**narrador**
street cleaner	**barredor de calles**
stretcher-bearer	**camillero**
structural engineer	**ingeniero de estructuras**
structural worker	**herrero de obra**
superintendent	**superintendente, inspector**
supervisor	**superintendente**
surveyor	**topógrafo**
swimmer	**nadador (-a)**
switchman	**guardagujas**
tailor	**sastre**
talent scout	**buscatalentos**
tanner	**curtidor**
tapestry maker	**tapicero**
tavern keeper	**tabernero, posadero**
tax collector	**exactor, recaudador de contribuciones**
taxidermist	**taxidermista**
taxi driver	**taxista, chofer de taxi** (Sp Am)
teacher	**maestro (-a), profesor, instructor**
teamster	**carretero**
technical adviser	**asesor técnico**

technician	**técnico, especialista, experto técnico**
technologist	**técnico, especialista; tecnólogo**
telegrapher	**telegrafista**
telephone operator	**telefonista**
teller	**pagador, cajero**
tentmaker	**tendero**
theoretician	**teórico**
therapist	**terapeuta**
ticket agent	**agente de viajes, taquillero**
ticket collector	**recaudador de boletos (billetes) de pasaje**
timberman	**entibador**
timekeeper	**cronometrador (-a)**
timeworker	**jornalero (-a); trabajador a destajo**
tinsmith	**hojalatero, estañero**
tobacconist	**tabaquero, estanquero**
topographer	**topógrafo**
toreador	**torero**
town clerk	**secretario de ayuntamiento**
town councillor	**concejal**
toy dealer	**comerciante en juguetes**
tracklayer	**tendedor de vía, instalador de carriles**
trackman	**guardavía**
tradesman	**tendero, comerciante al por menor**
trade unionist	**sindicalista**
traffic policeman	**policía de tráfico**
traffic engineer	**ingeniero de tránsito**
traffic manager	**jefe de despachos, director de tráfico**
train dispatcher	**despachador de trenes**
translator	**intérprete, traductor**
trapeze artist	**trapecista, gimnasta de trapecio**
travel agent	**agente de viajes**

treasurer	**tesorero (-a)**
tree surgeon	**curador de árboles**
trial lawyer	**abogado litigante**
trolleyman	**motorista, conductor de tranvía**
truck driver	**camionero, conductor de camíon**
trunk dealer	**baulero, cofrero**
trustee	**consignatario, fiduciario**
tumbler	**acróbata**
tutor	**preceptor, maestro particular**
typesetter	**compositor, tipógrafo**
typist	**mecanógrafo (-a), dactilógrafo (-a), tipiadora**
umpire	**árbitro**
undercover agent	**agente secreto**
undertaker	**funerario, agente de entierros**
underwriter	**suscriptor, asegurador**
unemployed	**cesante** (adj)
unionist	**sindicalista, gremialista**
unskilled laborer	**peón de pico y pala**
unskilled workman	**obrero no especializado**
upholsterer	**tapicero**
urbanist	**urbanista**
usher	**acomodador, ujier**
usurer	**usurero**
valet	**asistente personal**
varnisher	**barnizador, charolista**
vendor	**vendedor, buhonero**
versifier	**versificador, rimador**
veterinarian	**veterinario**
vice-president	**vicepresidente**
violinmaker	**fabricante de violines**
visiting professor	**profesor visitante**
vocalist	**cantante, vocalista**
waiter	**mozo, camarero, mesero** (Mex)
waitress	**moza de restaurante, camarera**
warden	**carcelero**

CRUCIAL VOCABULARY FOR MEDICAL PERSONNEL

warehouse keeper	**guardalmacén**
washerman	**lavandero**
washerwoman	**lavandera**
watchmaker	**relojero**
watchman	**sereno, guardián**
weatherman	**meteorologista**
weaver	**tejedor (-a)**
welder	**soldador**
wet nurse	**nodriza, ama de crianza**
white-collar worker	**oficinista profesional**
wholesaler	**mayorista** (Sp Am)
wholesale store keeper	**almacenista**
wigmaker	**fabricante de pelucas**
window dresser, trimmer	**escaparatista, decorador de escaparates**
wine dealer	**viñatero**
winegrower	**viñador, viñatero** (Arg, Chile)
wine merchant	**viñatero mayorista**
winepresser	**lagarero**
wine taster	**catavinos**
wiretapper	**persona que intercepta líneas telefónicas**
wood-carver	**tallista**
woodcutter	**leñador**
wood dealer	**maderero**
woodworker	**carpintero**
worker	**trabajador, obrero, operario**
workingman	**jornalero, obrero, trabajador, operario**
wrestler	**luchador**
writer	**escritor, autor**
yardman	**encargado del patio**
zoologist	**zoólogo**

COUNTRIES AND NATIONALITIES
PAISES Y NACIONALIDADES

Países	*Habitantes*[1]	*Capitales*	*Habitantes*
México ⎫ Méjico ⎭	mexicano ⎫ mejicano ⎭	Méjico	mejicano
Cuba	cubano	La Habana	habanero
Puerto Rico	puertorriqueño	San Juan	sanjuanero
La Republica Dominicana	dominicano	Santo Domingo	santodominicano
Guatemala	guatemalteco	Guatemala	guatemalteco
El Salvador	salvadoreño	San Salvador	sansalvadoreño
Honduras	hondureño	Tegucigalpa	tegucigalpense
Nicaragua	nicaragüense	Managua	managüense
Costa Rica	costarricense	San José	(san)josefino
Panamá	panameño	Panamá	panameño
Colombia	colombiano	Bogotá	bogotano
Venezuela	venezolano	Caracas	caragueño
El Ecuador	ecuatoriano	Quito	quiteño
El Perú	peruano	Lima	limeño
Bolivia	boliviano	La Paz	paceño
Chile	chileno	Santiago	santiaguino
(La) Argentina	argentino	Buenos Aires	bonaerense
El Uruguay	uruguayo	Montevideo	montevideano
El Paraguay	paraguayo	Asunción	asunceño
El Brasil	brasileño	Brasilia	brasileño
España	español	Madrid	madrileño

[1] Some nouns or adjectives of nationality—like nicaragüense—have only one form; others—like boliviano—change the masculine -*o* to -*a* for the feminine; those ending in a consonant add -*a* for feminine: español/española.

THE FAMILY   *LA FAMILIA*

Many nouns of relationship ending in -*o* change it to -*a* to form the feminine:

the grandfather **el abuelo**	the grandmother **la abuela**
the grandson **el nieto**	the granddaughter **la nieta**
the son **el hijo**	the daughter **la hija**
the brother **el hermano**	the sister **la hermana**
the uncle **el tío**	the aunt **la tía**
the nephew **el sobrino**	the niece **la sobrina**
the cousin (m) **el primo**	the cousin (f) **la prima**
the father-in-law **el suegro**	the mother-in-law **la suegra**
the brother-in-law **el cuñado**	the sister-in-law **la cuñada**
first cousin **el primo hermano**	the first cousin **la prima hermana**
the great grandson **el biznieto**	the great granddaughter **la biznieta**
the great grandfather **el bisabuelo**	the great grandmother **la bisabuela**
the great great grandson **el ta-taranieto**	the great great granddaughter **la tataranieta**
the great great grandfather **el ta-tarabuelo**	the great great grandmother **la ta-tarabuela**
the half brother **el medio hermano**	the half sister **la media hermana**
the husband **el esposo**	the wife **la esposa**
the stepbrother **el hermanastro**	the stepsister **la hermanastra**
the stepson **el hijastro**	the stepdaughter **la hijastra**
the bachelor **el soltero**	the bachelorette **la soltera**
the widower **el viudo**	the widow **la viuda**

Other nouns of relationship must be memorized:

adult **el adulto**	family name **apellido**
ancestor **el antepasado**	father **el padre**
baby **el bebé; la criatura; el(la) nene (-a); el(la) guagua** (Chile, Ec, Peru, Bol, Arg, Ur)	female **hembra**
	fiancé **el novio**
	fiancée **la novia**
dad **el papá; el tata**	first name **el primer nombre**
deceased **difunto**	foster child **hijo de leche**
dependent **dependiente** (m/f)	foster mother **ama de leche**
descendant **descendiente** (m/f)	friend **amigo**
divorced **divorciado (-a)**	girl **muchacha**

godchild **ahijado**

godfather **el padrino**

godmother **la madrina**

guardian **guardián**

little girl **niña**

little boy **niño**

lover **el amante**

mother **la madre**

mom **mamá**

maiden name **nombre de soltera**

male **el varón**

man **hombre**

marriage **el casamiento; matrimonio**

marital status **estado civil**

middle name **secundo nombre**

newly wed **recién casado**

nickname **mote; apodo**

orphan **huérfano (-a)**

older child **hijo mayor**

parenthood **paternidad**

puberty **la pubertad**

quadruplets **cuádruples**

quintuplets **quintillizos**

race **la raza**

relationship (family) **parentesco**

relatives **parientes; familiares**

stepfather **padrastro**

stepmother **madrastra**

surname **apellido**

survivor **sobreviviente**

triplets **trillizos**

twins **mellizos; gemelos**

under age **menor de edad**

virgin **virgen**

woman **mujer**

young person **joven**

youth **juventud**

NOTE: Nouns designating relationship are used in the masculine plural to denote individuals of both sexes:

the parents, the fathers **los padres**

the brothers, the brother and sister, the brothers and sisters **los hermanos**

PRACTITIONERS OF THE MAJOR RELIGIONS
PRACTICADORES DE LAS RELIGIONES PRINCIPALES

Agnostic	**agnóstico**
Anglican	**anglicano**
Atheist	**ateo**
Baptist	**bautista**
Buddhist	**budista**
Catholic	**católico**
Greek Catholic (Greek Orthodox)	**católico de rito griego**
Roman Catholic	**católico romano**
Christian	**cristiano**
Christian Scientist	**miembro de la ciencia cristiana**
Congregationalist	**congregacionalista**
Covenanter	**covenantario**
Evangelical Covenanter	**covenantario evangélico; miembro del Pacto**
Episcopalian	**episcopalista**
Evangelist	**evangelista**
Hindu	**hindú**
Jehovah's Witness	**testigo de Jehová**
Jew	**judío**
Lutheran	**luterano**
Methodist	**metodista**
Mormon	**mormón**
Moslem	**mahometano, musulmán, islámico**
Presbyterian	**presbiteriano**
Protestant	**protestante**
Quaker	**cuáquero, cuákero**
Seventh-Day Adventist	**adventista del séptimo día**
Shintoist	**sintoísta**
Taoist	**taoísta**
Unitarian	**unitario**
Zoroastrian	**zoroástrico**

FOODS AND MEALS	*ALIMENTOS Y COMIDAS*
Cooking terms	*Terminología de cocina*
agree, to	**caer bien**
appetite	**apetito** (m)
appetizing	**apetitoso** (adj)
aversion	**aversión** (f); **repugnancia** (f)
bake, to	**asar en horno; hornear; cocer en horno**
baked	**al horno; horneado** (adj)
beaten	**batido** (adj)
bitter	**amargo** (adj)
boil, to	**hervir**
boiled	**cocido** (adj); **hervido** (adj)
boil in water, to	**cocer**
breaded	**empanado** (adj)
breakfast	**desayuno** (m)
breakfast, to have, to eat	**desayunar (se)**
broiled	**asado; asado a la parrilla** (adj)
browned	**dorado** (adj)
calorie	**caloría** (f)
can	**lata** (f)
canned	**enlatado** (adj); **en conserva** (prep)
chew, to	**masticar**
chop, to	**picar**
cold	**frío** (adj)
cook, to	**guisar; cocinar**
cookbook	**libro (manual) de cocina** (m)
cooked	**cocinado** (adj)
crushed	**machacado** (adj)
cut, to	**cortar**
defrost, to	**deshelar**
delicacy	**golosina** (f)
delicious	**delicioso** (adj)
diced	**cortado en cuadritos**

diet	**dieta** (f); **régimen** (m)
diet, to	**estar a dieta**
dinner	**cena; comida** (f)
dinner, to have	**cenar**
dish	**plato** (m)
dredge, to	**espolvorear**
dry, dried	**seco** (adj)
eat, to	**comer**
eat heartily, to	**comer por cuatro**
enjoy eating or drinking, to	**saborear**
enriched	**enriquecido** (adj)
entrée	**principio** (m); **entrada** (f)
feed, to	**alimentar; dar de comer**
feeding	**alimentación** (f)
flavor	**sabor** (m)
food	**alimento** (m); **comestibles** (m, pl); **vianda** (f)
food stamps	**cupones de comida** (m)
fortify	**fortalecer**
freeze, to	**congelar; helar**
fresh	**fresco** (adj)
fricassee	**fricasé** (adj)
fried	**frito** (adj)
frosted	**azucarado** (adj)
frozen	**helado; congelado** (adj)
fry, to	**freír**
grated	**rallado** (adj)
gravy (au jus)	**salsa** (f)
greasy	**grasiento** (adj); **con grasa** (prep)
grilled	**asado a la parrilla** (adj)
grind, to	**moler**
ground	**molido** (adj)
heat, to	**calentar**
hot	**caliente** (adj)
juicy	**jugoso** (adj)

kosher	**cácher** (adj); **kosher** (adj)
larded	**mechado** (adj)
lean	**magro** (adj)
lunch	**almuerzo** (m)
lunch, to eat	**almorzar**
marinate, to	**marinar; escabechar**
mashed	**amasado** (adj); **majado** (adj)
measure	**medir**
medium	**medio** (adj)
mince, to	**desmenuzar**
mix, to	**mezclar**
mixed	**mezclado** (adj)
not agree, to	**caer mal**
nourish, to	**alimentar**
nourishment	**alimentación** (f); **alimento** (m)
nutricious	**alimenticio; nutritivo** (adj)
nutriment	**alimento** (m)
nutrition	**nutrición** (f)
peel, to	**pelar**
pickled	**encurtido; en escabeche** (adj)
poach	**escalfar**
poached	**escalfado** (adj)
pour, to	**verter**
precooked	**precocinado** (adj)
protein	**proteína** (f)
puree	**puré** (m)
put on weight, to	**engordar**
rare (meat)	**poco asado; poco frito; poco hecho; medio crudo; poco cocido** (adj)
raw	**crudo** (adj)
relish	**entremés** (m)
rind	**cáscara** (f)
rinse, to	**enjuagar**
ripe	**maduro** (adj)
roast, to	**asar**

roasted	**asado** (adj)
rough	**áspero** (adj)
round slice	**rueda** (f)
salty	**salado** (adj)
sauce	**salsa** (f)
sauté	**salteado** (adj)
scrape, to	**raspar**
scrub, to	**restregar**
season, to	**condimentar; sazonar**
shred, to	**desmenuzar**
sip	**trago** (m); **sorbo** (m)
sip, to	**sorber**
slice	**rebanada** (f); **tajado** (f)
slice, to	**rebanar; tajar**
smoke, to (food)	**ahumar**
smoked	**ahumado** (adj)
smooth	**blando** (adj)
snack	**merienda** (f)
soak, to	**remojar**
soft	**blando** (adj)
solid	**sólido** (adj)
sour	**agrio** (adj)
spicy	**picante; condimentado** (adj)
starch	**almidón** (m)
steamed	**cocido** (adj)
stew, to	**estofar; guisar**
stewed	**guisado** (adj)
strain, to	**colar**
stuffing	**relleno** (m)
supper	**cena** (f)
supper, to eat	**cenar**
swallow, to	**tragar**
sweet	**dulce** (m, adj)
sweetness	**dulzura** (f)
taste, to	**saborear**

tasteless	**sin sabor; insípido** (adj)
tender	**tierno** (adj)
temperature, at room	**al tiempo** (adj); **natural** (adj)
thaw, to	**deshelar**
thick (liquid)	**espeso** (adj)
toast, to	**tostar**
toasted	**tostado** (adj)
victuals	**viandas** (f)
wash, to	**lavar**
wean, to	**destetar**
well cooked	**bien cocinado** (adj)
well done (steak)	**bien frito** (adj); **bien asado** (adj); **bien cocido** (adj)
whipped	**batido** (adj)
wrap, to	**envolver**

Special diets

Dietas especiales

absolute diet	**dieta absoluta**
acid-ash diet	**dieta de residuo ácido**
alkali-ash diet	**dieta de residuos alcalinos**
balanced diet	**dieta balanceada**
bland diet	**dieta blanda**
diabetic diet	**dieta para los diabéticos**
diet to control weight	**dieta para controlar el peso**
diet to gain weight	**dieta para aumentar el peso**
diet to lose weight	**dieta para perder peso**
elimination diet	**dieta de eliminación**
fat-free diet	**dieta sin grasa**
gallbladder diet	**dieta para la vesícula**
high-carbohydrate diet	**dieta rica en carbohidratos**
high-fat diet	**dieta rica en grasas**
high-protein diet	**dieta rica en proteína**
iron-enriched diet	**dieta rica en hierro**
light diet	**dieta ligera**

liquid diet	**dieta de líquidos**
clear liquid diet	**dieta de líquidos claros**
full (nourishing) liquid diet	**dieta de líquidos nutritivos**
low-carbohydrate diet	**dieta baja en carbohidratos**
low-protein diet	**dieta baja en proteína**
low-residue diet	**dieta de escaso residuo**
mineral enriched diet	**dieta rica en minerales**
salt-free diet	**dieta desclorurada**
ulcer diet	**dieta para las úlceras**
vitamin-enriched diet	**dieta rica en vitaminas**
restricted diet	**dieta rigurosa**

Seasonings   *Condimentos*

anise seed	**anís** (m)
basil	**albahaca** (f)
bay leaves	**hojas de laurel** (f)
black pepper	**pimienta** (f)
butter	**mantequilla** (f)
catsup	**salsa de tomate** (f)
chile	**ají** (m); **chile** (m)
chile powder	**polvo de chile** (m)
cinnamon	**canela** (f)
cloves	**clavos** (m)
condiment	**condimento** (m)
corn oil	**aceite de maíz** (m)
cottonseed oil	**aceite de semillas de algodón** (m)
cumin seed	**comino** (m)
fat	**manteca** (f); **grasa** (f)
garlic	**ajo** (m)
ginger	**jengibre** (m)
grease	**grasa** (f); **manteca** (f)
honey	**miel** (f)
horse-radish	**rábano picante** (m)
hot sauce	**salsa picante** (f)
jelly	**jalea** (f)
lard	**manteca** (f)

lemon	**limón** (m)
margarine	**margarina** (f)
marjoram	**orégano** (m)
marmalade	**mermelada** (f)
mayonnaise	**mayonesa** (f); **salsa mayonesa** (f)
mushroom	**seta** (f); **hongo** (m)
mustard	**mostaza** (f)
nutmeg	**nuez moscada** (f)
oil	**aceite** (m)
olive oil	**aceite de oliva** (m)
paprika	**pimentón** (m)
red pepper	**pimiento** (m)
red pepper sauce (Mex)	**mole** (m)
saccharine	**sacarina** (f)
saffron	**azafrán** (m)
salt	**sal** (f)
sauce	**salsa** (f)
sesame oil	**aceite de sésame** (m); **aceite de ajonjolí** (m)
spice	**especia** (f)
sugar	**azúcar** (m)
tarragon	**tarrago** (m)
thyme	**tomillo** (m)
vinegar	**vinagre** (m)
Worcestershire sauce	**salsa inglesa** (f)

Soups   *Sopas*

broth	**caldo** (m)
chicken soup (with noodles)	**sopa de gallina (con fideos)** (f); **caldo de pollo (con fideos)** (m)
consomme	**consomé** (m)
cream of tomato soup	**crema de jitomate** (f)
onion soup	**sopa de cebollas** (f)
oyster soup	**caldo de ostras** (m); **sopa de ostiones** (f)
tomato soup	**sopa de tomate** (f)

vegetable soup	**sopa de vegetales** (f); **caldo de vegetales** (m)

Salads   *Ensaladas*

cucumber and tomato	**pepinos con tomates** (m)
fruit salad	**ensalada de frutas** (f)
lettuce with mayonnaise	**lechuga con mayonesa** (f)
mixed green salad	**ensalada mixta** (f)

Eggs and cereals   *Huevos y cereales*

barley	**cebada** (f)
bran	**acemite** (m)
cooked cereal	**cereal cocido** (m)
cornflakes	**copos de maíz** (m)
cream of wheat	**crema de trigo** (f)
dry cereal	**cereal seco** (m)
egg	**huevo** (m); **blanquillo** (m, Mex)
egg shell	**cáscara de huevo** (f)
egg white	**clara de huevo** (f)
egg yolk	**yema de huevo** (f)
fresh egg	**huevo fresco** (m)
fried eggs	**huevos fritos** (m)
hard boiled eggs	**huevos duros** (m); **huevos hervidos** (m); **huevos cocidos** (m)
omelette with ham	**tortilla con jamón** (f)
poached eggs	**huevos escalfados** (m); **huevos blandos** (m)
rotten eggs	**huevos podridos** (m)
scrambled eggs	**huevos revueltos** (m)
soft boiled eggs	**huevos pasados por agua** (m); **huevos tibios** (m)
hot cereal	**cereal caliente** (m)
oatmeal	**avena** (f)
rice	**arroz** (m)
wheat	**trigo** (m)

Breads and noodles	*Panes y pastas*
biscuit	**bizcocho** (m); **galleta** (f); **rosca** (f)
bread	**pan** (m)
bran bread	**acemita** (f)
corn bread	**pan de maíz** (m)
dark bread	**pan negro** (m); **pan moreno** (m)
French bread	**pan francés** (m)
fresh bread	**pan del día** (m); **pan tierno** (m)
home-made bread	**pan casero** (m)
rye bread	**pan de centeno** (m)
stale bread	**pan duro** (m); **pan sentado** (m)
white bread	**pan blanco** (m)
whole wheat bread	**pan de trigo entero** (m); **pan de grano integral** (m)
cracker	**galleta** (f); **galletica** (f)
soda cracker	**galleta salada** (f)
crumb	**miga(ja)** (f)
crust	**corteza** (f)
hot cakes	**queques** (m, pl, Mex); **panqueques** (m, pl, Sp Am); **tortitas calientes** (f, pl)
macaroni	**macarrones** (m, pl)
noodle	**fideo** (m); **tallarín** (m)
pasta	**pasta** (f)
roll	**panecillo** (m); **bollo de pan** (m); **bolillo** (m, Mex)
sandwich	**sandwich** (m); **emparedado** (m); **bocadillo** (m, Spain)
slice	**rebanada** (f); **tajada** (f)
spaghetti	**espaguetis** (m, pl); **tallarín** (m)
sweet roll	**pan dulce** (m, Mex)
toast	**tostada de pan** (f), **pan tostado** (m) **tostadas** (f, pl, Spain)
French toast	**tostada al estilo francés** (f)
waffles	**queques** (m, pl, Mex); **wafles** (m)

Butter and cheese	*Mantequilla y queso*
butter	**mantequilla** (f); **manteca de vaca** (f, Spain)
cheese	**queso** (m)
cottage cheese	**requesón** (m); **naterón** (m); **názula** (f)
cream cheese	**queso de crema** (m)
Dutch cheese	**queso de Holanda** (m)
Edam cheese	**queso de bola** (m); **queso de Edam** (m)
goat's cheese	**queso de cabra** (m)
headcheese	**queso de cerdo** (m)
Limburger cheese	**queso de Limburgo** (m)
parmesan cheese	**queso parmesano** (m)
Roquefort cheese	**queso de Roquefort** (m)
Swiss cheese	**queso de Gruyère** (m)
white cheese	**queso blanco** (m)
fat	**manteca** (f); **grasa** (f)
lard	**manteca** (f)
margarine	**margarina** (f); **mantequilla artificial** (f)
peanut butter	**mantequilla de maní** (f); **crema de cacahuete** (f); **crema de maní** (f); **mantequilla de cacahuete** (f)

Vegetables	*Legumbres y verduras*
artichoke	**alcachofa** (f)
asparagus	**espárragos** (m, pl)
avocado	**aguacate** (m)
bean	**haba** (f); **judía** (f); **habichuela** (f); **frijol** (m)
dried beans	**habichuelas secas** (f)
French beans	**habichuela** (f)
green beans	**habichuelas verdes** (f); **ejotes** (m)
kidney beans	**habichuela** (f); **frijol** (m)
Lima beans	**habas** (f, pl)
soy beans	**soya**; **soja** (f)
string beans	**habichuelas verdes** (f); **judías verdes** (f); **ejotes** (m, pl, Mex); **chauchas** (f, pl, Arg)

beet	**remolacha** (f); **betabel** (m)
broccoli	**brécol** (m)
Brussel sprouts	**col de Bruselas** (m)
cabbage	**col** (m); **repollo** (m)
carrot	**zanahoria** (f)
cauliflower	**coliflor** (f)
celery	**apio** (m)
chick pea	**garabanzo** (m)
corn	**maíz** (m)
green corn	**maíz tierno** (m)
corn on the cob (sweet corn)	**elote** (m, Mex)
sweet corn	**choclo** (m, SpAm)
cucumber	**pepino** (m)
eggplant	**berenjena** (f)
endive	**escarola** (f)
green pepper	**pimiento verde** (m)
green vegetables	**hortalizas de hoja verde** (f)
greens	**verduras** (f)
kale	**berza** (f); **col rizada** (f)
legumes	**legumbres** (f)
lettuce	**lechuga** (f)
maize	**maíz** (m)
onion	**cebolla** (f)
parsley	**perejil** (m)
pea	**guisante** (m); **alverjas** (f, pl, SpAm); **chícharo** (m)
green pea	**guisante** (m); **chícharo** (m)
pickle	**pepinillo** (m); **encurtido** (m); **picles** (m)
potato	**patata** (f); **papa** (f, SpAm)
baked potatoes	**papas asadas** (f)
fried (French fried)	**papas fritas** (f)
mashed potatoes	**puré de papas** (m); **puré de patata** (m)
sweet potato	**camote** (m, Mex); **batata** (f); **buniato** (m)
radish	**rábano** (m); **rabanito** (m)
sauerkraut	**berza** (f); **col agria** (f)

spinach	**espinaca** (f)
squash	**calabaza** (f)
tomato	**tomate** (m); **jitomate** (m, Mex)
stewed tomatoes	**puté de tomates** (m)
turnip	**nabo** (m)
turnip greens	**hojas de nabo** (f)
vegetables	**vegetales** (m); **hortalizas** (f); **legumbres** (f) **verduras** (f)
yellow vegetables	**vegetales de pulpa amarilla** (m)
water cress	**berro** (m)
yam	**batata** (f); **buniato** (m)

Meat   *Carne*

bacon	**tocino** (m)
barbecue	**barbacoa** (f)
beef	**carne de vaca** (f); **carne de res** (f)
beefsteak	**bistec** (m); **biftec** (m); **filete** (m); **bife** (m, Arg)
broiled (beef)steak	**churrasco** (m, Arg and Chile)
roast beef	**rosbif** (m); **carne asada** (f)
brains	**sesos** (m, pl.)
chop, cutlet	**chuleta** (f); **costilla** (f)
cold cuts	**fiambres** (m, pl)
frankfurter	**salchicha** (f)
giblets	**menudillo** (m)
ground meat	**carne molida** (f)
ham	**jamón** (m)
hamburger	**hamburguesa** (f)
hot dog	**perro caliente** (m)
kid	**cabrito** (m)
kidneys	**riñones** (m, pl)
lamb	**cordero** (m)
lamb meat	**carne de cordero** (f)
liver	**hígado** (m)
meatballs	**albóndigas** (f, pl)
meatpie	**empanada** (f)
meat stew and ají (Chile)	**ajiaco** (m)

mutton	**carnero** (m)
leg of mutton	**pierna de carnero** (f)
pork	**cerdo** (m); **carne de puerco** (f); **chancho** (m, SpAm)
stew of pork, corn and chile	**pozole** (m, Mex)
young pig	**lechón** (m); **lechoncillo** (m)
ribs	**costillas asadas** (f)
baked ribs	**costillas al horno** (f)
barbecued ribs	**costillas a la parrilla** (f)
roast	**asado** (m, adj)
sausage	**salchicha** (f)
blood sausage	**morcilla** (f)
Bologna	**salchichón** (m)
pork sausage	**chorizo** (m)
sirloin	**solomillo** (m)
stew	**cocido** (m); **estofado** (m); **guisado** (m)
sweetbreads	**mollejas** (f, pl)
tenderloin	**filete** (m)
tenderloin tips	**puntas de filete** (f)
tongue	**lengua** (f)
tripe	**mondongo** (m); **callos** (m, pl)
veal	**carne de ternera** (f)
breaded veal cutlet	**milanesa** (f); **ternera apanada** (f)

Poultry and game   *Aves y caza*

capon	**capón** (m)
chicken	**pollo** (m)
boiled chicken	**pollo cocido** (m)
breast of chicken	**pechuga de pollo** (f)
broiled chicken	**pollo a la parrilla** (m)
fried chicken	**pollo frito** (m)
roast chicken	**pollo asado** (m)
stuffed chicken	**pollo relleno** (m)
duck	**pato** (m)
wild duck	**pato silvestre** (m)
fowl	**ave** (f)
goose	**ganso** (m)
hare	**liebre** (f)
hen	**gallina** (f)

partridge	**perdiz** (f)
pheasant	**faisán** (m)
rabbit	**conejo** (m)
turkey	**pavo** (m); **guajolote** (m, Mex); **guanajo** (m, Cuba)

Fish and seafood

Pescado y mariscos

anchovies	**anchoas** (f)
bass	**mero** (m); **lobina** (f)
bluepoint	**ostra pequeña** (f)
caviar	**caviar** (m)
cod (fish) (baked)	**bacalao (guisado)** (m)
crab	**cangrejo** (m); **jaiba** (f, SpAm)
eel	**anguila** (f)
fish (living)	**pez** (m)
fish (already caught)	**pescado** (m)
pickled fish	**escabeche** (m)
fishbone	**espina** (f)
flounder	**lenguado** (m)
haddock	**róbalo** (m)
hake (a type of bass)	**merluza** (f)
herring (smoked)	**arrenque (ahumado)** (m)
lobster	**langosta** (f)
mackerel	**pejerrey** (m); **caballa** (f)
octopus	**pulpo** (m)
oyster	**ostra** (f); **ostión** (m, Mex)
perch	**percha** (f)
prawn	**langostino** (m)
red snapper	**huachinango** (m, Mex); **pargo** (m, Cuba)
roe	**nueva** (f)
salmon	**salmón** (m)
sardines	**sardinas** (f)
scallop	**pechina** (f); **venera** (f)
shellfish	**marisco** (m)
shrimps	**camarones** (m); **gambas** (f)
snapper	**pargo** (m)

sole	**lenguado** (m)
squid	**calamar** (m)
trout	**trucha** (f)
tuna fish	**atún** (m)
turtle	**tortuga** (f)
white fish	**corégono** (m)

Fruits — *Frutas*

apple	**manzana** (f)
apricot	**albaricoque** (m); **chabacano** (m)
avocado	**aguacate** (m, Mex and CentAm); **palta** (SpAm)
banana	**banana** (f); **plátano** (m)
blackberry	**zarza** (f)
blueberry	**vaccinio** (m)
cherry	**cereza** (f)
citrus fruit	**fruta cítrica** (f)
currant	**grosella** (f)
date	**dátil** (m)
grape	**uva** (f)
grapefruit	**toronja** (f); **pomelo** (m, Sp Am)
guava	**guayaba** (f)
lemon	**limón** (m)
lime	**lima** (f)
mango	**mango** (m)
melon	**melón** (m)
nut	**nuez** (f)
orange	**naranja** (f); **china** (f, PR)
papaya	**papaya** (f); **fruta bomba** (f, Cuba — AVOID use of *papaya* in this country!)
peach	**melocotón** (m); **durazno** (m)
pear	**pera** (f)
prickly pear	**tuna** (f)
pineapple	**piña** (f); **ananá** (m/f)
pit	**hueso** (m)
plantain	**plátano** (m); **banana** (m)

plum	**ciruela** (f)
pomegranate	**granada** (f)
prune	**ciruela seca** (f); **ciruela pasa** (f)
pumpkin	**calabaza** (f)
quince	**membrillo** (m)
raisin	**pasa** (f)
raspberry	**frambuesa** (f)
seed	**pepita** (f)
skin (of fruit)	**cáscara** (f)
strawberry	**fresa** (f); **frutilla** (f, SpAm)
tangerine	**mandarina** (f)
watermelon	**sandía** (f)

Desserts / *Postres*

bonbon	**bombón** (m)
cake	**torta** (f); **bizcocho** (m); **queque** (m)
cheese cake	**quesadilla** (f)
small pastry cake	**bollo** (m)
candy	**dulces** (m, pl); **confites** (m, pl)
chewing gum	**chicle** (m)
chocolate bar	**barra de chocolate** (f)
cookie	**galleta** (f); **galletica** (f); **pasta** (f)
custard	**flan** (m); **natilla** (f)
dessert	**postre** (m)
eclair	**pastelillo de crema** (m)
ice cream	**helado** (m); **mantecado** (m); **nieve** (f)
jello	**gelatina** (f)
lollipop	**caramelo en un palito** (m)
meringue	**merengue** (m)
nut	**nuez** (f)
pastry	**pasta** (f); **pastel** (m)
sweet pastry	**quesadilla** (f)
pie	**pastel** (m)
pudding	**pudín** (m)
rice pudding	**arroz con leche** (m)
sherbet	**sorbete** (m); **nieve** (f, Mex)

sweet	**dulce** (m)
syrup	**jarabe** (m)
tapioca	**tapioca** (f)
whipped cream	**nata batida** (f)

Beverages

Bebidas

alcohol	**alcohol** (m)
ale	**cerveza inglesa** (f)
beer	**cerveza** (f)
bottled beer	**cerveza embotellada** (f)
dark beer	**cerveza negra** (f)
draught beer	**cerveza de barril** (f)
light beer	**cerveza clara** (f); **cerveza blanca** (f)
beverage	**bebida** (f)
cold beverage	**refresco** (m)
brandy	**coñac** (m); **aguardiente** (m)
champagne	**champaña** (f)
chocolate	**chocolate** (m)
chocolate milk	**leche con chocolate** (f)
hot chocolate	**chocolate caliente** (m)
cocoa	**cacao** (m)
cider	**sidra** (f)
cane cider	**guarapo** (m)
fruit cider, fermented maize	**chicha** (f, SpAm)
coffee	**café** (m)
black coffee	**café solo** (m); **café puro** (m); **café tinto** (m, Col)
coffee with cream	**café con crema** (m)
coffee with cream and sugar	**café con azúcar y crema** (m)
coffee with milk	**café con leche** (m)
coffee with sugar	**café con azúcar** (m)
decaffeinated coffee	**café descafeinado** (m)
instant coffee	**café instantáneo** (m); **nescafé** (m)
strong coffee	**café fuerte** (m); **café cargado** (m)
weak coffee	**café débil** (m); **café claro** (m); **café simple** (m); **café suave** (m); **café ralo** (m)
cocktail	**coctel** (m)
cream	**crema** (f)

drink	**bebida** (f); **trago** (m, usually alcoholic)
carbonated drink	**gaseosa** (f)
cold drink	**bebida fría** (f)
hot drink	**bebida caliente** (f)
gin	**ginebra** (f)
juice	**jugo** (m)
apple juice	**jugo de manzana** (m)
cranberry juice	**jugo de arándano** (m)
grape juice	**jugo de uvas** (m)
grapefruit juice	**jugo de toronja** (m)
lemon juice	**jugo de limón** (m)
lime juice	**jugo de lima** (m)
orange juice	**jugo de naranja** (m)
pineapple juice	**jugo de piña** (m)
prune juice	**jugo de ciruela** (m)
tomato juice	**jugo de tomate** (m)
lemonade	**limonada** (f)
liqueur	**licor** (m)
milk	**leche** (f)
buttermilk	**leche agria** (f);); **suero de leche** (m)
condensed milk	**leche condensada** (f)
cow's milk	**leche de vaca** (f)
dry milk	**leche en polvo** (f)
evaporated milk	**leche evaporada** (f)
malted milk	**leche malteada** (f)
pasteurized milk	**leche pasteurizada** (f)
skim milk	**leche desnatada** (f); **leche sin crema** (f); **leche descremada** (f)
orangeade	**naranjada** (f)
pop	**soda** (f); **gaseosa** (f); **coca cola** (f)
punch	**ponche** (m)
refreshment	**refresco** (m)
rum	**ron** (m)
tea	**té** (m)
iced tea	**té helado** (m)
Paraguay tea	**yerba mate** (f, SpAm)
strong tea	**té fuerte** (m); **té cargado** (m)
weak tea	**té débil; té claro; té simple; té suave; té ralo** (m)

water	**agua** (f)
carbonated water	**agua gaseosa** (f)
drinking water	**agua potable** (f)
mineral water	**agua mineral** (f)
Seltzer water	**agua de Seltz** (f)
soda water	**agua de soda** (f)
whiskey	**whiskey** (m)
wine	**vino** (m)
Bordeaux wine	**vino de Burdeos** (m)
Burgundy wine	**vino de Borgoña** (m)
claret, red wine	**vino tinto** (m)
maguey wine	**pulque** (m, Mex)
pink wine	**vino rosado** (m)
port wine	**vino de Oporto** (m)
sherry wine	**vino de Jerez** (m)
sparkling wine	**vino espumoso** (m)
white wine	**vino blanco** (m)

Dishes and utensils

Loza y utensilios

bowl	**escudilla** (f)
salad bowl	**ensaladera** (f)
soup bowl	**sopera** (f)
sugar bowl	**azucarera** (f)
bread basket	**panera** (f)
china	**loza** (f); **porcelana** (f)
chocolate pot	**chocolatera** (f)
coffee pot	**cafetera** (f)
cup	**taza** (f)
small cup	**jícara** (f)
dish	**plato** (m); **platico** (m)
dessert dish	**plato de postre** (m)
pickle dish	**platico para encurtidos** (m)
sauce dish	**salsera** (f)
set of dishes	**vajilla** (f)
fork	**tenedor** (m)
dessert fork	**tenedor de postre** (m)
salad fork	**tenedor para la ensalada** (m)
frying pan	**sartén** (f)
glass	**vaso** (m)
jar	**jarra** (f)
jug	**jarra** (f)

knife	**cuchillo** (m)
table knife	**cuchillo** (m)
large knife	**cuchilla** (f)
small knife	**cuchilleja** (f)
ladle	**cucharón** (m)
lid	**cobertera** (f)
napkin	**servilleta** (f)
pepper shaker	**pimentero** (m)
plate	**plato** (m)
butter plate	**mantequera** (f)
dinner plate	**plato llano** (m)
salad plate	**plata de ensalada** (f)
service plate	**plato llano** (m)
small plate	**platillo** (m)
soup plate	**plato hondo** (m)
platter	**fuente** (f)
pot	**caldera** (f); **olla** (f); **puchero** (m), **pote** (m)
salt shaker	**salero** (m)
sauce pan	**cacerola** (f)
saucer	**platico** (m); **platillo** (m)
spoon	**cuchara** (f)
straw	**pajiza** (f); **popote** (m)
tablespoon	**cuchara grande** (f); **cuchara de sopa** (f)
teaspoon	**cucharita** (f); **cucharilla** (f); **cuchara de café** (f)
teapot	**tetera** (f)
toothpick holder	**palillero** (m)
tray	**bandeja** (f); **charola** (f); **charol** (m, SpAm)

CHAPTER

NINE

ESSENTIAL GRAMMAR
GRAMATICA BASICA

PARTS OF SPEECH
PARTES DE LA ORACION

In Spanish as well as in English there are eight parts of speech: nouns, pronouns, adjectives, verbs, adverbs, prepositions, conjunctions, and interjections.

Nouns   *Sustantivos*

A noun is the name of a person, place, or thing. A proper noun is the name of a specific person, place, or thing.

Méjico⎫
México⎬ Mexico
Juan John

María Mary
San Francisco San Francisco

A common noun is a common name for persons, places, or things that are of the same type or class.

muchacho boy
libro book

médico doctor
hospital hospital

Gender of Nouns   Género de los sustantivos

In English nouns are classified as masculine, feminine, or neuter. In Spanish ALL nouns are either masculine or feminine. There is no neuter gender.

Generally, nouns ending in **-o** or nouns referring to male beings are masculine.

un padre a father

el hijo the son

1. The masculine plural of certain nouns may denote both sexes:

los padres the parents (mother and father)
unos amigos some friends (girl and boy friends)

2. An important exception is **la mano** (the hand), which is feminine.

3. Nouns ending in **-ón, -el, -al, -ente, -ador**, and **-or** are usually masculine.

el hospital the hospital

4. The days of the week, months of the year, and names of languages are masculine.

el miércoles Wednesday
el abril April

el español Spanish

Nouns ending in **-a** or nouns referring to female beings are feminine.

la madre the mother

una hija a daughter

1. Nouns of Greek origin are an exception; they are masculine.

el día the day

el drama the drama

2. Nouns ending in -**tad**, -**dad**, -**ción**, -**sión**, -**tión**, -**ez**, -**ie**, -**ud**, and -**umbre** are usually feminine.

la deshidratación   the dehydration   **la edad**   the age
la tirantez   the tenseness   **la serie**   the series

Nouns not ending in -**o** or -**a** should be memorized with the definite article.

la sangre   the blood   **el pene**   the penis

Formation of the Plural of Nouns   *El plural de sustantivos*

A noun ending in a vowel forms the plural by adding -**s**; those ending in a consonant add -**es**.

el médico (the physician) → **los médicos** (the physicians)
el doctor (the physician) → **los doctores** (the physicians)

A noun ending in -**z** changes the -**z** to -**c**, and then adds -**es**.

la nariz (the nose) → **las narices** (the noses)

Nouns ending in a stressed vowel form the plural by adding -**es**.

el tisú (the tissue) → **los tisúes** (the tissues)

Nouns ending in unstressed -**es** or -**is** are considered to be both singular and plural. Number is expressed by the article.

el martes (Tuesday or on Tuesday)   **los martes** (Tuesdays or on Tuesdays)

Pronouns   *Los pronombres*

Personal Subject Pronouns   *Los pronombres personales nominativos*

A pronoun is a word that takes the place of, or is used instead of a noun. Subject pronouns are usually omitted in Spanish since their meaning is included in the meaning of the verb. They are used only for clarification or emphasis. The subject pronouns are:

yo   I   **nosotros (nosotras)**   we
tú   you (fam.)   **vosotros (vosotras)**   you (fam. pl.)
él   he   **ellos**   they
ella   she   **ellas**   they (feminine)
usted   you (form.)   **ustedes**   you (form., pl.)

The word *it* as the subject of a verb need not be translated:

Soy yo.   It is I.   **Está por aquí.**   It is through here.

Often the word *you* is expressed in Spanish by **usted** when speaking to one person, by **ustedes** when addressing more than one person. Both pronouns use the same verb endings as any other third person pronoun. The familiar form of address in Spanish, **tú**, derives from Latin. This form has a special conjugation, and the pronoun is usually omitted since the verb ending alone indicates the subject of the sentence. This form is generally reserved for close friends, relatives, children and pets, and, sometimes for social inferiors. The plural of **tú** is **vosotros**. This used to be used when speaking to a group of people who would be addressed individually with **tú**. However, all of Latin America and many parts of Spain use **ustedes** for the familiar plural as well as the polite plural. It should be noted that in Guatemala, El Salvador, Honduras, Nicaragua, Costa Rica, and parts of Colombia, Argentina, and Uruguay, **vos** is used as a singular familiar second person pronoun.

You may be translated into Spanish as follows:

	Familiar	Formal (Polite)
Singular	**tú** **(vos)**	**usted** (**Vd.** or **Ud.**)
Plural	**vosotros** **ustedes** (**Vds.** or **Uds.**)	**ustedes** (**Vds.** or **Uds.**)

Examples:
You are competent. **Tú eres competente.**
Vos eres competente.
Usted (Vd., Ud.) es competente.
Vosotros sois competentes.
Ustedes (Vds., Uds.) son competentes.

Direct Object Pronouns   *Los pronombres objetivos directos*

The direct object (noun or pronoun) of a sentence is acted upon by the subject; it directly receives the action of the verb. It answers "what" when it is referring to things.

The nurse prepares the booster shot.

What does the nurse prepare?   Answer: the *booster shot*; therefore, *booster shot* is the direct object noun.

My brother has bursitis.

What does my brother have?   Answer: *bursitis*; therefore, *bursitis* is the direct object noun.

The direct objects shown above are nouns. When a pronoun replaces each noun, the sentences read:

The nurse prepares *it*.   My brother has *it*.

In conversation, direct object nouns are not usually repeated after they have already been established; they are replaced with direct object pronouns. Since all nouns are either masculine or feminine in Spanish, object pronouns that agree both in number and gender must replace the direct object nouns. Spanish direct object pronouns for things are:

lo it (masculine)   **los** them (masculine)
la it (feminine)   **las** them (feminine)

The direct object can also refer to a person or persons. In this case it answers the question "Whom?"

Jane sees the nurse.

Whom does Jane see?   Answer: the *nurse*; therefore, *nurse* is the direct object noun.

Paul visits the patients.

Whom does Paul visit?   Answer: the *patients*; therefore, *patients* is the direct object.

In Spanish, whenever the direct object is a definite person noun, it is preceded by the personal **a** (See page 303)

Juana ve a la enfermera.   Jane sees the nurse.
Pablo visita a los pacientes.   Paul visits the patients.

If the direct object nouns are replaced with pronouns, the sentences will read:

Jane sees *her*.   Paul visits *them*.

The following are the direct object pronouns for persons:

Singular		*Plural*	
me me		**nos** us	
te you (familiar)		**os** you (familiar)	
le (preferred in Spain)	} him	**les, los** them (m)	
lo (commoner in Sp Am)		**las** them (f)	
la her		**los** (m), **las** (f) you	
le, lo (m), **la** (f) you			

Position of Object Pronouns   *El orden de los pronombres objetivos*

In English the noun's change to the pronoun does not affect the position of the direct object. It is in final position.

The doctor prescribes the medicine. (subject/verb/direct object noun)

The doctor prescribes it. (subject/verb/direct object pronoun)

In Spanish the direct object noun occurs at the end of the sentence as in English.

El médico receta la medicina. (Subject/verb/direct object noun)

The direct object pronoun does not follow the verb, except in three cases: the infinitive, the gerund and the direct affirmative command. (Notice the use of the accent mark over the syllable that normally takes the stress:)[1]

¡Lláme*me* a las dos! Call me at two!

Quiero ver*los*. I want to see them.

Estamos estudiándo*las*. We are studying them.

•Object pronouns immediately precede a conjugated verb:

Juan *la* toma. John takes it.

•Object pronouns immediately precede the conjugated form of the verb **haber** when dealing with the compound tenses.

Juan *la* ha recetado. John has prescribed it.

•Object pronouns may immediately precede the conjugated form of the verb **estar** or may be attached to the present participle when dealing with the progressive tenses.

Juan *la* está recetando.
Juan está recetándo*la*. } John is prescribing it.

Indirect Object Pronouns   *Los pronombres objetivos indirectos*

Indirect object nouns or pronouns name the person or persons to whom or for whom the subject gives or does something. Although in English it may be considered a prepositional phrase, in Spanish the indirect object is never considered as such. The indirect object answers the questions "to whom" or "for whom?"

Dr. Gómez writes John a prescription. *or* Dr. Gómez writes a prescription for John.

For whom does Dr. Gómez write a prescription?

Answer: for *John*; therefore, John is the indirect object.

She gives Paul a bedpan. or She gives a bedpan to Paul.

To whom does she give a bedpan?

Answer: to *Paul*; therefore, Paul is the indirect object.

---

[1] See page 300.

Upon substituting pronouns for nouns, the sentences will read:

Dr. Gómez writes *him* a prescription. *or* Dr. Gómez writes a prescription for *him*.

She gives *him* a bedpan. or She gives a bedpan to *him*.

Indirect object pronouns are expressed in English and Spanish as follows:

Singular		*Plural*	
me	me	**nos**	us
te	you (familiar)	**os**	you (familiar)
le	him, her, you	**les**	them, you

Since **le** has three meanings, the speaker may clarify further by adding a prepositional phrase **a Vd., a él,** or **a ella. Les** may also be clarified by adding **a Vds., a ellos,** or **a ellas.**

The position of indirect object pronouns in Spanish is the same as the position of direct object pronouns. (See above).

Double Object Pronouns   Dos pronombres objetivos

When there are two object pronouns the indirect always precedes the direct, and they both precede or follow the verb according to the rules.

Me las van a sacar.   They are going to take them out (of me).

If both object pronouns are in the third person (i.e., begin with **l-**) the indirect (**le, les**) changes to **se**:

Se la receto.   I prescribe it for you (for him, for them, for her, etc.)

Demonstrative Pronouns   Los pronombres demonstrativos

éste (m)   This one   **éstos** (m)   These
                    (near the speaker)

ésta (f)   This one   **éstas** (f)   These
                    (near the speaker)

ése (m)   That one   **ésos** (m)   Those
                    (near the listener)

ésa (f)   That one   **ésas** (f)   Those
                    (near the listener)

aquél (m)   That one   **aquéllos** (m)   Those
          (away from both speaker and listener)

aquélla (f)   That one   **aquéllas** (f)   Those
          (away from both speaker and listener)

Three neuter forms also exist: **esto** (this), **eso** (that), **aquello** (that).

Relative Pronouns   *Pronombres relativos*

Quien refers to persons only.
Que refers to persons or things, masculine or feminine, singular or plural.

El hombre *que* está allí es mi médico.	The man who is over there is my physician.

Interrogative Pronouns   *Los pronombres interrogativos*

«**Cuál**(**es**)?» meaning "which" refers to persons or things, and is used to choose one or more from a larger group.

¿Cuál es su enfermera?	Which (one) is your nurse?

«**¿Cuál?**» meaning "what?" precedes **ser**, except when definition is asked for, in which case «**¿qué?**» is used.

¿Cuál es su nacionalidad?	What is your nationality?
¿Qué es esto?	What is this?

«**¿Qué?**» translates the English interrogative "what?" in all other cases, except in idioms.

¿Qué estudia Vd.?	What are you studying?

«**¿Quién?**» or «**quiénes?**» meaning "who?" or "whom?" refer to persons only.

¿Quién tiene mi medicina?	Who has my medicine?
¿Con quiénes vive Vd.?	With whom do you live?

«**¿De quién?**» or «**¿De quiénes?**» meaning "whose?" is always followed immediately by the verb.

¿De quién es esta tarjeta verde?	Whose green card is this?

«**¿Cuánto (cuánta)?**» meaning "how much?" and «**¿cuántos (cuántas)?**» meaning "how many?" are used both as pronouns and as adjectives.

¿Cuántos van al hospital?	How many are going to the hospital?
¿Cuánto cuesta mi cuenta?	How much is my bill?

Possessive Pronouns   *Los pronombres posesivos*

A possessive pronoun agrees with the noun for which it stands in number and gender. The following are the forms used:

Singular	*Plural*	*Singular*	*Plural*	*English*
el mío	**los míos**	**la mía**	**las mías**	mine
el tuyo	**los tuyos**	**la tuya**	**las tuyas**	yours (fam)
el suyo	**los suyos**	**la suya**	**las suyas**	his
el suyo	**los suyos**	**la suya**	**las suyas**	hers

el suyo	**los suyos**	**la suya**	**las suyas**	yours
el nuestro	**los nuestros**	**la nuestra**	**las nuestras**	ours
el suyo	**los suyos**	**la suya**	**las suyas**	theirs (m)
el suyo	**los suyos**	**la suya**	**las suyas**	theirs (f)
el suyo	**los suyos**	**la suya**	**las suyas**	yours

To avoid confusion, instead of **el suyo** use **el de él, el de ella, el de Vd.**, etc. Instead of **la suya** use **la de él, la de ella, la de Vd.**, etc. Instead of **los suyos** use **los de él, los de ella, los de Vd.**, etc. Instead of **las suyas** use **las de él, las de ella, las de Vd.**, etc.

Adjectives   *Adjetivos*

An adjective is a word that modifies (limits or describes) a noun or a pronoun.

enfermo sick   **dolorido** painful

alta high   **amargo** sour

Agreement   Concordancia

Adjectives agree in number and gender with the nouns or pronouns that they modify.

el brazo roto the broken arm   **la tobilla rota** the broken ankle

Gender of Adjectives   Género de adjetivos

Adjectives ending in **-o** form the feminine by changing the **-o** to **-a**.

roto → rota = broken

Adjectives ending in **-e** or a consonant have the same form for both genders.

el hueso grande the large bone   **la glándula grande** the large gland

Adjectives (and nouns) of nationality ending in a consonant add **-a** for the feminine.

el médico español the Spanish   **la enfermera española** the Span-
physician   ish nurse

An adjective modifying two nouns of different genders is generally masculine.

las manos y los pies limpios the clean hands and feet

Adjectives ending in **-án, -ón, -or** add **-a** to form the feminine. (This does not apply to comparative forms ending in **-or**.)

holgazán, holgazana idle, lazy

el paciente llorón
la paciente llorona } the weeping patient

But:

el mejor paciente ⎫
la mejor paciente ⎭ the best patient

Formation of Plural of Adjectives   *Formación de los plurales de los adjetivos*

Adjectives form their plurals in the same way as nouns. If they end in a vowel, they form plurals by adding -s; if they end in a consonant, they form plurals by adding -es; if they end in -z, add -es after changing the -z to -c.

Masculine		Feminine		
Singular	*Plural*	*Singular*	*Plural*	*English*
blanco	**blancos**	**blanca**	**blancas**	white
grande	**grandes**	**grande**	**grandes**	large
español	**españoles**	**española**	**españolas**	Spanish
robusto	**robustos**	**robusta**	**robustas**	healthy

Position of Adjectives   *El orden de los adjetivos*

Limiting adjectives are numbers and other expressions of quantity, possessives, demonstratives, etc. They generally precede the noun that they modify.

muchos técnicos   many technicians

nuestro médico   our physician

ese hospital   that hospital

Descriptive adjectives are those that indicate color, shape, size, nationality, etc. They usually follow the noun that they modify.

muchas enfermeras buenas   many good nurses

el dolor torácico   the thoracic pain

Idiomatic Use of Adjectives   *Uso idiomático de adjetivos*

An adjective may be used as a noun.

El ciejo necesita primeros auxilios.   The blind man needs first aid.

Articles   *Los artículos*

In Spanish the (definite and indefinite) articles are adjectives and, thus, precede the noun they modify and agree with it in number and gender.

Definite Article   *El artículo definido*

The definite article (the) is translated in four different ways:

el   before a masculine singular noun   **El hospital**   The hospital

la   before a feminine singular noun   **La clínica**   The clinic

los   before a masculine plural noun   **Los hospitales**   The hospitals

las   before a feminine plural noun   **Las clínicas**   The clinics

NOTE: **El** is used in the singular instead of **la**, when the feminine noun begins with stressed **a** or **ha** and the definite article immediately precedes. This does not imply a change in the gender of the noun.

el acta de nacimiento   the birth certificate

las actas de nacimiento   the birth certificates

el hambre   the hunger

mucha hambre   very hungry (much hunger)

There are *only* two contractions in Spanish:

a + el = al (to the)   **de + el = del** (of/from the)

Voy al hospital, no a la clínica.   I am going to the hospital, not the clinic.

El viene del hospital, no de la clínica.   He is coming from the hospital, not from the clinic.

The Possessive Case   *El caso posesivo*

The possessive case (**el caso posesivo**) of nouns corresponding to the English *'s* or *s'*, is expressed in Spanish by means of the preposition **de** placed before the possessor.

la muestra del paciente   the patient's specimen/the specimen of the patient

el padre de las chicas   the girls' father/the father of the girls

Indefinite Articles   *Artículos indefinidos*

The indefinite article is translated as "a" or "an" in the singular, and "some" or "a few" in the plural.

un before a masculine singular noun   **unos** before a masculine plural noun

una before a feminine singular noun   **unas** before a feminine plural noun.

Normally an article is used before each noun and agrees in number and gender with the noun.

un ayudante   an orderly   **unas enfermeras**   some nurses

Omission of Indefinite Article   *Falta de artículo indefinido*

The indefinite article (**un, una, unos, unas**) is omitted

1. before unmodified predicate nouns indicating profession, occupation, political affiliation or nationality:

Es ayudante.   He is an orderly.

Mi amiga es enfermera.   My friend is a nurse.

Raúl es español.   Raul is Spanish.

but:

Mi padre es un buen médico.   My father is a good physician.

2. before **ciento, cierto, mil, otro:**

cien (mil) camas   a hundred (a thousand) beds

otro hospital   another hospital

3. after the exclamatory **¡qué!** (what a):

¡Qué error!   What a mistake!

Demonstrative Adjectives   Los adjetivos demonstrativos

Demonstrative adjectives are the same as demonstrative pronouns but lack a written accent mark.

Masculine (sing)	*Masculine (pl)*	
este hospital	**estos hospitales**	this (these) hospital(s)
ese hospital	**esos hospitales**	that (those) hospital(s)
aquel hospital	**aquellos hospitales**	that (those) hospital(s) (yonder)

Feminine (sing)	*Feminine (pl)*	
esta clínica	**estas clínicas**	this (these) clinic(s)
esa clínica	**esas clínicas**	that (those) clinic(s)
aquella clínica	**aquellas clínicas**	that (those) clinic(s) (yonder)

Apocopation of Adjectives   Apócope de adjetivos

Before a masculine singular noun the following adjectives drop the final **-o**:

primero (first)	**tercero** (third)	**bueno** (good)
malo (bad)	**alguno** (some)	**ninguno** (some)

Eres un buen técnico.   You are a good technician.

Grande becomes **gran:**

el gran médico   the great physician

but

el médico grande   the big physician (physically)

Ciento becomes **cien** before any noun:

Necesito cien dólares.   I need a hundred dollars.

Comparison of Adjectives   *Comparativo de adjetivos*

In English two ways exist to compare adjectives (and adverbs):

Positive	*Comparative*	*Superlative*
dark	darker	darkest
beautiful	more beautiful	most beautiful

In Spanish the comparison of adjectives is formed like the second example above. Regular adjectives add **más** (or **menos**) to the positive form for the comparative degree; **el más** (**la más**) or **el menos** (**la menos**) are added to form the superlative.

Positive	*Comparative*	*Superlative*
obscuro dark	**más obscuro** darker	**el más obscuro** darkest
rojo red	**menos rojo** less red	**el menos rojo** the least red

Some adjectives are irregular in their comparison:

Positive	*Comparative*	*Superlative*
bueno good	**mejor** better	**el mejor** best
malo bad	**peor** worse	**el peor** worst
grande large	**mayor** older	**el mayor** oldest[2]
pequeño small	**menor** younger	**el menor** youngest[2]

Este paciente es mayor que el otro, pero es más pequeño.
This patient is older than the other, but he is smaller.

In a comparative sentence the English word "than" is usually expressed in Spanish by **que**. However, before numbers, **de** is used.

Su presión arterial está más alta que la última vez.
Your blood pressure is higher than last time.

Un análisis de la orina necesita menos tiempo que un análisis de sangre.
A urinalysis takes less time than a blood chemistry.

Un cuarto doble debe costar más de cien dólares.
A semi-private room must cost more than $100.

The superlative form of the adjective generally follows the noun that it modifies.

El cirujano más importante acaba de llegar.
El más importante cirujano acaba de llegar.

The most important surgeon has just arrived.

---

[2] **Grande** and **pequeño** also compare regularly, in which case they retain the meanings of *larger* and *smaller*. Old (**viejo**) and young (**joven**) can also be compared regularly, but these are generally for animals and things.

In English the superlative is usually followed by *in*. This is translated by **de** in Spanish.

María es la mejor enfermera del hospital.

Mary is the best nurse in the hospital.

Absolute Superlative   El superlativo absoluto

This superlative is expressed in English when the adverbs *very*, *extremely*, or *highly* modify the adjective. The Spanish counterpart is formed by adding the suffix **-ísimo** to the adjective (or adverb).

hospitales modernísimos   extremely modern hospitals

Comparison of Equality   El comparativo de igualdad

In English the constructions "as . . . as" "as many . . . as," and "as much . . . as" are called the comparative of equality. In Spanish these forms are translated by:

tan . . . como	as . . . as
tanto (tanta) . . . como	as much . . . as
tantos (tantas) . . . como	as many . . . as

In the first case the comparison is of an adjective, and the word **tan** is an adverb and is invariable. In the other two, comparisons are of number and amount of nouns, and the words expressing the amount or number are adjectives, and therefore agree in number and gender with the word modified.

La dentistería es *tan* importante *como* la medicina.
Dentistry is *as* important *as* medicine.

Tengo *tantas* píldoras *como* Eduardo.
I have *as many* pills *as* Edward.

Hay *tanto* suero en este jarro *como* en aquél.
There is *as much* IV in this bottle *as* in that one.

Possessive Adjectives   Los adjetivos posesivos

Short Forms   *Ante el sustantivo*

Singular   Plural

mi	my		**mis**	my
tu	your		**tus**	your
su	his		**sus**	his
su	her		**sus**	her
su	your		**sus**	your
nuestro **nuestra**	} our		**nuestros** **nuestras**	} our

su their (m)		**sus** their (m)	
su their (f)		**sus** their (f)	
su your		**sus** your	

In Spanish the possessive adjectives agree in number and gender with the thing possessed rather than with the possessor.

mi seguro my insurance		**mis seguros** my insurances
mi enfermera my nurse		**mis enfermeras** my nurses
nuestra clínica our clinic		**nuestras clínicas** our clinics
nuestro hospital our hospital		**nuestros hospitales** our hospitals
su termómetro their thermometer		**sus termómetros** their thermometers.
su inyección his injection		**sus inyecciones** his injections

Possessive adjectives in the short form precede the nouns they modify, and are repeated before each noun.

Nuestra enfermera y su ayudante our nurse and their orderly

Su and **sus** have so many different meanings that they are often replaced by expressions that clarify the meaning. When a prepositional phrase is used for clearness, the definite article replaces the possessive adjective:

Tengo su medicina. I have his (her, your, their, etc.) medicine.

but

Tengo la medicina de él. I have his medicine.

Tengo la medicina de ella. I have her medicine.

Tengo la medicina de Vd. I have your medicine.

Tengo la medicina de ellos. I have their medicine.

Tengo la medicina de ellas. I have their medicine.

Tengo la medicina de Vds. I have your medicine.

Long Forms *Después del sustantivo*

These forms are the same as the possessive pronouns:

mío, mía, míos, mías my

tuyo, tuya, tuyos, tuyas your

suyo, suya, suyos, suyas his, her, its, your, their

nuestro, nuestra, nuestros, nuestras our

These stressed adjectives follow their nouns and are used to translate "of mine," "of his," etc., or "my" as used in an exclamation.

¡Dios mío! My goodness!

El doctor González es como un hermano mío. Dr. González is like a brother of mine.

Un primo nuestro es dentista. A cousin of ours is a dentist.

Verbs   *Los verbos*

A verb is a word that shows action, being, or state of being.

Dr. Jones *takes* my temperature.   *action*

Mary *is* a nurse.   *being*

Paul *is* sick.   *state of being*

Spanish verbs   *Los verbos españoles*

Spanish verbs are divided into three conjugations, according to the endings of their infinitives: **-ar**, **-er**, **-ir** verbs. Spanish verbs are conjugated by removing the final **-ar**, **-er**, or **-ir**, leaving a base or stem and then adding a series of endings, which express distinctions of person, number, tense and mood. The base, or stem, of the verb embodies the meaning of the verb. To conjugate in the present and past tenses, endings are added to the unchanged stem of the regular verb. To conjugate in the future and conditional tenses, endings are added to the entire infinitives.

Present Indicative Tense   El tiempo presente de indicativo

The present tense has three English meanings.

Estudio medicina. ⎰ I study medicine.
⎱ I do study medicine.
I am studying medicine.

Regular Spanish verbs are conjugated in the present tense by adding the following endings to the infinitive stem:

Subject pronoun	-AR	-ER	-IR
yo	-o	-o	-o
tú	-as	-es	-es
él, ella, usted	-a	-e	-e
nosotros (-as)	-amos	-emos	-imos
	—[3]	—[3]	—[3]
ellos, ellas, ustedes	-an	-en	-en

[3] As previously noted (see above p. 279), in all of Latin America and many parts of Spain the second person plural is replaced by the third person plural. Hence, this book will not show those verb forms.

The following IRREGULAR verbs are necessary for mastery of the Spanish language. They must be memorized since they do not follow the regular verb pattern. The English auxiliary verbs *do*, *does*, *am*, *are*, *is*, also apply to these verbs.

DAR *to give*

yo **doy**	I give, I am giving, I do give
tú **das**	you give, you are giving, you do give
él, ella, Vd. **da**	he, she, it gives; you give; he, she, it is giving; you are giving; he, she, it does give; you do give
nosotros (-as) **damos**	we give, we are giving, we do give
—	—
ellos, ellas, Vds. **dan**	they, you give, are giving, do give

DECIR *to say, to tell*

yo **digo**	I say, tell
tú **dices**	you say, tell
él, ella, Vd. **dice**	he, she, it says, tells; you say, tell
nosotros (-as) **decimos**	we say, tell
—	—
ellos, ellas, Vds. **dicen**	they, you say, tell

HABER *to have (auxiliary verb)*

yo **he**	I have
tú **has**	you have
él, ella, Vd. **ha**	he, she, it has; you have
nosotros (-as) **hemos**	we have
—	—
ellos, ellas, Vds. **han**	they, you have

Haber is always followed by the past participle and never stands alone.

Examples

Yo he vomitado mucho.	I have vomited a lot.
Ella ha comido uvas.	She has eaten grapes.
Nosotros hemos sufrido demasiado.	We have suffered too much.

HACER *to do, to make*

yo **hago**	I do, make
tú **haces**	you do, make
él, ella, Vd. **hace**	he, she, it does, makes; you do, make
nosotros (-as) **hacemos**	we do, make
—	—
ellos, ellas, Vds. **hacen**	they, you do, make

IR *to go*

yo **voy**	I go

tú **vas**	you go
él, ella, Vd. **va**	he, she, it goes, you go
nosotros (-as) **vamos**	we go
—	—
ellos, ellas, Vds. **van**	they, you go

Ir may be followed by **a** plus an infinitive. In this case it has the future meaning "to be going to do something."

Example

Voy a examinarle.	I am going to examine you.

OIR *to hear*

yo **oigo**	I hear
tú **oyes**	you hear
él, ella, Vd. **oye**	he, she, it hears; you hear
nosotros (-as) **oímos**	we hear
—	
ellos, ellas, Vds. **oyen**	they, you hear

PODER *to be able*

yo **puedo**	I can, am able
tú **puedes**	you can, are able
él, ella, Vd. **puede**	he, she, it can, is able; you can, are able
nosotros (-as) **podemos**	we can, are able
—	—
ellos, ellas, Vds. **pueden**	they, you can, are able

Poder is followed directly by an infinitive

Examples

Yo puedo comer ahora.	I am able to eat now.
Podemos estudiar más.	We can study more

PONER *to put, to place*

yo **pongo**	I put, place
tú **pones**	you put, place
él, ella, Vd. **pone**	he, she, it puts, places; you put, place
nosotros (-as) **ponemos**	we put, place
—	—
ellos, ellas, Vds. **ponen**	they, you put, place

QUERER *to want, wish*

yo **quiero**	I want, wish
tú **quieres**	you want, wish
él, ella, Vd. **quiere**	he, she, it wants, wishes; you want, wish
nosotros (-as) **queremos**	
—	—
ellos, ellas, Vds. **quieren**	we want, wish

Querer is followed by an infinitive.

they, you want, wish

Example

El médico quiere salir del hospital.

The physician wants to leave the hospital.

SABER *to know*

yo **sé**	I know
tú **sabes**	you know
él, ella, Vd. **sabe**	he, she, it knows, you know
nosotros (-as) **sabemos**	we know
—	—
ellos, ellas, Vds. **saben**	they, you know

Saber may be followed directly by an infinitive, in which case it has the meaning of "to know how to."

Example

Sé leer un libro español.

I know how to read a Spanish book.

SALIR *to leave*

yo **salgo**	I leave
tú **sales**	you leave
él, ella, Vd. **sale**	he, she, it leaves, you leave
nosotros (-as) **salimos**	we leave
—	—
ellos, ellas, Vds. **salen**	they, you leave

TENER *to have*

yo **tengo**	I have
tú **tienes**	you have
él, ella, Vd. **tiene**	he, she, it has, you have
nosotros (-as) **tenemos**	we have
—	—
ellos, ellas, Vds. **tienen**	they, you have

TRAER *to bring*

yo **traigo**	I bring
tú **traes**	you bring
él, ella, Vd. **trae**	he, she, it brings, you bring
nosotros (-as) **traemos**	we bring
—	—
ellos, ellas, Vds. **traen**	they, you bring

VENIR *to come*

yo **vengo**	I come
tú **vienes**	you come
él, ella, Vd. **viene**	he, she, it comes, you come

nosotros (-as) **venimos**	we come
—	—
ellos, ellas, Vds. **vienen**	they, you come

VER *to see*

yo **veo**	I see
tú **ves**	you see
él, ella, Vd. **ve**	he, she, it sees, you see
nosotros (-as) **vemos**	we see
—	—
ellos, ellas, Vds. **ven**	they, you see

*Some idiomatic uses of **hacer***   *Algunos usos idiomáticos de **hacer***

Hace + expressions of time = For (+ certain time)

An action that began in the past and is still going on now is expressed in English with the present perfect tense followed by the length of time: I have been sick for two days.

This concept is expressed in Spanish with **hace** + expression of time + **que** + the simple present tense of a verb. An alternative exists in which the verb precedes the time expression:

Present perfect English + for + time.	**Hace** + time expression + **que** + present tense verb.
	Present tense verb + **desde hace** + time expression.

I have been sick for two days.	**Hace** dos días **que** estoy enfermo.
	Estoy enfermo **desde hace** dos días.

The same pattern can be expressed in English in the pluperfect tense and in Spanish in the imperfect tense:

Pluperfect English + for + time.	**Hacía** + time expression + **que** + imperfect verb.
	Imperfect verb + **desde hacía** + time expression.

I had been sick for two days.	**Hacía** dos días **que** estaba enfermo.
	Estaba enfermo **desde hacía** dos días.

The preceding English sentences may be expressed in Spanish by a word for word translation, but the **hace** construction is preferable.

I have been sick for two days.	**He estado enfermo por dos días.**
I had been sick for two days.	**Hacía estado enfermo por dos días.**

A similar construction exists using **desde** alone and gives the idea of *since*:

How long have you been ill?	**¿Desde cuándo está Vd. enfermo?**
I have been ill since yesterday.	**Estoy enfermo desde ayer.**

Hace + expression of time = Ago

The only possible translation for the word *ago* is the idiomatic use of **hace**. In English the construction is the length of time + ago, whereas the Spanish construction is **hace** + time.

English past tense verb + length of time + ago.	Preterite main verb + **hace** + time. **Hace** + time + **que** + preterite verb.

She died five days ago.	Ella murió **hace** cinco días. **Hace** cinco días que ella murió.

SER and ESTAR

Both verbs translate in English as TO BE, but they are NOT interchangeable! Both are irregular in the present indicative tense:

SER	ESTAR	
yo **soy**	yo **estoy**	I am
tú **eres**	tú **estás**	you are
él, ella, Vd. **es**	él, ella, Vd. **está**	he, she, it is, you are
nosotros (-as) **somos**	nosotros (-as) **estamos**	we are
—	—	—
ellos, ellas, Vds. **son**	ellos, ellas, Vds. **están**	they, you are

Uses of Ser :   Usos de ser :

1. **Ser** expresses an inherent or relatively permanent quality:
Age—**Vd. es jóven.**   You are young.
Wealth—**La mujer es pobre.**   The woman is poor.
Size—**Mi hermano es alto.**   My brother is tall.
Shape—**La mesa es redonda.**   The table is round.
Color—**El traje es azul.**   The suit is blue.
Possession **El libro es mío.**   The book is mine.
Characteristic—**La nieve es.fría.**   Snow is cold.

2. **Ser** is used with predicate nouns, pronouns, or adjectives.
El es dentista.   He is a dentist.
¿Quién soy yo?   Who am I?
Somos católicos.   We are catholic.

3. **Ser** indicates origin, source, material, or ownership.
El ayudante es de Nueva York.   The orderly is from New York.
La bata es de algodón.   The bathrobe is cotton.
Las flores son de Vd.   The flowers are yours.

4. **Ser** tells time.
Es la una.   It is one o'clock.
Son las seis.   It is six o'clock.

Uses of Estar :   Usos de estar:

1. **Estar** expresses location (both temporary and permanent).
Chicago está en Illinois.   Chicago is in Illinois.
Yo estoy en la clase.   I am in class.

2. **Estar** expresses conditions of health.
¿Cómo está Vd.?   How are you?
Estoy muy bien.   I am fine.
Estamos enfermos.   We are ill.

3. **Estar** expresses a temporary quality or characteristic.
Ella está nerviosa.   She is nervous.
Estoy atenta.   I am attentive.
Vd. está ausente.   You are absent.

Some adjectives may be used with either **ser** or **estar**. The meaning of the adjective varies, however.

El paciente es aburrido.   The patient is boring.
El paciente está aburrido.   The patient is bored.

The Preterite Tense   El tiempo pretérito

The preterite tense expresses an action that began in the past and ended in the past. It is translated in English by the auxiliary *did*, or by the past of the verb in question.

The preterite tense is formed as follows for regular verbs:
For **-ar** verbs, remove the infinite ending (**-ar**) and add:

-é, -aste, -ó, -amos, –, -aron

For **-er** and **-ir** verbs, remove the infinite endings (**-er** and **-ir**)

and add: **-í, -iste, -ió, -imos, –, -ieron**

Subject Pronouns	EXAMINAR	COMER	SUFRIR
yo	examin**é**	com**í**	sufr**í**
tú	examin**aste**	com**iste**	sufr**iste**
él, ella, Vd.	examin**ó**	com**ió**	sufr**ió**
nosotros(-as)	examin**amos**	com**imos**	sufr**imos**
—	—	—	—
ellos, ellas, Vds.	examin**aron**	com**ieron**	sufr**ieron**

Thus, **examiné** means I examined, or I did examine.

The Imperfect Tense   El tiempo imperfecto

The imperfect tense is used in Spanish to represent an habitual state or continuous action in the past. It is expressed in English by *was* or *were* plus the present participle, or by *used to* plus the infinitive. Occasionally, this construction is translated by *would* plus the infinitive.

The imperfect tense is formed as follows for regular verbs:

For **-ar** verbs drop the **-ar** and add:

-aba, -abas, -aba, -ábamos, —, -aban

For **-er** or **-ir** verbs, drop **-er** and **-ir** and add:

-ía, -ías, -ía, -íamos, —, -ían

Subject Pronouns	EXAMINAR	COMER	SUFRIR
yo	examin**aba**	com**ía**	sufr**ía**
tú	examin**abas**	com**ías**	sufr**ías**
él, ella, Vd.	examin**aba**	com**ía**	sufr**ía**
nosotros (-as)	examin**ábamos**	com**íamos**	sufr**íamos**
—	—	—	—
ellos, ellas, Vds.	examin**aban**	com**ían**	sufr**ían**

Thus, **yo examinaba** means I was examining, I used to examine, or I would examine.

The Future Tense   El tiempo futuro

The future tense generally expresses a future action, and parallels English. In Spanish the future tense is formed by adding to the infinitive the following endings:

-é, -ás, -á, -emos, —, -án.

In English the future tense is rendered by *shall* in the first person, and by *will* in the second and third persons.

Subject Pronouns	EXAMINAR	COMER	SUFRIR
yo	examinar**é**	comer**é**	sufrir**é**
tú	examinar**ás**	comer**ás**	sufrir**ás**
él, ella, Vd.	examinar**á**	comer**á**	sufrir**á**
nosotros (-as)	examinar**emos**	comer**emos**	sufrir**emos**
—	—	—	—
ellos, ellas, Vds.	examinar**án**	comer**án**	sufrir**án**

Thus, **yo examinaré** means I shall examine or I will examine.

The Present Perfect Tense   El tiempo perfecto

The present perfect tense corresponds to the English present perfect. It is formed by the present of **haber** plus the past participle. The English equivalent is *have (has)* plus the past participle.

The *past participle* (**el participio pasivo**) in Spanish is formed by dropping the infinitive ending (**-ar**, **-er**, **-ir**), and replacing it by **-ado** or **-ido**.

examinar (to examine)	**examinado** (examined)
comer (to eat)	**comido** (eaten)
sufrir (to suffer)	**sufrido** (suffered)

Thus, the present perfect tense becomes:

yo he examinado	I have examined
él ha comido	he has eaten
nosotros (-as) hemos sufrido	we have suffered

Polite, Formal Command   El mandato formal

Polite, formal commands of most verbs are formed from the first person singular of the present indicative tense, provided that it ends in **-o**. The **-o** is dropped and the following endings are added:

For **-ar** verbs, **-e**; for **-er**, or **-ir** verbs, **-a**.

In *all* cases the plural of these commands will be formed by adding **-n** to the singular. Use **no** before the affirmative command to state the polite negative command.

Tome Vd. la medicina.	Take the medicine.
No tome Vd. la medicina.	Don't take the medicine.

Irregularities   Irregularidades

Certain orthographic changes are made for verbs ending in **–car** or **–gar** when forming polite commands. In order to retain the *k* sound in any verb ending in **car**, change the **c** to **qu** before adding **e** or **en**.

Búsquelo Vd.   Búsquenlo Vds. (buscar)   Look for it.

In order to retain the hard *g* sound in any verb ending in **–gar**, change the **g** to **gu** before adding **e** or **en**.

Pague Vd. ahora.   Paguen Vds. ahora. (pagar)   Pay now.

The following verbs are totally irregular in their polite commands and must be memorized:

		Singular	*Plural*
estar	to be	**esté Vd.**	**estén Vds.**
ser	to be	**sea Vd.**	**sean Vds.**
dar	to give	**dé Vd.**	**den Vds.**
ir	to go	**vaya Vd.**	**vayan Vds.**
saber	to know	**sepa Vd.**	**sepan Vds.**

Object pronouns—direct and indirect—are attached to the affirmative commands. Written accent marks are necessary in order to retain the original stress.[5]

Hábleme Vd.	Speak to me.
Dígamelo.	Tell it to me.

In the negative commands object pronouns precede the verb.

No me hable Vd.	Don't speak to me.

Reflexive Verbs   Los verbos reflexivos

In Spanish some verbs are called reflexive. These verbs can be recognized by their ending (**-se** attached to the infinitive). When conjugated in any tense they must be preceded by the appropriate reflexive pronouns. Reflexive pronouns are:

me	myself
te	yourself
se	himself, herself, yourself
nos	ourselves
—	—
se	themselves, yourselves

Remember, that a verb is reflexive when the subject acts upon itself, or does something to itself. Many Spanish reflexive verbs are not reflexive in English, and therefore cannot be literally translated into English:

yo *me* **llamo**	My name is (I call myself)
tú *te* **llamas**	your name is (you call yourself)
él, ella Vd., *se* **llama**	His, her, your name is (he, she, you call yourself)
nosotros (-as) *nos* **llamamos**	Our name is (we call ourselves)
—	—
ellos, ellas, Vds. *se* **llaman**	Their, your name is (They call themselves)

Adverbs   *Los adverbios*

An adverb is a word that modifies a verb, an adjective, or another adverb. It answers the questions "where?" "how?" or "when?"

después	afterwards	**casi**	almost
mucho	a lot	**ya**	already
antes, delante	before	**mal, malamente**	badly
mejor	better	**peor**	worse

[5] See above, page 281.

más more	**menos** less
nunca never	**siempre** always
bastante enough	**aquí** here

Camine *un poco*. Walk a little. (Modifies a verb)

Pablo está *muy* enfermo. Paul is very ill. (Modifies an adjective)

La clínica está *muy* cerca. The clinic is very near. (Modifies an adverb)

Many adverbs are formed by adding **-mente** (which corresponds to *-ly* in English) to the feminine singular form of the adjective:

lenta (slow)	**lentamente** (slowly)
rápida (rapid)	**rápidamente** (rapidly)

NOTE: The written accent mark of the adjective is kept in the new adverbial form (**rápidamente**).

Frequently an adverbial phrase is used instead of the adverb.

Adverb	Adverbial Phrase	English
cuidadosamente	**con cuidado**	carefully
finalmente	**por fin, al fin**	finally

In a series of two or more adverbs, both of which normally end in **-mente**, only the last adverb keeps the ending:

El opera lenta y cuidadosamente. He operates slowly and carefully.

Comparison of Adverbs   El comparativo de los adverbios

This is the same as for adjectives (see above) except that in the superlative case the definite article is omitted.

Positive	Comparative	Superlative
rápido (fast)	**más rápido** (faster)	**más rápido** (fastest)
despacio (slow)	**más despacio** (slower)	**más despacio** (slowest)

The comparison may be of a lesser degree rather than a greater degree. If this is so, the word **menos** replaces **más**. In the above examples the word **menos**, meaning *less*, could replace **más** giving the opposite idea.

There are four adverbs that are compared irregularly:

Positive	Comparative	Superlative
bien (well)	**mejor** (better)	**mejor** (best)
mal (badly)	**peor** (worse)	**peor** (worst)
mucho (much)	**más** (more)	**más** (most)
poco (little)	**menos** (less)	**menos** (least)

Absolute Superlative of Adverbs   El superlativo absoluto de los adverbios

The absolute superlative of adverbs is formed by adding the ending **-mente** to the feminine form of the absolute superlative of the adjective.

Trabaja diligentísimamente.   He works most diligently.

The same idea can be expressed by using the adverb **muy** before the adjective; however, the absolute form is more emphatic. **Muy** cannot be correctly used before **mucho** or any of its variants. Therefore, to translate the expression *very much*, **muchísimo** must be used.

Prepositions   *Las preposiciones*

A preposition is a word that shows the relation of a noun or pronoun following it to some other word.

a at	**de, desde** from
según according to	**hasta** until
entre between	**sobre, en, encima de** on
acerca de, alrededor de, con respecto a about	

Prepositional Pronouns   Pronombres preposicionales

Prepositional pronouns are the same as the subject pronouns with two exceptions—the first and second persons singular.

Singular	*Plural*
mí me	**nosotros (-as)** us
ti you (fam.)	**vosotros (-as)** you (fam.)
él him, it (m)	**ellos** them
ella her, it (f)	**ellas** them
Vd. you (formal)	**Vds.** you (formal)

Prepositional pronouns can never be substituted for the indirect object pronouns. The indirect object pronouns can stand alone; the prepositional pronouns cannot.

With the preposition **con** (with), the first and second person singular pronouns combine to form **conmigo** (with me) and **contigo** (with you).

*Use of preposition **de** to replace adjectival nouns   Uso especial de **de***

In Spanish a noun cannot be used as an adjective to show the material of which an item is made, as in English. In Spanish it is necessary to construct a prepositional phrase joining the material to the object by means of the preposition **de**.

English	*Spanish word order*	*Spanish translation*
a blue-eyed girl	a girl of blue eyes	**una niña de ojos azules**
the wheelchair	the chair of wheels	**la silla de ruedas**

*The personal **A***   ***A** personal*

The preposition **a**, untranslated, is always used before a direct object noun referring to a definite person or persons, or to a geographical location. It is also used before things that are personified, and before **nadie, alguno, quien,** etc., and at times to distinguish the noun object from the subject when both are things.

¿A quién ayuda Vd.?   Whom do you help?

Veo al ayudante.   I see the orderly.

La recuperación sigue a la operación. ⎫   Recuperation follows
A la operación sigue la recuperación. ⎭   the operation.

*Uses of **Por** and **Para***   *Usos de **por** y **para***

These two prepositions have more than one meaning. Each has definite uses and cannot be interchanged with the other without changing the meaning of the sentence.

When **por** and **para** both mean *for,*

1. **Para** means *for* in the sense of *destination* and *purpose,* or *use.*

El estudia para médico.   He is studying to be a doctor.

Mi marido salió para el hospital.   My husband left for the hospital.

Comemos para vivir.   We eat in order to live.

2. **Para** means *for* (by) when it indicates a definite point of time in the future.

Vd. tiene una cita en la clínica para el lunes.   You have an appointment in the clinic for Monday.

La cirugía para mañana es fácil.   The surgery for tomorrow is easy.

3. **Por** means *for* in the sense of *in exchange for, for the sake of, for a period of.*

¿Quiere Vd. hacerlo por mí?   Do you want to do it for me?

Trabajo por el doctor Gómez.   I work for (on behalf of) Dr. Gómez.

Para also means *in order to,* and is followed in Spanish by the infinitive.
Por is used idiomatically in the following expressions:

ir por   to go for

enviar por   to send for

venir por   to come for

Voy por la partera.   I am going for the midwife.

Envía por la medicina.   She sends for the medicine.

Viene por ayuda.   He comes for help.

Other meanings exist for both **por** and **para.**

Conjunctions   *Las conjunciones*

A conjunction is a word that links a word or group of words to another word or group of words.

porque   because

y   and

pero, más, sino   but

El estetoscopio *y* el espejo vaginal están aquí, *pero* el baumanómetro no está. The stethoscope *and* the speculum are here, *but* the sphygmomanometer isn't.

Interjections   *Las interjecciones*

An interjection is a word or group of words that express strong or sudden feeling.

¡Válgame Dios!   Good heavens!

¡Qué lástima!   What a shame!

ESSENTIAL GRAMMAR INDEX
INDICE DE GRAMATICA BASICA

para, 303

participle, 299

perfect indicative, 298f.

pero, 304

personal **a,** 303

personal pronouns
  direct object, 280
  indirect object, 282
  reflexive, 300
  subject, 278f.

plural
  adjectives, 285
  nouns, 278

por, 303

position
  adjectives, 285
  object pronouns, 281, 282

possession, 286

possessive adjectives, 289ff.

possessive pronouns, 283f.

prepositions, 302f.
  por and **para,** 303

present indicative, 291ff.

preterite, 297

pronouns
  demonstrative, 282
  direct object, 280
  indirect object, 282
  interrogative, 283
  order, 282
  possessive, 283f.
  reflexive, 300
  relative, 283
  se for **le** or **les,** 282
  subject, 278f.

punctuation, 20

¿qué?, 283

que

para, 303

participio, 299

tiempo perfecto, 298f.

pero, 304

a **personal,** 303

pronombres personales
  objeto directo, 280
  objeto indirecto, 282
  reflexivo, 300
  nominativo, 278f.

plural
  de adjetivos, 285
  de sustantivos, 278

por, 303

posición
  de adjetivos, 285
  de pronombres objetivos, 281, 282

posesión, 286

adjetivos posesivos, 289ff.

pronombres posesivos, 283f.

preposiciones, 302f.
  por y *para*, 303

tiempo presente de indicativo, 291ff.

tiempo pretérito, 297

pronombres
  demostrativos, 282
  objetivos directos, 280
  objetivos indirectos, 282
  como interrogativos, 283
  orden de, 282
  posesivos, 283f.
  reflexivos, 300
  relativos, 283
  conversión de *le* **o** *les* **en** *se*, 282
  nominativos, 278f.

puntuación, 20

¿qué?, 283

que

INDEX

English Index

Indice Español

NOTES

NOTES

NOTES

NOTES

NOTES

NOTES

NOTES

NOTES

post partum cramps = entuertos

rash - erupsión